Fight to the Finish

Fight to the Finish

The Inside Story of our Rollercoaster 2011-12 Season

WITH
STEVE BARTRAM

SIMON &
SCHUSTER

London · New York · Sydney · Toronto · New Delhi

A CBS COMPANY

First published in Great Britain by Simon & Schuster UK Ltd, 2012
A CBS COMPANY

1 3 5 7 9 10 8 6 4 2

Simon & Schuster UK Ltd
1st Floor
222 Gray's Inn Road
London
WC1X 8HB

www.simonandschuster.co.uk

Simon & Schuster Australia, Sydney
Simon & Schuster India, New Delhi

All photographs © Manchester United/Getty Images

A CIP catalogue for this book is available from the British Library.

ISBN: 978-1-84983-732-3

Typeset by M Rules
Printed and bound by CPI Group (UK) Ltd, Croydon, CR0 4YY

Contents

Introduction

Never dull, is it? A season that began with hope rather than expectation for many Manchester United supporters quickly scaled the peaks of realism, ploughed the odd trough and then looked set for an unfathomable success, only to be snatched away at the very last moment when it seemed as though the Reds had retained the title against the odds.

Transition is a term often over-used in football. After all, isn't every team in perpetual transition as it develops and evolves over time? At the start of the 2011-12 campaign, Sir Alex Ferguson's squad wasn't so much in transition as amid wholesale renovations. The trade of buckets of experience for silos of promise was an exciting one, as shown in the unbridled joy both on and off the field as United's youngsters tore through the August and September fixture list.

Inexperience does, of course, invite harsh lessons, and there were plenty of those during the season. From the jaw-dropping horror of a biggest Manchester derby defeat at Old Trafford since 1926, to early exits from four cup competitions, Sir Alex's new-look side took plenty of hefty blows on the chin.

Incredibly, the start of 2012 heralded a storming run of Premier League results that, coupled with the apparent collapse of long-term league leaders Manchester City, put the Reds on the brink of a successful title defence. A 20th crown, secured despite such squad upheaval and a vexing run of misfortune with injury, looked set to be one of the club's outstanding achievements as the finishing line loomed large.

Then, through little more than carelessness in three games, the title was gone. A poor concession at Wigan, two late lapses at home to Everton and lax defending from a set-piece at the Etihad Stadium contrived to secure a dramatic eight-point swing that took the title over to Roberto Mancini's City. As lessons go, they come no harsher, but they beg learning.

Top scorer Wayne Rooney, now team talisman of the burgeoning Reds, bristles with intent as he reflects on a season that could have a long-term impact on the squad. 'I think we've all learned a lot,' he admits. 'There have been a lot of games this season where you get a feeling afterwards that you never want to have again, and hopefully we can get hold of that feeling and make sure it doesn't happen again.

'Just look at all the young players in the squad: they've played a lot of games, had a lot of ups and downs, and most of them are already getting selected now for their national teams. That's all going to help them. The next two or three years will be a big test for them, and I'm sure we'll all pull through it.'

The spectre of trying to overthrow the limitless spending power and growing presence of Manchester City is an imposing one, but after a season conducted on a steep learning curve, everybody at Old Trafford and Carrington is united in shooting towards that tantalising goal. The battle may have been lost, but the wider war has only just begun.

Steve Bartram, Manchester, 14 May 2012

1

Pre-season –
Getting Ready for Action

Manchester United has never been a football club content to dawdle on the shifting sands of time. Sir Alex Ferguson has masterminded the club's evolution over a glorious quarter-century, ensuring sustained success through constant fine-tuning, punctuated by the occasional shredding of blueprints. And few overhauls have been as dramatic as that enforced upon the Reds ahead of the 2011-12 season.

The stalwart trio of Gary Neville, Edwin van der Sar and Paul Scholes all retired, while new challenges beckoned the experienced John O'Shea, Wes Brown and Owen Hargreaves, trimming the United squad of a group with 2,338 Reds appearances between them.

Despite bagging a record-breaking 19th English league title and reaching a third Champions League final in four seasons in 2010-11, the Reds needed to undergo extensive renovations following these departures. Ascending to the role of the squad's eldest statesman, Ryan Giggs had seen enough change during his epic Reds career to simplify the situation. 'Getting players in like-for-like is impossible,' he said. 'But the club has to go on. We have to evolve. That is the Manchester United way.'

In time-honoured fashion, Sir Alex placed his faith in youth. Goalkeeper David De Gea arrived from Atlético Madrid with a burgeoning reputation reflected by a sizeable transfer fee, yet at just 20, the Spaniard was only half the age of his predecessor. Teenage talent Phil Jones further freshened an already youthful defence upon arriving from Blackburn Rovers, while England winger Ashley Young left Aston Villa and marched into comparative seniority at just 25.

As ever, there were also in-house talents to promote. Danny Welbeck and Tom Cleverley returned from promising loan years at Sunderland and Wigan respectively and quickly applied the improvements they'd made to their game, while Sir Alex was able to draw on another clutch of FA Youth Cup winners fresh off the Academy conveyor belt.

The exploits of five of the Reds' fledglings – De Gea, Cleverley, Welbeck, Jones and Chris Smalling – at the UEFA Under-21 European Championships meant that they would return to Carrington later than their colleagues, as would Javier 'Chicharito' Hernandez after his part in Mexico's Gold Cup campaign.

The sextet holidayed while the Reds jetted out for a three-week pre-season tour of America – United's second successive trip Stateside to prepare for the new campaign. Darren Fletcher was also absent, apparently after a recurrence of the mystery virus that had laid him low during the latter stages of the 2010-11 campaign. The reality of his situation, however, would emerge during the coming months.

With reinforcements due to bolster the squad along the way, Sir Alex took a 21-man squad comprising three goalkeepers (Anders Lindegaard, Ben Amos and Sam Johnstone), six defenders (Rafael, Fabio, Nemanja Vidic, Jonny Evans, Patrice Evra and Rio Ferdinand), seven midfielders (Michael Carrick, Nani, Anderson, Ryan Giggs, Ji-sung Park, Gabriel Obertan and Ashley Young) and five strikers (Mame Biram Diouf, Federico Macheda, Wayne Rooney, Michael Owen and Dimitar Berbatov).

The Reds had enjoyed just a week of fitness work before jetting off to sweltering Boston, and the breathless preparations continued, as Sir Alex immediately rushed to a press conference with Steve Nicol, the ex-Liverpool defender who had taken charge of New England Revolution, United's first opponents.

'It doesn't seem so long ago we were fighting out for the European Cup final,' admitted Sir Alex, before quickly stressing that he would have high expectations of his side. 'It's difficult for us to play friendly games because of the expectation on us. Even if we lose a friendly there's criticism, from the press, our own fans, our own staff. We can't go into any game not wanting to win. That will be the case against the Revolution.'

For the majority of the assembled press – particularly those who had flown over from England – the commencement of pre-season preparations on the field was secondary to the Reds' recruitment drive off it. Rumours had abounded for weeks that Sir Alex was aiming to recruit a long-term replacement for Paul Scholes, with Internazionale's Wesley Sneijder and Arsenal schemer Samir Nasri strongly linked with the club.

'Nasri? No, I don't think he's coming to United,' said the boss. 'I think he's agreed to go somewhere else. But how do you replace somebody like Paul Scholes? It's very difficult. If you bracket four of the best midfield players in the world, he'd be alongside Xavi and Iniesta and then you take your pick. In my mind he's one of the top four players in the world. Maybe the next few weeks will help us overcome it. Maybe somebody will emerge out of the youth team or one of the young players emerges, and then we carry on.'

The contenders' first opportunity would come at the Gillette Stadium, but it was the strikers who stole the show for United. Michael Owen opened the scoring before a quickfire brace from Kiko Macheda, and Ji-sung Park rounded off a comfortable 4-1 win and a highly satisfactory start to the pre-season preparations for the Reds.

Next stop, Seattle. A new base, but familiar issues for Sir Alex, whose next press conference was conducted amid a frenzy of whispers linking the Reds with Inter star Sneijder. When asked about the situation regarding a potential move for the Dutchman, the manager retorted: 'I couldn't tell you. I've not really been involved in it since we've come to America. There's no real interest at this moment in time in Wesley Sneijder for a lot of reasons. There's nothing I can tell you about it.'

While uncertainty reigned around the Reds' ongoing hunt for new recruits, the need to prepare thoroughly for the coming campaign was cast-iron. A fringe benefit of touring the United States was the access to some of the world's most cutting-edge training facilities, and the players and staff were blown away by the Virginia Mason Athletic Center, home of the Seattle Sounders, the Reds' next opponents.

As he and his fellow coaches looked to step up the players' preparations, first team fitness coach Tony Strudwick was delighted. 'You've got everything you need in these facilities,' he said. 'The priority in the first week was to expose the players back to football and integrate that with the levels of conditioning. Much of the conditioning work is completed within a football environment. The classic pre-season of running up hills and running for eight miles is out of the window. Now it's all about base work in a football environment, and these facilities let you do that perfectly.'

Preparations on tour invariably allow for a little more razzmatazz than usual. The pre-match coin toss for the Sounders clash took place the day before the game, with skippers Nemanja Vidic and Kasey Keller performing the honours atop the world-famous Space Needle. Meanwhile, several players partook in fish tossing at the renowned Pike Place Market – where they hurled fish across thoroughfare areas from one stall to another – and Reds legends Bryan Robson and Andy Cole joined the club mascot, Fred the Red, to parade the Premier League trophy around the city.

In their role as club ambassadors, Robson and Cole were chiefly responsible for appearing at such functions – both on tour and year-round at a host of worldwide locations – to represent United with the same distinction which underscored their playing days at Old Trafford. The newest ambassador, Gary Neville, would join up with the travelling party later in the tour, long after the Reds' young quintet – Tom Cleverley, David De Gea, Phil Jones, Chris Smalling and Danny Welbeck – had arrived in Seattle.

None had done enough training to be considered for the clash with the Sounders, but their collective absence was rendered irrelevant as United strode to a 7-0 win at CenturyLink Stadium. Michael Owen hit the only goal of the first period, but a Wayne Rooney hat-trick, allied to further strikes from Mame Biram Diouf, Ji-sung Park and Gabriel Obertan, completed a stylish end to the Reds' stay.

A flying visit to Chicago was altogether more breathless – not least because of the searing heat. 'We've come from a nice cool atmosphere in Seattle to a furnace in Chicago,' remarked the manager, who confirmed that he would be handing David De Gea his first outing with the Reds. 'He's had a few days' training and he's done fine,' said the boss. 'He has terrific composure, he's quick, his use of the ball is excellent. He has good ingredients for our club. Hopefully they'll show as we get to the start of the season.' It would be a baptism of fire for the young Spaniard, as the Reds faced Chicago Fire at Soldier Field Stadium.

The hosts made a bright start and took an early lead, but United responded in the second period by levelling through Wayne Rooney, before late strikes from Rafael and Nani secured a comeback rendered all the more impressive by the tourists' fitness levels. After such a strenuous outing, the entire touring party – players, coaches and staff – were granted a day off once they had touched down in New Jersey for the penultimate leg of the tour.

Suitably refreshed by a selection of pastimes including golf, shopping and sightseeing, the squad were quickly back on the training field and were joined by the final member of the touring party: Chicharito, who had finished as the tournament's top scorer in Mexico's Gold Cup triumph one month earlier.

The familiar faces came in a procession. First Gary Neville, then

Chicharito, then David Beckham, who partook in a pre-match press conference ahead of the Reds' meeting with the MLS All-Stars. United had become the first team to beat the All-Stars a year earlier, though this year America's finest would be bolstered by both Beckham and ex-Arsenal star Thierry Henry.

'We've got a lot of young, good talent in this team, as well as players who have been at the top of their game for a long time,' said Beckham, before smiling. 'These players are good players. I think we have a chance.' Chicharito was in agreement. 'We're looking forward to it and we need to play a good game,' said the Mexican. 'They have a lot of good players.'

Hernandez's slim hopes of gaining some game time on tour were hit when he suffered concussion after being hit on the head by a ball in training. The striker was taken to hospital as a precaution and stayed overnight before being released, and Sir Alex quickly confirmed that the little speedster would be allowed to take his time. 'We won't be rushing him back,' he said. 'I'll only bring him back when the doctor tells me I can bring him back.'

Though the Mexican, who announced himself as a United player against the MLS All-Stars a year earlier, was side-lined for the sides' reunion at the Red Bull Arena, the Reds made light work of their hosts. Anderson, Ji-sung Park, Dimitar Berbatov and Danny Welbeck all struck in a comprehensive 4-0 victory, before the touring party made their way to Washington DC for the final leg of the excursion.

One of the underpinning themes of the players' downtime between matches was the running battles on video games; primarily FIFA 2012. Inevitably, conflicting reports emerged as to which players excelled at the expense of others.

'Me and Wayne play together and our record at the moment is won sixteen, drawn one and lost one,' claimed Rio Ferdinand, mid-tour. 'And, saying that, we lost with an own goal when we were down to ten men. It takes somebody a lot of luck to beat us. We were beaten by Fabio and Rafael. Nani and Kiko are like a married couple – they argue all the time. Gaby Obertan and Ashley Young, or Ashley Young and Ando … they promise a lot but haven't produced yet. Berba and Vida are solid too – they're waiting to catch fire. Me and Wayne are the top dogs, though.'

Nani had his own thoughts on the matter, opining: 'Wazza's the best. He and Rio play together. Rio just follows Wazza. He passes to Wazza, Wazza does the skill and then scores.' The Portuguese also emphatically smashed suggestions that Ferdinand ruled the roost when it came to table tennis; another of the squad's collective pursuits.

'At that I was the best, one hundred percent,' he protested. 'Second best you could say is Rio – but I'm not going to say that because he played one or two games, won, and then ran away! Then he came back again and won one game. That's not the best player. The best is the one who wins, plays with everyone, loses some, but wins the most.'

Collectively, United were still clutching a perfect record when they landed in Washington. Undoubtedly, however, the tour's sternest test awaited: Pep Guardiola's Barcelona, whose claim to be named the greatest side in history had been further strengthened two months earlier by their convincing Champions League triumph over the Reds.

'When I play against a team like that, I just want to beat them,' grinned Patrice Evra, at a pre-match press conference. 'For the moment they are the best team in the world, but it's difficult for us to accept that because we want to be the best team in the world. That's why we want to play against Barcelona again and make sure we beat them.'

Though United's resolve to exact a modicum of revenge for Wembley was glaring, there was still time for a memorable excursion in the build-up to the game. Sir Alex, his staff and players were given a behind-the-scenes tour of the White House. Though US President Barack Obama was unable to meet the group, the experience was unforgettable. 'It was fantastic,' said the manager. 'It was fascinating. I'd been before but it still excites. It's such a historic and incredible place. We all enjoyed it – it was good.'

Were an example needed of the high-security measures in place around the White House, it was provided when Rio Ferdinand Tweeted a picture of the building's security staff, only to have it mysteriously vanish from his account within moments. 'My pic of the security was removed quick, rapido, sharpish, fast . . . they don't play here in DC . . . I feel like I'm on *24* right now,' the defender soon posted to his personal audience.

Ferdinand was given the night off as United rounded off the cross-Atlantic trip with an impressive victory over the reigning European champions at FedEx Field. Nani capped an exceptional personal display with the opening goal and, although Thiago levelled midway through the second period, Michael Owen strode through on goal and clinically sealed victory for the Reds with 14 minutes remaining.

Five wins from five games, 20 goals scored, packed stadiums and a host of invaluable charity and commercial ventures conspired to total an unquestionably successful trip for the Reds. Now, the real work would begin.

2

August – Looking Past the Present, to the Future

While August traditionally heralds new beginnings in football, United began the opening month of the season with two poignant and significant farewells to consider. Edwin van der Sar and Paul Scholes had been key to the Reds' recent (and in the latter's case, distant) success under Sir Alex Ferguson; they were fixtures in the first team for six and 16 years respectively, and the club was keen to serve up a proper send-off for the two old stagers.

Sir Alex and first team coach Rene Meulensteen agreed to manage a composite XI chosen by van der Sar to go up against a side of legends from the Dutch goalkeeper's first professional club, Ajax, in the Amsterdam ArenA.

Rio Ferdinand, Nemanja Vidic, Michael Carrick, Ryan Giggs and Wayne Rooney joined Edwin's dream team, alongside ex-Reds Gary Neville and Louis Saha. Van der Sar declared pre-match that the occasion would be 'the perfect way to say goodbye', and enjoyed an emotional evening in the stadium where he began his professional career.

Scholes, meanwhile, was given his send-off at Old Trafford. Having retired just two days after the Reds' Champions League final defeat to Barcelona, the midfield string-puller had barely kicked a ball since. As his sold-out testimonial against New York Cosmos loomed, Scholes began running to regain his fitness. Though he enjoyed mixed results (he lost interest during one long-distance jog and ended up walking home), he was soon ready for the occasion.

The midfielder's retirement had deprived the United arsenal of a tried and trusted attacking weapon, yet Eric Cantona – back in Manchester as Cosmos' director of soccer – insisted that the club would carry on regardless.

'You can replace any player, especially at a club like Manchester United, with a great manager like Alex Ferguson,' the Frenchman told reporters. 'Every time a player leaves, you think the club won't win any more. But they still do. They are very strong and have a great history, and they work a lot every day so any player can be replaced. Paul is still a great player. But I left, Ronaldo left, Hughes left, Beckham left, and United are still one of the best clubs in the world.'

Cantona's admiration for the Reds was only strengthened by their resounding victory over the Cosmos. Fittingly, the first goal in a 6-0 win for the hosts was thundered home by Paul Scholes. The man of the hour smashed in a trademark 25-yard scorcher and afterwards admitted: 'Over the last sixteen or seventeen years, the fans have always been great to me. I just want to say "thank you" to everyone. It's about memories; I just hope I've given the fans some decent memories.'

Scholes' impact on supporters' memory banks had long-since been assured, and the Reds' collective efforts in obliterating the Cosmos provided further assurances ahead of the looming season, according to Sir Alex.

'You can see the appetite for the game is still there for the players,' said the manager. 'No matter what they achieved last season or the season before, they want to win again. They want to win this league again. If the supporters wanted to know that, they've got evidence tonight.'

Even before a ball had been kicked in competitive anger, United would have the opportunity to lay down a marker for the new season with a Community Shield clash against Manchester City. The Blues' FA Cup semi-final win in 2010-11 over the Reds had further fuelled suggestions that Roberto Mancini's side were ready to make use of their spectacular funding and mount a sustained challenge for the Premier League title, but Sir Alex was keen to avoid the hype around the game and rather focus on the fixture's true value.

The United manager, for whom Chicharito, Darren Fletcher and Antonio Valencia missed out said: 'It's very easy to get emotional about this type of game. I don't think we'll be changing our policy. I've always viewed the Community Shield as a stepping stone for the first game of the season, and there are two or three players who will need a game.'

Community Shield

7 August 2011 | Wembley Stadium | Kick-off 14:30 |
Attendance: 77,169

Manchester United 3 (Smalling 52, Nani 58, 90)
Manchester City 2 (Lescott 38, Dzeko 45)

A stepping stone? A fitness exercise? The scenes of wild celebration that met the dramatic climax of this particular Community Shield victory betrayed the ever-increasing stakes of the Manchester derby. United roared back from two goals down to take the Shield in stoppage time, as Manchester City were overrun by a stunning second-half display from the Premier League champions.

Quickfire goals between the interval and the hour-mark from Chris Smalling and Nani turned around a two-goal deficit and seized back the momentum from a Blues side who had grasped control of a tight game with two goals at the end of the first period through Joleon Lescott and Edin Dzeko. As the game seemed set for a decisive penalty shootout, Nani charged down a Vincent Kompany clearance and bore down on goal before rounding Joe Hart and sliding home a finish to secure the season's first piece of silverware.

Despite their half-time deficit, the Reds actually began brightly at Wembley, going close when Smalling volleyed just off-target and enjoying the bulk of possession. Inevitably, both sides looked to impose themselves physically in a well-contested opening, though City's Micah Richards was fortunate to avoid a red card for his lunging challenge on Ashley Young.

It took a set piece to open the scoring. David Silva curled an unplayable ball towards David De Gea's goal and into the path of the onrushing Lescott, who headed home to send the Blue half of Wembley wild. Their joy was enhanced when, in the dying seconds of the first period, Bosnian striker Dzeko was allowed to advance and unleash a dipping, long-range effort that eluded De Gea's dive.

Sir Alex Ferguson's response was to hand Tom Cleverley and Phil Jones their Reds debuts, with Michael Carrick and Nemanja Vidic replaced, while Rio Ferdinand made way for Jonny Evans. The response was emphatic. United soon wrested back the initiative, and were level before the hour. First Smalling reached Young's free-kick ahead of Hart to prod home, then Nani capped a stunning, intricate team move with an impudent clipped finish. Suddenly it was the Red half of Wembley that was revelling in the occasion.

City steadied themselves and substitute Adam Johnson drew a smart save from De Gea with 15 minutes remaining, before United piled on the pressure once more for a late winner. Penalties seemed inevitable, until Nani charged down Kompany's clearance, kept his cool and sealed the shield for the reigning champions.

The Teams

Manchester United: De Gea; Smalling, Ferdinand (Jones 46), Vidic (Evans 46), Evra (Rafael 72); Nani, Carrick (Cleverley 46), Anderson, Young; Rooney, Welbeck (Berbatov 89)

Subs not used: Lindegaard, Park
Booked: Evra, Anderson

Manchester City: Hart; Richards, Kompany, Lescott, Kolarov (Clichy 74); Milner (Johnson 67), De Jong, Y.Toure, Silva; Balotelli (Barry 59), Dzeko
Subs not used: Taylor, Savic, Wright-Phillips, Aguero
Booked: Richards, Y.Toure, Milner, Dzeko

'This is United,' grinned Nani. 'We always play until the last minute. I think with the attitude from the young lads in the second half, everyone believed we could score. The manager said we just needed to score the first goal and the game would be easier for us, and we did well. It's good to play against Man City and win like that. I think the fans are proud of us and it's a beautiful day. Now we just enjoy.'

Sir Alex Ferguson could be forgiven for enjoying it most of all. 'It was a great performance,' he beamed. 'We were always going to make changes. I wanted to expose Jones, Evans and Cleverley to a situation like today. It was a big challenge and they have done well. We are confident in this group of players.

'For us it just confirms what I thought about the squad. People have been saying we are not the best United squad. But you have to remember we have a lot of young players, who will improve. The addition of Jones and De Gea gives us a good future.'

'You can't ask for any more than beating City to win a trophy in your first United appearance,' says Jones, looking back on his competitive debut. 'The way we played was fantastic. It was an incredible match and the football on show was unbelievable at times – when we play like that other teams cannot live with us. Our supporters were so passionate and they made so much noise, which was really inspiring and they played a major part.'

Another youngster with cause for celebration was Tom Cleverley. Far beyond finally making his first senior Reds appearance – after featuring in three other pre-season campaigns – the Basingstoke-born midfielder was handed his first call-up to Fabio Capello's senior England squad to face the Netherlands at Wembley.

Not for the last time during 2011-12, however, Cleverley would be dealt a cruel hand by fate. A short-lived but dangerous wave of riots in London spread across the country and prompted the Football Association to postpone the fixture, depriving the 21-year-old of the experience. He wasn't the only United player to spend the international break at Carrington.

Michael Carrick and Danny Welbeck had already withdrawn from the England squad through injury before the riots began, while Patrice Evra missed France's friendly due to a tweaked knee. All three were doubts for the Reds' Premier League curtain-raiser against West Bromwich Albion at The Hawthorns, with Chicharito, Darren Fletcher, Michael Owen and Antonio Valencia already ruled out with an assortment of ailments. Rafael, meanwhile, joined the walking wounded during training the day before United were due to head to the Midlands, after he won a tackle, stumbled and fell on his shoulder, dislocating it badly enough to require an operation.

Contract extensions for Valencia and Ji-sung Park provided welcome news before the commencement of the season proper, but Sir Alex retained clarity about the task that faced his re-jigged squad over the coming months.

'I trust them and have confidence in the ability of the players,' he said. 'But you can never be confident in the Barclays Premier League. It is such a difficult league. Six teams could be challenging for the title. You know by the very experience of going through league campaigns how difficult it is. It will be difficult next season.'

Looking shorter-term was skipper Nemanja Vidic, who warned the Baggies: 'I don't think we have hit top form quite yet, but I think we've done a very good job in pre-season and, fitness-wise, we're ready. Now we have to do all we can to win three points, which is the most important thing. It's not about how we play the game or whether or not we play good football – it's all about winning.'

Barclays Premier League

14 August 2011 | The Hawthorns | Kick-off 16:00 |
Attendance: 25,360

West Bromwich Albion 1 (Long 37)
Manchester United 2 (Rooney 13, Reid 81 (og))

United kicked off their defence of the Barclays Premier League title with a hard-fought victory at The Hawthorns, snatching the points nine minutes from time, when Steven Reid deflected Ashley Young's cross past Ben Foster. The Reds had moved into an early lead through Wayne Rooney's low shot, only for the hosts to draw level when Shane Long's bobbling effort evaded David De Gea. Chances were spurned by the champions – who were hindered by injuries to Nemanja Vidic and Rio Ferdinand – before Reid's decisive late intervention.

A bright start from Sir Alex Ferguson's energetic young side yielded quick rewards, as Rooney traded passes with Young before drilling a low, left-footed effort beyond Foster from just outside the area.

United threatened to bury the game inside the opening 20 minutes, as Rooney then fired off-target and Nani twice shot over from inviting positions, but the hosts gradually worked their way into the game. Paul Scharner's shot brought a fine reaction stop from De Gea but, two minutes later, the Spaniard was left embarrassed as the Baggies levelled.

There seemed little danger when Republic of Ireland striker Long cut in from the left flank. Less still when his half-hit shot trundled towards the far corner, yet it slipped under De Gea's grasp and nestled in the bottom corner to the delight of the home support. There were hands on heads throughout the United ranks, and the pepped-up hosts came close to moving ahead before the break through Chris Brunt and Somen Tchoyi.

Half time brought respite, however. United bossed a low-key

second half for long periods, despite losing Vidic and Ferdinand, who both limped off during the course of the second 45 minutes. Rooney glanced a header off-target, but it was the lively Young who looked likeliest to inspire victory; and so it proved. Substitute Dimitar Berbatov fed the winger on the left flank, and his charge into the Baggies' box culminated in a cross that clipped Gabriel Tamas, then struck Reid before nestling in Foster's bottom corner.

Though West Brom endeavoured to level in what little time remained, they failed to forge a noteworthy opening and the champions posted a winning start to their title defence. The Hawthorns had been a launchpad for success at the start of 2011 – and an away win on the opening day augured well for the season ahead.

The Teams

West Bromwich Albion: Foster; Reid (Jara 85), Tamas, Olsson, Shorey; Brunt, Scharner, Mulumbu, Morrison, Tchoyi; Long (Cox 87)
Subs not used: Fulop, Dawson, Dorrens, Thorne, Fortune
Booked: Cox, Reid, Scharner

Manchester United: De Gea; Smalling, Ferdinand (Jones 75), Vidic (Evans 52), Fabio; Nani, Cleverley, Anderson, Young; Rooney, Welbeck (Berbatov 65)
Subs not used: Lindegaard, Giggs, Park, Carrick
Booked: Anderson, Young

A winning start to the season came at a sizeable cost, with Rio Ferdinand and Nemanja Vidic limping into the Carrington treatment room within three days of Rafael being ruled out until November.

'We've had a torrid two or three days with injuries,' winced Sir Alex Ferguson, who was similarly frank when discussing David De Gea's unfortunate concession of Shane Long's trickling shot. 'I think it was just a bit of concentration there,' he said. 'I patted him on the head and said: "Welcome to English football," because he took a battering in the second half. He should have maybe been protected more by the referee, but he withstood it and it was a good experience for him. David is only twenty years of age. We expect a learning process at the moment and we'll see it through.

'Ours is a different type of game for goalkeepers coming in from Europe. [Peter] Schmeichel was the same when he came. Wimbledon away on a Wednesday night was his first away game and they gave him a torrid time. Then, in the home game on the following Saturday against Leeds, he lost a really bad goal, but Peter went on to be possibly the greatest goalkeeper of all time.'

The intervention of another new signing, Ashley Young – supplier of the cross for Steven Reid's own-goal – ensured victory, and the summer arrival was already aware of his new club's age-old penchant for late drama.

'We had to grind it out,' he said. 'We have got that never-say-die attitude and we keep going until the final whistle, and we got the rewards at the end of the day when we got the winner. That is the way we are drilled and worked: to play until the final whistle. That is what we did and we knew we'd get another couple of chances. Luckily mine went in and it was nice to get the win.'

Though United's growing injury list provided cause for concern, especially with ambitious Tottenham due at Old Trafford eight days later, Chris Smalling felt the summer exertions of the club's burgeoning talents provided ample cause for optimism.

'It's unfortunate to see your big players go down injured,' he said. 'But the manager has shown all pre-season he's willing to give the young players a go and he's thrown them in to big games. So it's great to see them step up. Everyone's really gelling. If you do well, the manager will keep you in the team. It's a big marker to all the other players and the rest of the squad that, if you play well, it doesn't matter how old you are. If you've got that ability, the manager is going to put you in.'

Smalling also gave his considered reaction to knee-jerk media condemnation of David De Gea's early-season form. 'Some of the media criticism has been a bit judgmental, given that he has only played a couple of games for United,' said the defender. 'He played some massive games for Atlético Madrid – including the Europa League final – and performed well. The manager has obviously put a lot of faith in him by making him first choice and I think he is going to be a great goalkeeper for us. He is showing his quality in training and it is only a matter of time until the whole world sees it too.'

The young Spaniard would get his next chance to showcase his talents under the glare of the Old Trafford floodlights, as Harry Redknapp brought his Tottenham side north for their first league game of the campaign. Spurs' scheduled league opener against Everton had fallen foul of the Tottenham riots, so they would be playing catch-up from week one of the season. They would also have to do it amid public agitation from playmaker Luka Modric, who had formally requested to join Chelsea before the transfer window closed. The Croatian schemer was a doubt to miss the United clash as a result. Redknapp admitted: 'His head's not in the right place.' Meanwhile, Tom Huddlestone, Steven Pienaar, Jermaine Jenas and William Gallas were all major injury doubts.

Sir Alex Ferguson was juggling mixed news with his own squad. Rio Ferdinand's hamstring injury was less severe than feared, but Nemanja Vidic's calf strain looked set to rule him out for six weeks.

'The team on Monday will be a very young defensive line-up, with Jones and Evans in the centre and Smalling at right-back,' shrugged the manager. 'But Patrice Evra will be back for Spurs, which gives us experience. It's a very young team at the moment, but it's a team full of energy and it's a team of great ability. I'm enjoying watching them at the moment. I'm not worried about the young players filling in at the back; no issues whatsoever with playing those guys. We're happy with the age of the squad.'

Youth would be given its chance. Not for the first time, it would take it.

Barclays Premier League

22 August 2011 | Old Trafford | Kick-off 20:00 |
Attendance: 75,498

Manchester United 3 (Welbeck 61, Anderson 76, Rooney 87)
Tottenham Hotspur 0

The clamour around Sir Alex Ferguson's newest iteration of Manchester United grew from a rumble to a roar after the Reds registered a superb victory over Tottenham at Old Trafford. Harry Redknapp's side were worn down and spectacularly put to the sword as Danny Welbeck nodded home Tom Cleverley's cross, before teeing up Anderson with an impudent back-heel to make the game safe. Wayne Rooney then capped a fine personal display by heading in a late third goal.

At 30, captain-for-the-night Patrice Evra was by far the eldest statesman of the fresh-faced side – United's second-youngest in the Premier League era – and the hosts began in suitably energetic fashion. The deadlock was almost broken after seven minutes, only for Cleverley's curling, side-footed effort to be brilliantly brushed around the post by Spurs debutant Brad Friedel. It may have been a new club, but they were familiar Old Trafford heroics from the veteran American.

At the opposite end of the field, David De Gea's every move attracted scrutiny after the obsessive media coverage of his early displays as Edwin van der Sar's replacement. The Spaniard showed no adverse effects, comfortably fielding efforts from Gareth Bale, Nico Kranjcar and Rafael van der Vaart.

In the closest call of the half, Ashley Young's looping header drifted just wide, with Friedel beaten. The interval came and went with an engaging game finely poised. In the second period, however, there was even greater purpose in United's play, as the hosts were increasingly first to every ball and Spurs struggled to match the Reds' movement.

It took a fabulous example of United's youthful link-up to break the visitors' resistance. Cleverley bent an unplayable cross in between Michael Dawson and Younes Kaboul, straight onto the head of Welbeck, who powered his effort into Friedel's bottom corner.

Already playing with great liberty, there was a sudden abandon about United's play. The second goal, coming 15 minutes later, could be conceived only by the unshackled mind and spirit. A neat passing move culminated in Anderson releasing Welbeck deep inside the Spurs area but, rather than shoot, the Longsight trickster served up a tap-in for the Brazilian with a jaw-dropping back-heel.

Spurs' final route back into the game came and went when Jermain Defoe thundered against the post after De Gea had spilled a deep cross from Vedran Corluka. Shortly afterwards, Rooney set the seal on United's victory by emphatically heading home substitute Ryan Giggs' beautifully weighted cross.

By the time referee Lee Probert sounded the final whistle, excitement for the short term and far beyond had gripped Old Trafford and all onlookers of a Red persuasion. The future suddenly gleamed brighter than ever.

The Teams

Manchester United: De Gea; Smalling, Evans, Jones, Evra; Nani, Cleverley (Giggs 81), Anderson, Young (Park 81); Rooney, Welbeck (Hernandez 81)
Subs not used: Lindegaard, Berbatov, Carrick, Fabio
Booked: Evans

Tottenham Hotspur: Friedel; Walker (Corluka 46), Dawson, Kaboul, Assou-Ekotto; Lennon, Livermore (Huddlestone 74), Kranjcar (Pavlyuchenko 74), Bale; van der Vaart; Defoe
Subs not used: Gomes, Jenas, Bassong, Townsend
Booked: Dawson, Defoe

The sense of pride within Old Trafford after the resounding result was heightened by both the manner of the victory and the starring role of home-grown produce within it. Tom Cleverley's assist for Danny Welbeck's all-important opener was the result of a decade's work by the club's coaching staff, and a success to revel in collectively.

'Tom and I have been playing with each other since we were little kids,' says Welbeck, looking back. 'The coaches take credit for everything. From the Under-nines coach, Eddie Leach, up to Paul McGuinness with the Under-eighteens and Warren Joyce with the Reserves, they've all taught us our trade. Just for us to come through to the first team is a big positive. We're good friends and we've built up an understanding over time. He knows my game and I know his, and I think you can see that whenever we play together.

'Personally, I felt I'd really come into my own at the start of the season. When the chance came along, I wasn't going to sit back. I didn't really think: "This is my chance," I just played my normal game and thankfully I got the rewards for that. I loved scoring against Spurs; there's no better feeling than scoring in front of the Stretford End.'

Immediately after the Tottenham game, the Longsight striker came in for glowing praise from his manager. 'He's got a great future, the lad,' said Sir Alex. 'Danny made slow progress because when he was growing he had Osgood-Schlatter's, the knee-growth condition, and it was always a case of we're going to have to wait for him. When we put him on loan to Sunderland [in 2010-11], I think that's when he became a man. He's still only twenty years of age. He's a big rangy, long-legged boy who can gallop really quickly. Once he gets his legs going, he's quick. He's a good footballer; he's got a great attitude when he loses the ball and a tremendous attitude to win it back.'

The ongoing excellence of Welbeck, Cleverley and the rest of the fledgling talents on show against Tottenham validated the manager's continued use of them, and stand-in skipper Patrice Evra made no attempt to disguise his admiration for the bright young things glowing around him.

'The young players deserve this and you have to give them a lot of credit,' he beamed. 'A lot of people talk about the Academy and they showed tonight what they can do. It's amazing. In the Community Shield, and against West Brom, the boss showed he is not afraid to play young players.

'They have such composure. They want to prove to the manager that they are ready to play in the team. It's good for us because we need some energy and they have that. We have lost a lot of experienced players, like Edwin van der Sar, Paul Scholes and Gary Neville, but you can see now that the team is very fresh, it has a lot of energy and the football is quick. The young players just have to keep going and it's up to players like myself, Rio and Vidic to make sure they keep developing.'

Phil Jones, named man of the match in his first start for the club, revelled in making the step up from representing Blackburn Rovers, an established Premier League side, but one more accustomed to battling in its lower reaches. 'The fans were unbelievable,' he reflected. 'I knew it would be like this. I was just excited to be out there and I'm pleased with the three points in the end. I think it's the tempo of the game that's the biggest difference. No disrespect to Blackburn, I enjoyed my time there, but it's the speed at which we play. The gaffer and Rene Meulensteen have been saying how much energy we've got in the side, and that showed.'

Energy levels looked potentially problematic for the Reds' next opponents, Arsenal. The injury-ravaged Gunners had endured a torrid opening to the season, drawing at Newcastle and losing at home to Liverpool, while also losing Cesc Fabregas to Barcelona as the midfielder's much-mooted transfer was finally completed. Speculation around Samir Nasri's future had also proven disruptive, and the Frenchman penned a deal with Manchester City on the eve of Arsenal's Champions League qualifying win at Udinese.

The Gunners' victory and subsequent progress to the group stages put them in the same draw as United, who were handed a seemingly kind group alongside Portugal's Benfica, Basel of Switzerland and

Romanian champions Otelul Galati. The switch of attentions was only fleeting, with such a tantalising domestic fixture looming large, and Sir Alex was keen to back his opposite number at the Emirates Stadium.

'I think the work Arsène Wenger has done in the fifteen years he's been at the club is the best in Arsenal's history,' said the United boss. 'Yes, he's not won a trophy in six years, but what does that mean? The quality in his side has not been reduced. He's still had great quality in his teams in that period. It's a cynical world and supporters are far less easy to please than they were twenty years ago. It's disappointing.'

The boss also empathised with the enforced departure of Nasri, who moved to the Etihad Stadium rather than run down his contract with the Gunners. 'Today the situation is difficult because when a player gets to the last two years of his contract, you have an issue,' he explained. 'Two years out, you can try to persuade him to sign a new deal. But if he doesn't want to sign it, and you get to that last year then it's almost inevitable you will have a problem. We're all in the same boat and we at United have had the same issue at times with players getting into their last year.

'If you do get to that final part, you can do what Arsène nearly did with Nasri – keep him for another year, then not get anything – or capitalise and get the money a year ahead. So I think Arsène was sensible with that deal, because if the player isn't going to sign a new contract with you, why throw away money?'

The departures of Fabregas and Nasri, allied to injuries to Jack Wilshere and Thomas Vermaelen and suspensions for Alex Song, Emmanuel Frimpong and Gervinho, meant the Gunners were looking especially threadbare ahead of their trip north. Nevertheless, they would not be taken lightly by their hosts.

'I think it's going to be a much more difficult game than everyone is thinking,' said Jonny Evans. 'Arsenal are a fantastic team and, no matter who plays for them, Arsène Wenger has got unbelievable ability to bring through young lads.

'I know they've got a lot of suspensions, but the lads who come in will be so well integrated into how the Arsenal system works. They do have a distinct style of play that they very rarely change from, so I think that helps. When they come through the Arsenal youth or reserve teams, they know exactly how to play. He's still got a big squad there. Obviously, they've lost two great players in Nasri and Fabregas, but they've got great strength in depth in their squad. It's going to be a tough game.'

The unforgettable events that followed would spectacularly suggest the opposite.

Barclays Premier League

28 August 2011 | Old Trafford | Kick-off 16:00 |
Attendance: 75,448

Manchester United 8 (Welbeck 22, Young 28, 90, Rooney 41, 64, 82 (pen), Nani 67, Park 70)
Arsenal 2 (Walcott 45, van Persie 74)

United heaped more misery on beleaguered Arsenal with an eight-goal annihilation which instantly took its place in the Old Trafford hall of fame. A Wayne Rooney hat-trick, Ashley Young's stunning brace and single strikes for Danny Welbeck, Nani and Ji-sung Park extended the Reds' mesmerising start to the season, but also embossed a swaggering display that blew away Arsène Wenger's depleted side.

For so long the closest of rivals in pursuit of silverware, never before have United and Arsenal been so disparate. Manchester City's earlier 5-1 destruction of Tottenham had nudged the Reds off top spot, but it was quickly reclaimed in awesome circumstances.

From the off, the lively Welbeck appeared intent on wreaking havoc, and it didn't take long for his presence to cause confusion in the visitors' unfamiliar backline, who dithered deep inside their own area and allowed the United striker to gently nod home Anderson's bouncing ball.

Old Trafford was briefly silenced when Jonny Evans held Theo Walcott to concede a penalty, but David De Gea's plunging save from Robin van Persie's spot-kick merely cranked up the volume. The din reached new levels when, from United's next attack, Young collected a loose header from Armand Traore and bent an inch-perfect effort into Wojciech Szczesny's top corner from 25 yards out.

Though Welbeck's afternoon was curtailed when he pulled up with a hamstring strain, the Reds' momentum remained unstoppable as Rooney joined the scoring spree in spectacular fashion by curling home a 20-yard free-kick. Arsenal rallied before the break and reduced their deficit when Walcott powered a low finish through De Gea, but the Spaniard redeemed himself with a superb reflex stop from van Persie's volley early in the second period.

The dam broke, however, when Rooney whipped home another superb free-kick shortly after the hour mark, sparking a frenzied 25-minute spell which yielded five more goals and a sending-off.

Rooney sprang a bedraggled Arsenal offside trap to release Nani, who clipped an outrageously cheeky finish over Szczesny, substitute Ji-sung Park drove in a low, left-footed shot and van Persie restored a modicum of pride with an emphatic finish after United's defenders had been caught upfield.

The visitors' misery was heightened when rookie defender Carl Jenkinson received a second yellow card for bundling Javier Hernandez over, then Walcott tripped Patrice Evra inside the box to give Rooney the opportunity to clinically complete his hat-trick from the penalty spot.

Young curled in another majestic effort in injury time to secure United's demolition job; it was only the 11th time the Reds had ever mustered an octet of goals. For Arsenal, the damage had even greater historical significance, confirming their worst defeat since 1896.

The Teams

Manchester United: De Gea; Smalling, Jones, Evans, Evra; Nani (Park 68) Cleverley, Anderson (Giggs 68), Young; Rooney, Welbeck (Hernandez 35)
Subs not used: Lindegaard, Ferdinand, Berbatov, Fabio
Booked: Evans, Young

Arsenal: Szczesny; Jenkinson, Djourou, Koscielny, Traore; Walcott (Lansbury 83), Rosicky, Ramsey, Coquelin (Oxlade-Chamberlain 62), Arshavin; van Persie (Chamakh 83)
Subs not used: Fabianski, Miquel, Ozyakup, Sunu
Booked: Arshavin, Djourou, Jenkinson
Sent off: Jenkinson

'It's unusual because you don't expect it,' puffed a somewhat dazed Sir Alex Ferguson. 'We've scored six against them twice in the past, so maybe when we hit form like that somebody suffers. When you see Arsenal's team like that, we do expect to score goals. I felt all their quality was in the forward positions and they were a threat at times. They could have scored more than two goals. It was a funny game, a strange result, but we can only do our jobs and I think the players kept it professional that way and did their best. We're showing great energy at the moment and great enjoyment in our game, and that's important.'

The boss was also quick to try to pick up the man most floored by the champions' display: Arsène Wenger. 'He's a great football man,' said Sir Alex. 'He's done an incredible job for Arsenal for fifteen years; he's given them a quality of football that they've never experienced. He's brought some exciting players to his club and he deserves respect for that, especially from myself.'

Nevertheless, the rare opportunity to savour an eight-goal demolition job of a title rival – regardless of their obvious weakening – could not be passed up by Ashley Young, one of the stars of the show and scorer of his spectacular first United goals.

'We went about our job from the first minute all the way through to the last,' said the winger. 'We were terrific. We found an Arsenal team who weren't so good on the day and we've punished them. You see the way we go forward at pace and we're always looking to create chances from the first minute right to the end. We were terrific, from the goalkeeper to the front man. It was a great team performance and hopefully we can continue that form we've shown so far and take that right the way through the season.'

Young's instant chemistry with leading man Wayne Rooney had been a feature of the Reds' storming start to the campaign, and the winger also took time to salute United's number 10 for his eye-catching treble. 'The boys are delighted for him to get the hat-trick,' he said. 'I think he even wanted to give up the penalty to Giggsy, which just shows what kind of person he is and it was brilliant for him.'

Sir Alex, meanwhile, could only agree. 'He's thriving in his role of leader of the front players,' said the manager. 'Welbeck's young, Hernandez is young, Ashley Young has just joined and Wayne's thriving in the responsibility and I think that's important.'

Rooney's form was merely a continuation of his strong finish to the 2010-11 season, a taxing campaign in which he came close to leaving Old Trafford, before a last-minute about-turn prompted him to sign a new contract – a decision which he continued to reflect on with relief.

'I'm thankful I stayed and signed,' said the striker. 'I said at the time, after I signed my contract, that I had made a mistake. I owed performances and goals to the fans for what happened. For me, it's the best decision I've made in my football career. I am enjoying it and I am in a happy place both on and off the pitch. I am looking forward to every game that comes. I feel good. I think there have been times when I have been more aggressive on the pitch and gone in for silly challenges, but I'm not really doing that any more and I'm feeling more relaxed on the pitch. Sometimes it happens and it's hard to control but, if you stay more controlled, your performances will certainly be better.

'I feel strong and fit. We're playing well and enjoying it as a team. I'm extremely confident in what we do now and I believe I can help us be successful with the players around me. There is a lot of movement and energy – that helps you get in more space and influence the game more. That is what I seem to be doing.'

Rooney was among a clutch of players who ended August away from Carrington, as the season's first competitive international break required a dozen senior figures to report for their respective nations. In their absence, Sir Alex and his coaching staff could gather themselves in the calm, after the storming manner in which the Reds had commenced the campaign proper.

3

September –
And the Beat Goes On

As a new month began, the legacy of August lived on, with Sir Alex Ferguson collecting his 26th Barclays Manager of the Month award in appreciation of United's rip-roaring opening to the campaign. Most of the Reds' playing staff were abroad when their manager received his award, and the gaffer's attentions were unyieldingly centred on how his squad's fitness would bear up during the stresses of international football and its associated globetrotting.

'You've just got to accept it,' he sighed. 'There's nothing you can do about it. Over the last year, we had Paul [Scholes], Gary [Neville], Ryan [Giggs] and Edwin [van der Sar] who had retired from internationals, so we had the benefit of having those players for weekends. Now those players, bar Giggsy, are away from us, so most of the players are going to internationals.

'We have to keep our fingers crossed that they come back healthy. Sometimes we're lucky, sometimes we're not. It's not in our hands. The only benefit is the internationals are now Tuesday fixtures and that gives us an extra day to prepare for weekend games.'

The manager and his coaching staff would have to ready the squad for the perennially taxing trip to Bolton's Reebok Stadium. With United's youthful and unfamiliar back five in his sights, Trotters skipper Kevin Davies gave an insight into his own plans ahead of the game – especially with Phil Jones earning rave reviews.

'I relish these kind of challenges,' said Davies. 'Jones is coming on as a player, but he's still young, so I'll be looking to give him a going-over. There will be a few crosses flying in. I played against him last year. He's a big strong boy, so it's the kind of game I'll look forward to.' The Bolton striker's desire to impose himself on the game would become glaringly evident.

For all the bluster coming from the Reebok Stadium, however, United's cause was aided by a clean bill of health after the international double-header. Most notably, Chicharito picked up some invaluable playing time with Mexico, prompting Sir Alex to beam: 'It's terrific for him. He's ready and has trained very well. The only concern was the rest time he needed after the concussion in the US. Otherwise he was fine. Rio Ferdinand's available, but none of the back four deserve to be dropped, so I don't anticipate many changes in the team.'

The continued absence of Danny Welbeck had propelled Chicharito back into contention for a regular starting berth alongside Wayne Rooney, with whom the Mexican had formed a deadly strike partnership during the 2010-11 season. As such, Rooney was predictably delighted to have the double-act restored.

'He was a young lad in his first season [in 2010-11] and I probably didn't think he was going to play as many games as he did,' said the England striker. 'Once he got into the team, he took his chance and the manager kept him in. He repaid the manager with goals and was brilliant for us last season – a big reason why we won the league.

'I'm looking forward to him doing the same, if not scoring more goals for us, this season. Of course people know about him now but, if you look at all the top players around the world, people know how they play and it's still difficult to stop them. I'm sure people will know a bit more about him this year, but his movement is so good it's difficult to defend against. It won't be easy for players to defend against him whether they know about him or not.

'He's a lovely lad who is great for us around the dressing room. Me and him do a lot of finishing after sessions to try to keep progressing and getting better. It's great to have a lad who has just come into the team, who speaks good English and is always smiling. It's great for him and for me to have someone like that. I think we can both learn from each other.'

In the end, it was Bolton who would be taught a lesson by the Anglo-Mexican axis.

Barclays Premier League

10 September 2011 | Reebok Stadium | Kick-off 17:30 |
Attendance: 25,944

Bolton Wanderers 0
Manchester United 5 (Hernandez 5, 58, Rooney 20, 25, 68)

United's mesmerising start to the season continued with a five-goal stroll at Bolton's Reebok Stadium, as Javier Hernandez struck his first goals of the campaign and Wayne Rooney extended his fine form with a second successive hat-trick. The Reds turned in a devastating showcase of finishing, bagging three goals inside the first half-hour and a further pair after the break, and also demonstrated admirable defensive resolve in the face of a characteristically direct bombardment from the hosts.

The only sour note of the afternoon was a derivative of the Trotters' trademark vigour, as Tom Cleverley left the Reebok Stadium on crutches after a heavy challenge from Bolton skipper Kevin Davies, having apparently suffered a damaged ankle. Cleverley's injury prompted the introduction of Michael Carrick, ringing an early alteration to a side that otherwise featured only two changes to that which obliterated Arsenal, with Chicharito and Rio Ferdinand starting in place of Danny Welbeck and Chris Smalling.

In keeping with their start to the season, the Reds began on the front foot and forged ahead inside five minutes. As a United attack built on the right wing, with Rooney releasing Nani, Chicharito outwitted Gary Cahill by shaping to move to the near post, feinting to the back and then sprinted forward just in time to redirect Nani's centre past the sprawling Jussi Jaaskelainen.

By that point, Cleverley was receiving treatment for an ankle injury after a poor challenge from Davies. Bolton had their best opening of the half while Cleverley was en route to the dressing room, but Rooney was on hand to hack Chris Eagles' volley off the line after a goalmouth scramble. Carrick was duly introduced to restore equality in personnel and wrest back the initiative. United retained it thereafter, with Phil Jones at the heart of a devastating spell for the visitors.

The right-back first arced an unplayable cross into the heart of the Bolton area, where the onrushing Rooney needed only to brush the ball with the studs of his right boot to double United's lead, then ploughed through the Bolton defence five minutes later. Though Jones' shot was well saved by Jaaskelainen, Rooney carefully tucked the rebound between the desperate lunges of Cahill and Dedryck Boyata to heap further misery on the hosts.

The game lulled until half time, but United emerged clearly intent on more goals in the second half. Chicharito duly ensured victory by sliding home from close range after Carrick's shot had rolled through a thicket of bodies, before Nigel Reo-Coker crashed Bolton's best effort against David De Gea's crossbar from 20 yards.

The final word belonged to Rooney, who completed his second successive hat-trick by striding onto Nani's rolled pass and curling an unstoppable shot into Jaaskelainen's bottom right-hand corner.

Another week, another sensational performance. Early days, yes, but caution was becoming harder by the week.

The Teams

Bolton Wanderers: Jaaskelainen; Boyata, Knight, Cahill, Robinson; Eagles (Pratley 62), Reo-Coker, M.Davies, Petrov; K.Davies (Ngog 65), Klasnic (Tuncay 75)
Subs not used: Bogdan, Muamba, Wheater, Kakuta
Booked: K.Davies, M.Davies

Manchester United: De Gea; Jones, Ferdinand, Evans (Smalling 62), Evra; Nani, Cleverley (Carrick 8), Anderson, Young (Giggs 61); Rooney, Hernandez
Subs not used: Lindegaard, Berbatov, Park, Fabio

'When I saw the programme to begin with, I thought it would be tough,' admitted Sir Alex Ferguson, post-match. 'But the boys are coping with it very well.' A perfect record after four games, with 18 goals scored, exceeded all expectations within the United camp.

Certainly, nobody could have budgeted for Wayne Rooney's consecutive hat-tricks. 'It's down to maturity,' said Sir Alex, of a player not only scoring the goals, but pulling the strings in attack. 'He's in his mid-twenties and I always think when players get to this age they get more authority in their game, their timing is better and their control of games is better. His presence is getting bigger in every game. He's looking fantastic.'

The striker attributed his storming start to a rare summer devoid of injury or international commitments. 'I had a long time to rest,' he conceded. 'I wanted a good pre-season under my belt and thankfully I've done that, steered clear of injuries and it's helped me for the start of the season.

'We always know Bolton's a difficult place to come, but we got an early goal and kicked on from there. Thankfully, the win was a bit easier than we thought, but we still had to work hard for it. We controlled the game and I think it could have been a lot more, but obviously I'm delighted to score a hat-trick again. First start with Chicha and we both scored, so it's great.'

Amid the overflowing positives, however, were some important negatives. The cost of the trip to the Reebok Stadium could be counted in the Reds' post-match injuries. Having confirmed that Tom Cleverley would miss at least a month after Kevin Davies' lunging challenge, Sir Alex added: 'Jonny Evans is doubtful for Wednesday [at Benfica] – he got a knee in the hip in the second half which was pretty painful, while Patrice got a kick on the kneecap. We'll have a look at them tomorrow – it's too early to say [how serious the injuries are].'

There was plenty of time, however, for United's youngsters to get giddy about their first collective venture into the Champions League arena, with their Group C opener at Benfica looming large. 'I'm looking forward to it,' enthused Phil Jones. 'It is one of the main reasons why I came to Manchester United – to play Champions League football and test my ability against some of the best players in the world. If I get picked, I'll look forward to the challenge.'

Therein lay a dilemma: persist with the free-flowing youngsters, surfing the crest of a wave, or hand some much-needed playing time to some of the squad's under-utilised, yet vastly more experienced, members.

Though Rio Ferdinand was rested for the trip and remained in Manchester, the travelling party retained a blend of youth and experience – including Evans and Evra, who were both suitably recovered from their knocks to travel. Having touched down in Lisbon, with Portugal amid a heat wave, Sir Alex was playing it cool in his pre-match press conference, claiming: 'I haven't picked my team yet.'

Whichever end of the age scale the manager chose to stock his starting line-up, the subject of much pre-match debate centred around a player in between: Wayne Rooney. Benfica boss Jorge Jesus made no attempt to disguise his admiration for the United striker, purring: 'Rooney is the best British player, but doesn't seem like a British player. He's like an Argentinian or Brazilian. He can decide the match in the final third and so we have to pay special attention to him.'

While Jesus' counterpart remained unconvinced about the South American traits of Rooney's game, Sir Alex was happy to heap further praise on his line-leading sensation. 'I think Wayne is a typical British player,' he said. 'But there have been British players who have great qualities that make them great players. Players like Paul Gascoigne, George Best, Bobby Charlton and Denis Law. The similarities are that the boy has great courage. He wants to play all the time. He has incredible stamina. These are added extras to the talent he has. Pelé was a very aggressive attacker who could look after himself. So can Rooney. There are similarities that way in strength and speed, determination. But he is white, completely white!'

As United prepared to open their European campaign with what appeared to be their toughest group fixture, all eyes were on who would join 'the White Pelé' in the United line-up: the young or the old?

Champions League Group C

14 September 2011 | Estadio da Luz | Kick-off 19:45 |
Attendance: 59,671

Benfica 1 (Cardozo 24)
Manchester United 1 (Giggs 42)

For the first time in 2011-12, United's youngsters stood aside to let some of their senior peers clock up some match time, and it was the Reds' eldest statesman, Ryan Giggs, who made the telling contribution to an entertaining evening in Portugal.

Benfica had moved ahead midway through the first period when Oscar Cardozo latched on to Nicolas Gaitan's pass, turned neatly and rifled a finish on the run past Anders Lindegaard. A baying home support had the Estadio da Luz rocking, but they were quietened by Giggs' stunning leveller: a thunderous 20-yard effort which came at the climax of a trademark surging run from the Welshman.

Giggs, making his first start of the season, headed a long list of changes to the side that had trounced Bolton. Anders Lindegaard, Ji-sung Park, Darren Fletcher, Michael Carrick and Antonio Valencia all enjoyed their first starts of the campaign, which made early signs of ring-rust wholly understandable.

Benfica drove at the visitors from the first whistle, with Gaitan particularly influential, and the Argentine drove one scorching shot narrowly wide before Cardozo tested Lindegaard for the first time with a well-struck shot from the edge of the area. The Paraguayan would not be thwarted shortly afterwards, however, as he controlled Gaitan's incisive diagonal ball, turned sharply away from Jonny Evans and thundered a shot across Lindegaard with his weaker right foot.

Buoyed by their backing, Benfica sought to press home their dominance, but solid, calm defensive work from United repeatedly denied the hosts, and an incisive break yielded parity shortly before the interval, as Valencia fed Giggs, who made straight for goal and crashed home a superb finish.

Suitably lifted by the half-time score, United began the second period in more menacing mood, and both Rooney and Giggs narrowly failed to convert Valencia's drilled cross shortly after the restart.

Despite United's galvanised approach, however, it was the hosts who always looked more likely to pinch a winning goal. Pablo Aimar came close from 25 yards, before Lindegaard contorted brilliantly to plunge to his left and fend away a close-range effort from substitute Nolito. The Dane then tipped away Gaitan's curling shot and, while only a sharp stop from home goalkeeper Artur denied Giggs a late winner, the Reds could reflect on a hard-earned point to start their latest Champions League assault.

The Teams

Benfica: Artur; Maxi Pereira, Garay, Luisao, Emerson; Amorim (Nolito 56), Aimar (Matic 75), Javi Garcia, Witsel, Gaitan (Cesar 90); Cardozo
Subs not used: Eduardo, Rodrigo, Saviola, Jardel
Booked: Aimar, Pereira, Gaitan

Manchester United: Lindegaard; Fabio (Jones 78), Smalling, Evans, Evra; Valencia (Hernandez 69) Fletcher (Nani 69), Carrick, Park; Giggs; Rooney
Subs not used: De Gea, Owen, Anderson, Berbatov
Booked: Rooney, Carrick

'The lads have started the season fantastically and the manager's obviously made a few changes with one eye on the match against Chelsea on Sunday,' said Darren Fletcher, fresh from his first 90-minute senior outing since the final Premier League game of 2010-11. 'I think he said at the beginning of the season that once the Champions League starts everyone would be involved. That's when the squad game comes into play.

'We came for the three points and we're disappointed not to get them. But I think a point, away here against a good Benfica side after going a goal down, is a decent point. We expected Benfica to start quick when we saw the stadium and their passionate fans. Obviously, we went a goal down but we showed good character to respond and we got a foothold in the game.

'After we equalised, I felt we controlled the match without getting the chances our possession deserved. There were a few half-chances here and there, but I felt with our possession that we would go on to get the winner. Unfortunately that didn't happen. That's something we'll need to work on.'

United's tangible reward stemmed from Ryan Giggs' stunning equaliser, a record-breaking goal for the winger-turned-midfielder, who had scored in 16 successive Champions League campaigns, 17 years to the day since his first and second goals in the competition, which came against IFK Gothenburg in 1994.

'Giggsy scored a fantastic goal,' said Fletcher. 'He's an inspiration to all of us. He's got so much experience, he never misses a day's training, he's always in. He was fantastic on the pitch tonight. He just keeps going and getting better and better, which is a credit to him and great for Manchester United.'

The conversely inexperienced Anders Lindegaard had caught the eye in his first European outing for the Reds, and the Danish international revelled in the cauldron of the Estadio da Luz. 'I had great fun and that is the most important part of why I play football,' he smiled. 'I enjoyed it very much and it was a great night. It is a great stadium to play in with a very loud audience. I could also hear our fans, which was nice. This is why I came to United: to play in these kind of games.

'I have said one thousand times before – I am not here to pick my nose. Although I came from a small team in Norway called Aalesunds, I am here because I want to play, not because I want to sit on the bench.'

Sir Alex Ferguson, while full of praise for Lindegaard's display, rejected suggestions that the Dane had played his way ahead of David De Gea for United's next game: the visit of Chelsea.

'David will play on Sunday,' said the boss. 'That was the understanding we had before the Benfica game and it doesn't change.' Days later, as widespread media reports continued to suggest that the Spaniard's United career was already in jeopardy, Sir Alex once more sprang to his stopper's defence.

'There's obviously an agenda on De Gea,' he stated. 'We've experienced that in the press for some reason. They seem desperate for the boy to fail. That's the impression I get and I don't understand it. It's nothing to do with his age. They never did that with [Chelsea's] Petr Cech.

'I think they will all want interviews with him when he's doing well. He doesn't speak English, was looking for a house but has got one now, and is learning to drive in England. He's twenty years of age and doesn't know the culture of the country. I think that's a lot to deal with, but he's shown great composure about the whole thing. He's not got himself flapping about the goalmouth. I think he's absolutely outstanding – the boy is tremendous.

'Anders has done well in the sense that he's bided his time. He's been patient and understands the situation. When we signed him, he knew we were going to sign another keeper. Last January, that was put to him at the time that he would come in next season in a position where he had to challenge for a place. He was happy with that and delighted to join United.

'He showed he's a very good keeper and a good thing about the two of them is their use of the ball is terrific. You've got a sweeper you can play the ball back to all the time, knowing they're going to deliver accurate passes to the back four and midfield and be confident about it. I think it's a fabulous asset in the modern game.'

Looking back, De Gea feels the intense scrutiny under which he was placed merely hastened his adaptation to life with the champions. 'The criticism I received only served to make me a stronger person,' he says. 'It helped me to reflect and think. It encouraged me to keep fighting and work. English football is a little bit more physical and maybe a bit more aggressive. The challenges you face up to are tougher and referees let play go on more here than they do in Spain. The important thing is not to let yourself get down because you can turn it around.'

The forensic tendencies of Britain's media were also being felt by Andre Villas-Boas, newly installed manager of United's next visitors, Chelsea. The Portuguese, just 33 when he took the Stamford Bridge hot-seat, had tackled a sizeable job head-on: looking to overhaul an ageing squad while still delivering the success unyieldingly demanded by Blues owner Roman Abramovich.

Villas-Boas' side had taken ten points from their opening four league games, and had the chance to leapfrog United with victory at Old Trafford. With the league's youngest and oldest managers going head-to-head, the topic of age inevitably cropped up in pre-match debate.

'It's slightly strange, I suppose, seeing managers younger than me,' laughed Ryan Giggs. 'I mean, he's obviously had a successful time at Porto and Pep Guardiola is only forty, so it might be a trend that is starting to happen.' Fronted with the suggestion that Villas-Boas could guide a side of perennial challengers to the title, Sir Alex admitted: 'It will be an incredible achievement. That somebody so young could go and do that would be incredible. You can't dispute that.'

Rio Ferdinand, meanwhile, refused to rule out the chances of Chelsea once again mounting a strong title challenge, having spent almost a decade pushing for domestic rule. 'I'd say they have experienced players in vital areas, which is exactly what you need in a championship-winning team,' said the defender. 'I'd put them side by side with Manchester City. I don't think anybody else is capable of winning the league, but those two are definitely strong enough and it will be a good battle between us all.'

All the more reason, then, to lay down a marker at Old Trafford.

Barclays Premier League

18 September 2011 | Old Trafford | Kick-off 16:00 |
Attendance: 75,455

Manchester United 3 (Smalling 8, Nani 37, Rooney 45)
Chelsea 1 (Torres 46)

A baffling, nerve-shredding game swung the way of the champions as first-half strikes from Chris Smalling, Nani and Wayne Rooney exploited Chelsea's woeful finishing at Old Trafford.

Fernando Torres' neat strike gave the visitors hope, but the Spaniard spurned a glut of chances, including an open goal, in a thrilling encounter in which the momentum fluctuated wildly between two sides devoted only to attacking. United could even afford the luxury of a missed penalty from Rooney and a host of late missed chances en route to chalking up a fifth straight victory in the Barclays Premier League and firmly grasping top spot.

The game began in whirlwind fashion and rarely lulled over the course of the afternoon. David De Gea alertly kicked away Ramires' volley before United forged ahead as Smalling – lurking fractionally offside – powerfully headed home his first league goal for the Reds from Ashley Young's superb free-kick.

Such an early boon seemed to breed overconfidence, however, and United were fortunate to escape with their lead intact when Torres slid off-target after being presented with the ball by Anderson, and then De Gea flung himself to prevent Ramires from tapping home a simple finish.

United needed a second goal as Andre Villas-Boas' side continued to jostle for a route back into the game. Nani duly provided it, and in sensational fashion. The Portuguese collected Jonny Evans' diagonal pass, skipped away from Juan Mata and cracked an unstoppable, 30-yard effort high past the motionless Petr Cech.

The momentum returned to the hosts, who established an even healthier lead in the final moments of the first period. A rampaging run from Phil Jones caused panic in the Chelsea area and, when the ball ricocheted off Nani, Rooney was on-hand to casually slot home a simple finish and send Old Trafford wild once again.

Yet, as the first 45 minutes had shown, the game could easily swing back and forth. Under a minute of the second period had passed when Nicolas Anelka, on as a substitute, threaded a sublime ball into the path of Torres, who scooped an impish finish over De Gea. Game on.

The outcome could have been put beyond doubt when Nani was bundled over by Jose Bosingwa as he tried to follow up his initial effort, which had thudded against Cech's bar. In scenes reminiscent of John Terry's infamous Moscow miss, however, Rooney lost his footing and sent his spot-kick horribly off-target.

Rooney then skewed another shot against the post, while Chicharito was heavily challenged by Ashley Cole in the ensuing mêlée. The England defender escaped serious punishment, with neither another penalty nor a red card dished out – instead Cole was booked. At the other end, Torres lashed over after his initial shot had been beaten out by De Gea, then rounded the United stopper with seven minutes left, but inexplicably shot wide of the empty net with his left foot.

That miss sucked all the remaining fight from the visitors, who might have conceded again in injury time as Rooney and Dimitar Berbatov broke together, but the Bulgarian's strike was cleared off the line by Cole in a fittingly breathless end to a dizzying day's entertainment.

The Teams

Manchester United: De Gea; Smalling (Valencia 62), Evans, Jones, Evra; Nani, Fletcher, Anderson (Carrick 63), Young; Rooney, Hernandez (Berbatov 79)
Subs not used: Lindegaard, Giggs, Park, Fabio
Booked: Fletcher, Valencia

Chelsea: Cech; Bosingwa, Ivanovic, Terry, Cole; Ramires, Lampard (Anelka 46), Meireles (Mikel 79); Sturridge (Lukaku 68), Mata; Torres
Subs not used: Turnbull, Romeu, Malouda, Luiz
Booked: Ramires, Cole, Terry

A mood of confusion gripped the tunnel after a discombobulating game. Delight at victory was tempered by the nerve-jangling manner of its attainment, while Sir Alex openly rued Ashley Cole's reckless challenge on Chicharito.

'To me, it was a shocking tackle,' complained the boss. 'An absolutely shocking tackle. The referee's booked him and, if he's booked him, I don't know why it wasn't a penalty. I must ask him [referee Phil Dowd]. We don't know how Hernandez will be. We're going to have to wait until the morning but, at the moment, his leg is very numb. He's hardly got any feeling in it so he could be out for a couple of weeks.'

The boss also confirmed that goalscorer Chris Smalling had suffered a groin strain, but looked past the potential ramifications for his forthcoming selections by reflecting on a curious victory. 'I think for the neutral it was a fantastic, open match,' he said. 'It was strange because games against Chelsea over the years have always been tight affairs. This was a very, very open match.

'Some of our football was terrific at times. But I thought we created our own problems for ourselves by giving the ball away so many times in attacking areas and they kept counter-attacking against us. In the first half they could have scored two or three.'

That guarded assessment was mirrored by Patrice Evra, who continued to stand in as skipper in the absence of Nemanja Vidic. The Frenchman lamented: 'Maybe for the first time, we didn't control all the game. Five wins is a good start, but I always want more. I'm happy to win but I hope in the next league game, against Stoke, we create more and not try to rush things. I think we tried to rush things and gave the ball away too easily. It's why I'm not so happy. I'm happy because there are a lot of positive things and we scored three times against Chelsea but, if we want to win the league and win every game, we have to perform better than on Sunday.

'We were lucky to be in front three-nil at half time, so I said to the players: "Forget the first half and try to play like a team in the second half." It was like a boxing fight, I give you and you give me back. I have a lot of respect for Chelsea. People talk about City and us, but I always say Chelsea are our most difficult opponents, as you can see. They didn't come here just to defend, but they attacked and looked to score goals and create chances. I couldn't believe the goal didn't go in from Fernando Torres. Maybe God was with us.'

If United needed time to regroup after such a taxing success, the resumption of the Carling Cup and its associated squad rotation meant that the majority of the Reds' first-team squad could enjoy a midweek break. For those selected, however, the hostile hotbed of Elland Road awaited. Pitted against Leeds United in a cup competition for the second time in three seasons, United had the chance to avenge their 2010 FA Cup third round humbling at the hands of the Whites, then of League One.

'That was a bad day for us,' winced Michael Carrick. 'But that's gone now. We're looking forward to going there this time. I'm guessing it will be a full house. It will be a nice hot atmosphere.'

With the squad so shorn of fit defenders, Carrick's cool head and versatility would prove useful. Sir Alex admitted he was pondering how best to approach his team selection – especially with the ever-tough Premier League trip to Stoke coming hot on the heels of the Elland Road flashback. 'There'll be a sprinkling of experience,' hinted the manager. 'But the area of worry for me will be picking a back four, because we've still got Vidic and Rafael injured. I'm not well off for defenders and there are players who could have helped who are out on loan. But that's part of it and I'll hopefully pick the right team.'

Carling Cup third round

**20 September 2011 | Elland Road | Kick-off 20:00 |
Attendance: 31,031**

**Leeds United 0
Manchester United 3** (Owen 15, 32, Giggs 45)

In a one-sided war of the Roses, Leeds wilted as Sir Alex Ferguson's much-changed side strolled to a comprehensive victory in the Elland Road cauldron. The Reds were home and hosed by half time, as a clinical pair from Michael Owen was capped by a solo effort from

Ryan Giggs just before the interval. Leeds, for their part, rarely threatened in a one-sided victory for the visitors.

That it was achieved with a dramatically reshuffled pack spoke volumes for the resources at Sir Alex's disposal. Michael Carrick joined debutant Zeki Fryers at centre-back, with Antonio Valencia and Fabio at full-back. A front six of Giggs, Kiko Macheda, Ji-sung Park, Mame Diouf, Dimitar Berbatov and Owen operated in two banks of three and never gave the hosts any respite.

Nevertheless, the rotated Reds had to survive an early scare as Tom Lees' powerful header was blocked by Berbatov, Ben Amos repelled the defender's follow-up and Berbatov was again on hand to thwart Ross McCormack's attempts to turn in the loose ball.

That was as good as it got for Simon Grayson's side, and United's growing authority quickly yielded a lead. Berbatov slid an inch-perfect pass into the path of Park, who fed Owen. The striker controlled with his right foot, then rolled a neat finish in between Aidan White's legs and into the bottom corner, via the base of Andy Lonergan's left-hand post.

The veteran striker was soon at it again, taking a pass from Diouf in his stride before rifling an unstoppable finish into Lonergan's top corner with hardly any backlift. For all the scrutiny afforded to his shock signing in 2009, Owen continued to demonstrate his predatory instincts whenever given the chance.

He and United were suddenly rampant. Valencia slid an effort horribly wide from the six-yard box, but a third goal finally arrived when Giggs took a short corner to Park, received the ball back and nutmegged Snodgrass, before advancing into the box and stabbing a finish which nicked Luciano Becchio's shin on its way past Lonergan.

That was Giggs' final act, and he made way for Paul Pogba during the interval. The French midfielder entered the fray for his Reds debut, as did fellow substitute Larnell Cole during the second period. Their cameos provided warming highlights of a second half coldly killed off by the Premier League champions.

The Teams

Leeds United: Lonergan; Lees, White, O'Dea, Bromby; Howson,
Clayton, Snodgrass, Keogh (Vayrynen 52); McCormack (Nunez 66),
Becchio (Forssell 52)
Subs not used: Rachubka, O'Brien, Brown, Taylor
Booked: O'Dea, Snodgrass

Manchester United: Amos; Valencia, Carrick, Fryers, Fabio; Diouf
(Welbeck 70), Giggs (Pogba 46), Park; Macheda (Cole 77),
Berbatov, Owen
Subs not used: De Gea, Brown, W.Keane, Thorpe
Booked: Diouf, Fabio

Upon picking up his Man of the Match award from Sky Sports, two-goal hero Michael Owen conceded that he was obliged to deliver the goods whenever selected. 'The pressure's on,' said the striker. 'You don't get many chances and when you do get a chance, you have to perform because it's going to be a couple of months before you see a pitch again. It's nice to prove to yourself and everyone that you can still contribute, still play well. It's always nice to score, obviously, that's what my game has been about all over the years. I also try to contribute in other areas as well and I was pleased to get the goals.

'At thirty-one I've still got a few years left in me. There are different roles you have throughout your career, and at the minute I'm doing that. I'm comfortable and trying to be a bit of an example to young kids to help them through. We're coming into a good part of the season now, with the games coming thick and fast, so hopefully the games will be shared round a bit.'

As ever, the Carling Cup's provision of a platform for the younger players had provided an engaging subplot to the game, and Zeki Fryers, Paul Pogba and Larnell Cole all picked up invaluable experience on their Reds debuts.

'It was a massive night for me,' grinned Fryers, conducting his first senior interview while United's locked-in away support provided an overpowering background din. 'It was quality and a massive step up, so I was happy to get eighty minutes in. I had to come off with a bit of cramp, so now it's all about working hard with the Reserves and getting fitter so that I'm ready for whenever these chances might come again. It was good to have Larnell and Pogba alongside me when they came on. We have been playing together for a long time, so this was massive for all of us.'

Fryers' late withdrawal with cramp facilitated an unlikely switch to defensive duties for Dimitar Berbatov, who joined Michael Carrick and Antonio Valencia in moonlighting at the back. According to Owen, though, the Bulgarian was hardly a novice in the role.

'He does it all the time in training, so we know he's capable of it,' said the striker. 'He thinks he can play centre-half, so he was probably first to lift his hand when we lost Zeki. It was no surprise to see Berba at the back! Fair play to Zeki, though, I thought he was fantastic. He put in a great performance and he should be delighted with himself.'

Though the Manchester-born youngster had grabbed his chance in the limelight, Sir Alex Ferguson was eager to have an altogether more experienced defender available for his side's trip to Stoke City. Having withstood an aerial assault at the Reebok Stadium a fortnight earlier, the Reds knew the importance of being able to compete physically with imposing opponents.

'I'm hoping Rio will be okay for Saturday,' said the manager. 'When you go to Stoke you need a bit of experience. Rio came into the team when we played at Bolton and gave us that experience, so we hope he'll be fit for Saturday.'

Chris Smalling remained a doubt, however, while the champions' preparations were also hampered by a tight hamstring for Wayne Rooney. When Jonny Evans sustained an ankle injury in training, the Reds' hopes of extending their perfect Premier League record against the Potters looked an increasingly tall order.

Only Chicharito's sharpish recovery from the leg injury he suffered against Chelsea provided any relief. Just as the Carrington treatment room began to fill, ex-Red Owen Hargreaves publicly questioned the treatment he had received during his injury-hit time at Old Trafford. United's response was brisk, insisting in a club statement that there was no validity in the Manchester City midfielder's comments.

Sir Alex, meanwhile, was similarly defiant in his response, declaring: 'As far as I'm concerned, my medical staff are one of the main reasons Manchester United has been so successful. We've got fantastic medical staff and great sports scientists. Do you think we'd be successful if we didn't have an operation that wasn't a hundred percent and handled absolutely brilliantly? The doctor and his five physios and sports science guys are fantastic. That's my opinion on Manchester United and that's more important than what anyone else has got to say about it.'

The boss also sought to share his opinion on Stoke City, who welcomed United to the Britannia Stadium after earning an impressive draw in their Europa League visit to Dynamo Kiev, a result that illustrated their evolution under Tony Pulis.

'You can see the progress the team is making,' said the manager. 'They've signed two or three players, they're playing European football and they're having a right go. They have a great attitude in their team and their support is brilliant. I've never criticised it [Stoke's style of play]. I think everyone plays to their strengths and that's what they do. There's absolutely nothing wrong with that. I see Stoke becoming quite an important side. The progress they have made over the last few years is phenomenal.'

Barclays Premier League

24 September 2011 | Britannia Stadium | Kick-off 17:30 |
Attendance: 27,582

Stoke City 1 (Crouch 52)
Manchester United 1 (Nani 27)

United's lightning start to the defence of their title slowed for the first time, as Stoke City pegged the champions back in a gritty draw at the Britannia Stadium. Nani's superb first-half opener gave an injury-hit Reds side a lead that was preserved by heroics from David De Gea, before Peter Crouch levelled matters shortly after the interval with his first goal for the Potters.

United's cause was hardly helped by the loss of Jonny Evans and Javier Hernandez to injury, during the warm-up and in the third minute respectively, while referee Peter Walton twice ignored strong penalty claims from the visitors. The loss of Evans to a foot injury in the warm-up prompted a reshuffle for Sir Alex Ferguson, with Phil Jones alongside Rio Ferdinand at centre-back and Antonio Valencia in at right-back, while Dimitar Berbatov replaced the injured Wayne Rooney up front.

The champions were baying for a spot-kick in the third minute, when Darren Fletcher's pass was deflected in behind the Stoke defence. Chicharito raced onto the loose ball and was bundled to the ground by Jonathan Woodgate. Although the defender made scarcely detectable contact with the ball, referee Walton declined to award the penalty and Chicharito, who had collided heavily with Potters goalkeeper Asmir Begovic after the challenge, had to be replaced by Michael Owen.

The two sides postured without the deadlock seeming to be under threat, until an act of brilliance from Nani shattered it. Just in from the right flank, the Portuguese sized up his options, swapped passes with Fletcher, meandered into a packed penalty area and squeezed a low, left-footed shot underneath the challenge of Ryan Shawcross and just inside Begovic's left-hand post.

In the face of a defiant response from the hosts, De Gea sprung to the fore with two world-class saves: firstly to instinctively fling up an arm and turn Andy Wilkinson's rocket onto the crossbar, then to plunge to his right and turn Jonathan Walters' powerful effort past the post with his fingertips.

Stoke were pushing for parity and, in the early stages of the second half, it arrived. Matthew Etherington swung in a tantalising corner, and the onrushing Crouch stole between Ferdinand and Jones to power a header past De Gea.

The duel between United's goalkeeper and Stoke's star signing continued apace. Ferdinand missed a lofted ball, leaving Crouch through on goal, but De Gea was off his line sharply to deflect the striker's shot over the bar. Before long, the Spaniard had to clear the ball from Crouch's feet as Stoke pressed. De Gea then beat away a ferocious free-kick from Marc Wilson, before United were denied what looked to be a clear penalty.

A breakaway culminated in Ashley Young's shot being parried out by Begovic. The winger headed the rebound across to Patrice Evra, whose goal-bound shot struck Shawcross' raised arm inside the area. But no penalty was given.

Crouch passed up two more openings, heading wide and then dragging a close-range shot off-target, but the clearest opening of the dying stages fell to substitute Ryan Giggs in injury time. Nani's superb floated cross begged for a back-post conversion, but the veteran could only skew his close-range volley past the gaping goal. Any frustration at that missed opportunity, however, could make way for a sense of satisfaction at having taken tangible reward from one of the most inhospitable away fixtures of the season.

The Teams

Stoke City: Begovic; Wilkinson (Huth 83), Woodgate, Shawcross, Wilson; Pennant (Jerome 89), Delap (Whitehead 85), Whelan, Etherington; Walters, Crouch
Subs not used: Sorensen, Upson, Palacios, Shotton
Booked: Whelan

Manchester United: De Gea; Valencia, Jones, Ferdinand, Evra; Nani, Fletcher, Anderson, Young (Welbeck 70); Hernandez (Owen 11), Berbatov (Giggs 70)
Subs not used: Lindegaard, Park, Fabio, Macheda

Though the champions' winning start had been curtailed, Patrice Evra was unmoved by the concession of two points. 'I will be honest, it was a good point,' said the Frenchman. 'It is really difficult to go to Stoke and get three points. Big teams come here and only get a point. It was not an easy game and it finished with a draw. We are disappointed because we conceded a goal from a set piece, but after the game you feel strong. The boss told us he needed men before the game and I think all the lads showed character and personality. It was a shame we didn't win the game, but it is not easy to play at Stoke.'

Both Evra and his manager went on to celebrate the contribution of David De Gea, who embossed a commanding display with a string of top-drawer saves. 'I think David is doing really well and his confidence is growing,' Evra observed. 'You can see how all of the players are happy for him when he makes a great save. We support him. That is United. He had a difficult start, but if you saw the game against Chelsea, you'll know he made some great saves, and he made some more against Stoke. I'm really confident with him and you know he gets a lot of support from the players and the manager. He can be one of the best.'

'He had a couple of great saves in the first half and looked very confident,' added the boss. 'He has terrific composure, nothing disturbs him. He just sailed through the game.'

The Spaniard's first shot at Champions League football would be his reward, with Basel returning to Old Trafford for their second visit. The Swiss champions had visited M16 just once before, on a poignant night for Darren Fletcher.

The Scot, who made his senior bow against Basel in 2003, admitted: 'It does bring back memories of making my debut in the Champions League, which I was very fortunate to do. I just remember thinking about all the people who'd had a massive influence on me getting to that point in my career – school teachers, coaches, parents, family, all the coaches at United, the manager – people who had put in a lot of work and effort to help me. Then you've got all the pressure of playing for United and the fact you're desperate to do well. Sometimes that can be a hindrance and I remember a lot of the experienced lads telling me just to play my own game.'

Now among the squad's elders, Fletcher would be dispensing the advice as Sir Alex sought to introduce some of his younger players to the rigours of Champions League football. 'Maybe I'll use some of them against Basel,' confirmed the manager. 'I do need to get all the squad moving. I think there will be changes on Tuesday.

'I think we got a positive result against Benfica. Hopefully, we can strengthen our position. Basel are a decent side, though. Thorsten Fink [manager of the Swiss champions] was a substitute in the final for Bayern Munich in 1999 when he came on for Lothar Matthäus. I spoke to him at the UEFA conference and he's done a good job.

'If you get to ten points, you know you're into the next stage, but we'd like to win the group anyway. If we win our next three games, we can utilise the squad. It would definitely help and we've done that over the years. It's sometimes backfired – I played a fresh team over in Fenerbahce [in 2004] and they beat us three-nil. Although I want to make changes, I don't want an embarrassment. So changes have got to be made with a mind of still winning the game.'

Ashley Young headed a list of Champions League greenhorns aiming to make their mark on a competition his manager termed 'the best in the world'. The winger joined Sir Alex for the pre-match press conference at Old Trafford, and told the assembled media: 'When you come to a club like Manchester United, you are going to be challenged. I am definitely someone who wants to challenge myself at the top level and being able to play in the big competitions at club level is every boy's dream.

'I'm looking forward to playing in the Champions League. We know it is going to be a tough game, but I'm sure if we impose ourselves on the game as we have done in every other game this season we'll get the three points. Hopefully I'll be selected and can play a part in the game.'

He was, and he did – though hardly in a capacity anybody would have envisaged beforehand.

UEFA Champions League Group C

27 September 2011 | Old Trafford | Kick-off 19:45 |
Attendance: 73,115

Manchester United 3 (Welbeck 16, 17, Young 90)
FC Basel 3 (F.Frei 58, A.Frei 60, 76 (pen))

If any reminder was required about the unforgiving nature of the Champions League, the frantic salvaging of a point against unfancied Swiss champions Basel provided it.

Having established a two-goal lead inside 20 minutes through Danny Welbeck's quickfire brace, United reached and passed the interval in relative comfort, surviving a clutch of missed chances from the visitors. In a madcap 18-minute spell, however, Basel were suddenly level, then closing in on a stunning victory after the conversion of a controversial late penalty. The shock startled United back into life, and the Reds' trademark spirit and resolve shone through as Ashley Young headed a last-minute leveller, before both Welbeck and substitute Dimitar Berbatov came close to snatching victory.

It was a breathless end to a game that began promisingly. Basel served notice of their attacking intentions when midfielder Fabian Frei blazed off-target after striding through on goal, but close calls for Antonio Valencia and Young warned the visitors of United's intent. Before long, the Reds broke the deadlock.

Fabio burst into the Basel area and squared for Ryan Giggs, who in turn teed up Welbeck. The striker's first-time effort was only half-hit, but the shot contained sufficient power to dribble goalwards and spin inside Yann Sommer's left-hand post.

Welbeck had barely finished celebrating his first Champions League goal, when his second arrived – in far crisper style. Giggs was again the architect, spotting the striker in space at the back post and finding him with a perfect, low pass, which was promptly side-footed home with minimal fuss.

The quickfire burst perhaps worked to United's detriment, as operating with an early cushion appeared to blunt the hosts' early edge. Basel's failure to convert presentable chances for Alexander Frei and Jacques Zoua meant slack defensive play went unpunished before the break, but that changed just before the hour mark.

David De Gea, fresh from brilliantly turning Marco Streller's close-range effort to safety with his outstretched leg, parried away the striker's near-post header from the subsequent corner, but was helpless to prevent Fabian Frei from lashing home the rebound. Two minutes later, the Spaniard was left exposed as the goalscorer curled in a marvellous cross, which Alexander Frei emphatically headed home.

With Old Trafford stunned and the Reds reeling, events took a further twist when referee Paolo Tagliavento penalised Valencia for a tangle with Streller from which the Ecuadorian emerged with the ball. When Alexander Frei hammered home the spot-kick, United suddenly reverted to type: pressed by the need to chase a seemingly lost cause at the Stretford End.

Welbeck came close to equalising when he narrowly missed Nani's right-wing cross, but Young went one better in the final minute, clinically nodding the Portuguese's deep centre inside Sommer's near post in the final minute of normal time.

In keeping with the previous 90 minutes, injury time managed to serve up further drama. Welbeck headed narrowly wide and substitute Berbatov hammered a shot into the side netting, while Aleksander Dragovic's gargantuan clearance bounced just wide of De Gea's goal. While the points were shared, the relief was monopolised by the hosts.

The Teams

Manchester United: De Gea; Fabio (Nani 70), Jones, Ferdinand, Evra; Valencia, Carrick, Anderson (Berbatov 82), Giggs (Park 61), Young; Welbeck
Subs not used: Lindegaard, Owen, Fletcher, Diouf

FC Basel: Sommer; Park, Dragovic, Abraham, Steinhofer; F.Frei
(Chipperfield 77), Cabral, G.Xhaka, Zoua; A.Frei (T.Xhaka 89),
Streller (Pak 81)
Subs not used: Colomba, Ajeti, Schurpf, Kovac
Booked: G.Xhaka, A.Frei

'We said at half time that the game wasn't over,' shrugged a stunned
Michael Carrick. 'It was a bit of a shock to find ourselves three-two
down after being two-nil up. We've no excuses – we threw it away.
It's not like us at all, but what we expect of ourselves really is to keep
going. We believe that if we get a chance, we'll score. Thankfully,
Ashley Young put it away and we might even have nicked a win in
the end when Berba had half a chance. But that was probably asking
too much.

'It's not the end of the world, but it's not ideal either. We've
given ourselves a lot of hard work, but we're capable of doing it. We
were looking to win those two Galati games anyway, so if we can
approach them as we normally do then we're confident we can pull
through. Tonight we'll take a draw yet it still feels a bit like a defeat.
But we'll not get too down about it; we'll move on and bounce back.
We have to.'

For Danny Welbeck, scoring his first European goals in a shock
concession of points represented an evening of mixed emotions. 'To
get two goals in the Champions League, I'm over the moon with
that,' said the striker. 'But it's a team game and I'm disappointed.

'Manchester United should be finishing teams off. In the second
half, we didn't start as brightly as we should have. They gradually
worked their way into the game and pulled two goals back quickly.
They played it from the back well and we found it difficult. We're
really disappointed with the result today, but we just have to get back
into training and get on with it.'

For Patrice Evra, there was concern to be found in the manner
with which United fell apart before Young's late salvage act. 'We have
to press more like we did in the first few games and not let other

teams have time to play,' said the Frenchman. 'When they come to Old Trafford they have to be scared and know they will not enjoy their football and they will find it hard.

'It's not difficult to get the balance right. None of our games have been easy, but we made them look easy at the beginning of the season because we worked hard, we were compact and everything about our shape was right. I think if we just go back to that we're going to resolve the problem. It's not a disaster; it's just a good warning and a wake-up call. We are beautiful when we make the game easy, but we can be ugly if we don't make the effort and do what we need to do!'

Having dished out plenty of lessons in the opening weeks of the campaign, it was time for the Reds to show over the coming months that they could also take heed of warnings.

United States: The Reds pose for a squad picture in New York, amid a gruelling three-week pre-season tour.

Rafael, Fabio and Mame Biram Diouf enjoy a day off at Seattle's Pike Place Market, hurling fish from stall to stall in traditional fashion.

Paul Scholes takes to the field for his testimonial against New York Cosmos, shortly before opening the scoring with a trademark blockbuster.

Nani completes a delightful move to draw United level with Manchester City, and later caps the comeback with an injury-time Wembley winner in the Community Shield.

On his long-awaited Premier League bow for the Reds, Tom Cleverley excels in midfield as United make a winning start to the season at West Brom.

Sorry about that: Hat-trick hero Wayne Rooney offers Wojciech Szczesny a smile and a handshake after United's 8-2 rout of Arsenal.

Ryan Giggs hits home the equaliser to ensure a solid start to the Reds' Champions League campaign at Benfica. It was the 16th successive season he had scored a goal in the tournament.

Chris Smalling scores his first league goal for United in the 3-1 thriller against Chelsea in September.

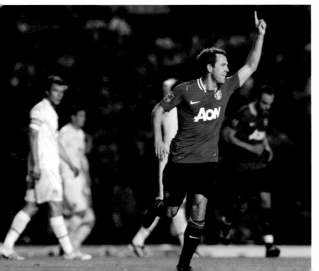

Arch poacher Michael Owen celebrates his first start of the season with a brace, as Leeds are routinely bypassed in the Carling Cup at Elland Road.

Danny Welbeck opens his European account and sets the Reds on their way against Basel, but the Swiss champions fight back in a thrilling encounter.

A dramatic denouement at Anfield, as substitute Chicharito heads a late leveller to give United a share of the spoils.

A dark day: Jonny Evans is red-carded during the Manchester derby; after which City run amok and notch up a 6-1 win on a dismal afternoon for the Reds.

Below the club's lasting tribute to him, Sir Alex Ferguson celebrates 25
years in charge of United with a narrow win over Sunderland.

United's post-derby recovery gathers momentum, as Chicharito's solitary strike posts
an invaluable win at Swansea's Liberty Stadium.

Rio Ferdinand protests against the award of a penalty that gave Newcastle United an equaliser, as United squander a succession of chances to drop two points.

The players line up to pay their respects to the late Gary Speed, ahead of a narrow, but important victory at Villa Park.

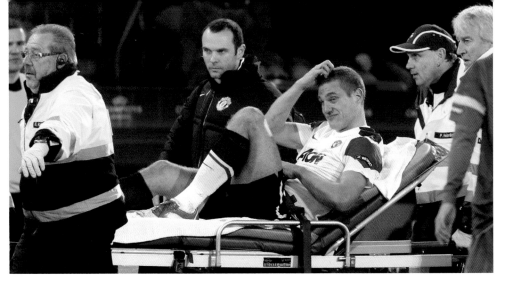

Nemanja Vidic is stretchered from the field with cruciate knee ligament damage, during the Reds' shock Champions League exit at Basel.

Having scored an impressive brace, Nani looks to the heavens during United's win over Wolves on 10 December.

Michael Carrick scores a rare, but superbly taken, goal against Queens Park Rangers at Loftus Road.

Danny Welbeck, Nani and Phil Jones pose for photos during the squad's annual gift-bearing Christmas visit to the Royal Manchester Children's Hospital.

Antonio Valencia flashes a smile after smashing home United's fourth goal in a 5-0 romp over his former side, Wigan Athletic.

Sir Alex laments a missed opportunity on his 70th birthday, as the Reds slip to a shock defeat to bottom-placed Blackburn at Old Trafford.

4

October –
The Dark Before the Dawn

After an adrenaline-fuelled August and September, the season was beginning to settle down into a truer rhythm as October arrived. The manner of United's see-saw draw with Basel had underlined the trade-off for playing with youthful verve: inexperience and occasional rashness could occasionally lead to the side being exposed at the top level. Whether those lessons had been learned would be tested by Norwich City, acquitting themselves impressively despite being freshly promoted from the Championship.

Helmed by Paul Lambert – another Glaswegian manager in the Premier League – the Canaries had lost just twice in their opening six league matches, and arrived at Old Trafford on the back of successive wins over Bolton Wanderers and Sunderland. Though Norwich failed to equal the pre-match billing of Tottenham, Arsenal and Chelsea – all beaten in M16 already – on-song midfielder Anderson warned that United had to be ready for all-comers, even as they stood on the brink of a potential Premier League record 19th successive home victory.

'It doesn't matter who you play in the league, you always have to play well,' said the Brazilian. 'I haven't seen much of Norwich, but I know they are a strong team who will come here and battle. Whenever you play at home you have to perform and we are always confident at Old Trafford in front of our fans. It's important to be strong at home and our record has been amazing for a long time now. You feel more relaxed, more comfortable when you're at home and you have that extra spring in your step. It's important we show that on Saturday and keep our good run going.'

Barclays Premier League

1 October 2011 | Old Trafford | Kick-off 15:00 |
Attendance: 75,514

Manchester United 2 (Anderson 68, Welbeck 87)
Norwich City 0

United were made to sweat for victory in the unseasonable October warmth, but second-half goals from Anderson and Danny Welbeck gave the Reds a hard-earned victory over an impressive Norwich City side.

Paul Lambert's team not only showed enough defensive resolve to provoke a jittery atmosphere inside Old Trafford, they also provided plenty of scares at the other end, where wasteful finishing and the efforts of Reds goalkeeper Anders Lindegaard somehow contrived to give the hosts a clean sheet. The Canaries' wastefulness was punished by Anderson's close-range header with 22 minutes remaining, before substitute Welbeck reached Ji-sung Park's pull-back to slide home a late clincher.

It was the visitors who made the brighter start, as Bradley Johnson charitably returned a weak shot when Lindegaard had fluffed his clearance, before Phil Jones crucially snuffed out the danger posed by Elliott Bennett's surging run. As United continued to toil in the sunshine, the troublesome Steve Morison evaded Jonny Evans with his chest control and pulled his finish wide.

In time, the champions began to get to grips with the challenge they faced. Marc Tierney volleyed away when Darren Fletcher flicked a Nani corner goalwards, Wayne Rooney headed another Nani corner off target and the Portuguese rounded off a lacklustre half for United by firing well wide from distance.

The Reds upped the ante after the break with spells of sustained pressure, but the visitors had clearly readied themselves for counter-attacking bursts and it took fine last-ditch interventions from Jones and Lindegaard to deny Morison and Anthony Pilkington respectively. Then followed the game's decisive period.

Antonio Valencia, again operating as a makeshift right-back, showed his unfamiliarity in the role by dwelling in possession, allowing Pilkington to nick the ball and bear down on Lindegaard before inexplicably side-footing his effort past the far post. Within three minutes, United were ahead.

Ryan Giggs, part of a double substitution with Welbeck, took a deep corner from the left that was headed around the area, helped on by Jones and then Rooney, before the unmarked Anderson took advantage of lax marking to nod past John Ruddy from close range.

Despite the breakthrough, Norwich remained undeterred. Pilkington again caused panic in the United box when his left-footed shot deflected off Anderson's shoulder, looped against the inside of Lindegaard's post and rebounded into the grateful Dane's arms. It took a second goal finally to kill off the visitors' challenge, and it was provided by substitute Welbeck, who played in Park and met the South Korean's unselfish return with a close-range finish at the Stretford End.

The Teams

Manchester United: Lindegaard; Valencia, Evans, Jones, Evra; Nani (Giggs 64), Fletcher, Anderson (Ferdinand 76), Park; Rooney, Hernandez (Welbeck 65)

Subs not used: De Gea, Owen, Berbatov, Carrick
Booked: Welbeck

Norwich City: Ruddy; Martin, Naughton, Barnett, Tierney; Pilkington, Hoolahan (C.Martin 85), Bennett (Crofts 74), Fox (Jackson 74), Johnson; Morison
Subs not used: Rudd, Drury, Holt, Surman

'You don't expect Ando to score with a header, do you?' grinned Sir Alex. 'But you take a goal from anyone. You couldn't say that was a good performance, but it was gritty and determined as we always are and we never give in, which is a fantastic quality. Our home record has been fantastic over the last year. Only the draw against West Brom [in October 2010] has spoiled it a bit. It would have been a really fantastic record otherwise. We still remain undefeated at home in the league [since Chelsea's 2-1 win in April 2010].'

For Phil Jones, the manner with which the dogged visitors were gradually ground down provided evidence of welcome substance to complement the Reds' unquestioned style. 'It was a difficult game,' the defender conceded. 'Norwich came here with a game-plan and stuck to it. It made it difficult for us to break them down, but we showed signs of champions in getting two goals late on.

'As champions, fans expect you to turn up and be the best every week, but we know football isn't like that and it was proved today. Norwich's game-plan worked well for them before we broke them down in the end. They made it difficult and we had to be patient; that's what the manager said at half time: move the ball quicker, but be patient.

'They're dangerous with a few good players up front who are sharp and lively. We had to watch out for that – perhaps I was needed too many times, when I wasn't expected to be, but that's what I'm there for. It's been difficult, not having a settled back four all season, but all the lads are capable of switching around and it again shows the sign of champions, coming into positions and still proving you're good enough.'

Despite his absence from the victory over the Canaries, Tom Cleverley's early input had been one of the talking points of the season to date, and United moved quickly to secure the midfielder's long-term future at Old Trafford, despite his ongoing injury-enforced absence.

Upon announcing the midfielder's new, four-year extension, Sir Alex declared: 'Tom is one of the brightest prospects in the English game. For a young boy, he has a good footballing brain which, when coupled with his energy and ability, makes for a player with a fine future ahead of him. It's the United way to encourage our young players to make their mark in the first team and Tom has grabbed that chance with both hands.'

'I was due to be out of contract at the end of the season,' reflects Cleverley. 'I had a good start to the season and I wanted to commit my future to the club. I've been here a long time and finally getting into the first team has been like a dream come true for me. I was happy to commit myself and hopefully I'll be here for many more years to come – hopefully I can go on as long as Giggsy!'

In the same week that United assured themselves of the services of Cleverley for the foreseeable future, the man at the uppermost end of the age scale on the Reds' playing staff, Ryan Giggs, briefly jetted off to Monaco to be presented with the Golden Foot, an award for players over the age of 29 who are recognised with a footprint on Monte Carlo's 'Champions Promenade'.

Upon collecting his prize, the veteran winger quickly paid tribute to the man who had overseen his entire time at the club. 'I've been fortunate to play for the greatest manager,' he said. 'He's hard but fair. He demands a lot from his players as he does from himself. He is the best manager and it's great to have had him there throughout my career.

'It's a great honour to win such an award and to have my footprints alongside some of the greatest football players is a real privilege. I have been fortunate to play alongside great players, play for the greatest manager and play for the best club in the world. At the moment I am still enjoying my football, so I have not thought about what I will do when I finish, but if it all finished tomorrow I could say that I have had a fantastic career and wouldn't swap it with anybody.'

Giggs was among a host of players who briefly took leave of Manchester after the win over Norwich, with the vast majority bound for international duty, with some key Euro 2012 qualifying matters to settle. Not in their midst were Anders Lindegaard and Jonny Evans, who both remained at Carrington for treatment on injuries sustained against the Canaries. Free time is a rare luxury amid the pressures of the football season, but for a number of the United squad, welcome relaxation can be sought in another sport: golf.

'In my spare time, when the weather's good I like to try to play golf,' says Evans. 'Not as much as I can, because obviously you've got to be wary of taking too much out of yourself, but especially when the weather's nice, a good game of golf is enjoyable. Most of the time a few of the lads get together, which is handy because we all know not to take it too mad and make sure we don't tire ourselves out.

'I think I'm up there, I have to say, out of the lads! Michael Carrick's decent. I've only seen Giggsy once or twice so I can't judge him. I did play with Michael Owen once at Mere, and I was impressed by him. Wazza is a bit of a bandit. We played in the Foundation event at the end of the last season and I think he played off a twenty-eight handicap, which meant he ended up finishing with a ridiculously low points total, so he was the clear winner on the golf day. He should really be off about eighteen. I did get longest drive on that day, though, and I've still got the trophy from it!'

Silverware is never far from the thinking among those at Carrington, and fixtures between United and Liverpool have proven pivotal in its destination down the years. With a trip to Anfield awaiting after the international break, the anticipation was becoming palpable.

'We've been poor there of late,' conceded Sir Alex. 'Our record hasn't been great. On a couple of occasions, we've been outfought by them, which has been disappointing. The atmosphere always plays a part. Of course, every time we go there it's as if it's the biggest game of the century. But we need to be better than we have been in recent seasons, and this team can do that.

'It's an important contest that's been going on for a long time. But even when Liverpool were in their pomp – in the 1980s – United would regularly beat them there. If you look at what was happening then, Liverpool were winning league titles but United were winning the matches between us and them. It's been the other way around in the last few years. My thinking, though, is that I'd rather be winning the league come May than worry too much about dropping three points at Anfield. Of course, that doesn't mean I'm okay with losing the game. Far from it – it's never nice to be beaten by Liverpool. But at the end of the day, I'd prefer to win the Premier League.'

The United manager would make the short trip to Anfield pondering the inclusion of Wayne Rooney, who had been ruled out of England's opening three games at Euro 2012 after being sent off against Montenegro and was, in the manager's eyes, struggling under a mental burden as a result. Sir Alex was also uncertain over the availability of Nemanja Vidic, who completed his first full game of the season in Serbia's midweek outing, but was able to call upon Jonny Evans after some much-needed rest. Tom Cleverley and Rafael continued to miss out, but Fabio, Ashley Young and Patrice Evra were all in contention after overcoming minor knocks.

For the latter, this particular trip to Anfield would prove more eventful than any other.

Barclays Premier League

15 October 2011 | Anfield | Kick-off 12:45 |
Attendance: 45,065

Liverpool 1 (Gerrard 68)
Manchester United 1 (Hernandez 81)

Chicharito leapt from the substitutes' bench to procure an invaluable late point for United, whose carefully contrived tactical approach looked set to be wrecked by Steven Gerrard's free-kick for the hosts.

The Liverpool skipper took advantage of a gaping hole in the Reds' defensive wall to fire his side into the lead midway through the second period, only for United's super-sub to head home from close range after Danny Welbeck had flicked on Nani's corner.

Sir Alex Ferguson surprised many with a team selection that left the Portuguese winger and Wayne Rooney on the bench, with a set-up designed to neutralise Liverpool's central midfield strength and build a platform for victory. Phil Jones stuck to Charlie Adam like a limpet as the Reds' third middle man, while Welbeck ploughed a lone furrow in attack.

A disjointed opening to the game was characterised by sloppy passing from both sides, but Welbeck's industry led to the first opening of the afternoon when he fed Patrice Evra to cross for Jones, who headed into Pepe Reina's side-netting.

Liverpool's first chance came shortly before the break, when Adam's shot bounced kindly into the path of Luis Suarez, who turned Jonny Evans but could only shoot straight at David De Gea, who deflected the ball to safety.

After a dour first 45 minutes, the second period began with a greater ebb and flow. Ashley Young chanced his arm three times in the opening six minutes, while De Gea comfortably fielded another Suarez effort. Then, just as Sir Alex was poised to go for the kill, with Rooney and Nani lined up ready for their introduction, Liverpool struck.

Adam tumbled theatrically under a challenge from Rio Ferdinand, just outside the United area. Gerrard – just as he had at Old Trafford 13 months earlier – found a gap in the Reds' wall and curled his finish past the exposed De Gea. As Anfield revelled, Rooney and Nani immediately replaced Young and Ji-sung Park.

The response wasn't a long time coming. Nani's corner from the left was headed on by Welbeck for fellow sub Javier Hernandez to divert instinctively into the net and plunder the equaliser with nine minutes left. But, just as it seemed United were best placed to push for victory, Liverpool finished the game stronger.

De Gea marvellously turned away Kuyt's close-range volley and acrobatically clawed away Jordan Henderson's measured lob, before Martin Skrtel slashed over from inside the six-yard box and Henderson glanced a header onto the roof of the United goal. Despite riding their luck in the final few minutes, the champions could consider a point fair reward for the way they adapted their game-plan after such a damaging setback.

The Teams

Liverpool: Reina; Kelly, Carragher, Skrtel, Jose Enrique; Kuyt, Gerrard, Lucas (Henderson 57), Adam, Downing; Suarez
Subs not used: Doni, Agger, Carroll, Spearing, Bellamy, Robinson
Booked: Henderson

Manchester United: De Gea; Smalling, Ferdinand, Evans, Evra; Park (Rooney 69), Fletcher, Jones (Hernandez 76), Giggs, Young (Nani 69); Welbeck
Subs not used: Lindegaard, Anderson, Carrick, Valencia
Booked: Evra, Ferdinand, Young

The general consensus post-match was that a share of the spoils had been a fitting outcome. 'I'm happy with a point in the end,' admitted Rio Ferdinand, while Sir Alex Ferguson reflected: 'It was probably a typical United–Liverpool game and the result was fair.' Phil Jones, meanwhile, added: 'It's a hostile fixture and a tough one, but we knew that and expected it.'

Nobody, however, could have predicted the mid-match experiences of Patrice Evra, whose afternoon would emerge as the real story of the day. After the final whistle, the Frenchman and Sir Alex Ferguson visited referee Andre Marriner to report racist comments made towards Evra by Liverpool striker Luis Suarez. The United defender, who captained the Reds at Anfield, alleged that the Uruguayan had referred to his skin colour in a 58th-minute argument in the build-up to a Liverpool corner in front of the Kop. Referee Marriner and his fourth official, Phil Dowd, took statements from parties on both sides of the incident.

Evra had also mentioned the events during a post-match interview with French TV station Canal Plus, and the story spread like wildfire. United were soon en route to Romania for their Champions League clash with Otelul Galati but, upon touching down in Bucharest, Sir Alex confirmed that the serious allegation would be pursued.

'We spoke to Patrice today and he was adamant he wanted to follow it up,' said the manager. 'It's not an easy one because everybody knows Manchester United and Liverpool have great responsibilities in terms of what happens on and off the pitch. Incidentally, I thought Saturday was terrific – both sets of fans were good and there was none of the silly chanting we've had in previous years. This isn't something we want to level against Liverpool, and it's not against Liverpool, but obviously Patrice feels very aggrieved by what was said to him. Now it rests in the hands of the FA.'

While the authorities investigated the incident, United's focus remained on events on the field. After drawing their opening two Group C games, victory was imperative against the unfancied Romanian champions, while the subsequent Premier League summit meeting with title rivals Manchester City at Old Trafford also loomed into view.

'If you come out of this week with two wins, you have had a fantastic week and the confidence goes sky high,' admitted Rio Ferdinand. 'But it can go the other way. That is what you are up against. That is what the demands of this club are. If you can't deal with those demands, the manager won't have you here for long. We have a massive week, but one we are relishing.'

The England defender had been left back at Carrington to ensure his availability for the Manchester derby, but the return of Nemanja Vidic as his replacement in the Reds' travelling party substantially softened the blow, and Sir Alex confirmed that he was planning to utilise the Serbian's steel in Bucharest. 'Rio played very well on Saturday,' said the boss, 'but we have Vidic with us here and I felt it was a good opportunity to give Rio a break – playing three games in seven days is a lot to ask.'

Wayne Rooney was also set to return, after being deployed from the bench at Anfield. 'I think Wayne's ready,' said Sir Alex. 'When he came on [at Liverpool] I thought he was bubbly, full of energy and enthusiasm. He was desperate to get on, which was good.'

With Rooney champing at the bit, United's European season was ready to belatedly get off the ground.

UEFA Champions League Group C

18 October 2011 | National Stadium | Kick-off 19:45 | Attendance: 49,500

Otelul Galati 0
Manchester United 2 (Rooney 64 (pen), 90 (pen))

After opening their Champions League assault with two draws, three much-needed points were duly secured against Otelul Galati by Wayne Rooney's pair of second-half penalties. On an attritional evening in the Romanian capital, United's task was encumbered by a harsh red card for skipper Nemanja Vidic, but their hosts lacked the sufficient quality to pose their visitors any major problems.

Despite controlling the first period, the Reds rarely mustered sufficient tempo to stretch the well-drilled hosts. Galati were even able to spring forward and register all the noteworthy attempts on goal, albeit without troubling Anders Lindegaard, until Rooney finally worked Branko Grahovac with a tame free-kick on 31 minutes.

A spell of concerted United pressure followed, with Patrice Evra and Nani again testing Grahovac, before Michael Carrick blotted an otherwise accomplished display with a wayward finish after good work by Anderson and Nani.

Clearly, Sir Alex demanded more of his troops at the interval and the second half became more of a spectacle as United turned the screw. With just over 25 minutes remaining, Sergiu Costin cut out Rooney's square ball to the unmarked Javier Hernandez with a blatant handball. Rooney calmly sent Grahovac the wrong way from the spot to become the highest-scoring Englishman in the history of the Champions League.

With the deadlock broken, it should have been plain sailing for the Reds, but an unexpected twist arose when Vidic was sent off for a robust – but hardly dangerous – challenge on Gabriel Giurgiu; a decision made even more perplexing considering that Costin had only been booked for an obvious case of denying a goalscoring opportunity.

Carrick slotted in at the back seamlessly before Jonny Evans could be introduced, but the Romanians recognised their opportunity and attacked with renewed belief. Ioan Filip lashed an ambitious drive off-target, substitute Marius Pena headed over and Branislav Punosevac volleyed Filip's cross just wide.

United were able to draw on vast reserves of experience, and the visitors' task was made easier when Milan Perendija earned a second yellow card for cynically dragging down Hernandez to rule himself out of an appearance at Old Trafford in the sides' November reunion.

Back on level footing in terms of personnel, the Reds looked to make the points safe and, after Nani rapped a left-footed drive against an upright, Rooney won a second spot-kick by drawing a careless foul out of Liviu Antal. This time, Grahovac guessed correctly but the shot went in the same corner with the same result to put some gloss on a hard night's work.

The Teams

Otelul Galati: Grahovac; Rapa, Costin, Perendija, Salageanu;
Filip, Giurgiu, Neagu (Pena 72), Antal, Frunza (Ilie 83); Punosevac
(Viglianti 87)
Subs not used: Branet, Skubic, Iorga, Sarghi
Booked: Rapa, Costin, Giurgiu, Neagu
Sent off: Perendija

Manchester United: Lindegaard; Fabio (Jones 76), Smalling, Vidic,
Evra; Valencia (Evans 71), Carrick, Anderson, Nani; Rooney, Hernandez
Subs not used: De Gea, Owen, Berbatov, Welbeck, Fletcher
Booked: Carrick
Sent off: Vidic

'It was very bitty,' admitted Michael Carrick, United's outstanding
performer in a game suited to those of patient dispositions. 'It was
good at times and not so good at others. We expected a tough game,
though. People expected us to come here and score a lot of goals and
for it to be an easy night, but we knew it was going to be tough. We
had to be patient and in the end we came through. We are delighted
with the three points. It's a much-needed win and it's been a long
time coming. We're up and running now and hopefully we can keep
the momentum up.'

Carrick was also required to fill in at centre back following the
sending off of Nemanja Vidic, a decision the midfielder labelled:
'Dubious at best, really. We are disappointed with that. It was all
hands to the pump for a few minutes and I thought I might have
played at centre-half for a bit longer, but the boss changed it and after
that we were pretty comfortable and managed to get the second goal.'

Job done, victory secured, attentions could immediately switch
to the Manchester derby against a City side who headed the table
by two points, having comfortably won all but one of their opening seven games. Having finally discovered their continental mojo,

however, the Reds were perfectly prepared for Roberto Mancini's men, according to Nani.

'It was important to win in the Champions League on Tuesday and go with confidence into a big league game like Sunday's match,' explained the Portuguese winger. 'Everyone is ready to contribute to the game.

'It is too early to say it is just going to be about Manchester United and Manchester City for the title. I think they are one of the teams who have been doing fantastic since the season started. Of course, there are a lot of teams who are doing well. Chelsea are doing fantastic, too. But these are the games that always get the team motivated. When we play these games, the team has a different attitude and a different motivation. Of course, we like to play big games like that.

'City have a fantastic team at the moment with fantastic players. They play a lot of good stuff. It will be difficult to play against them. But we should not forget, we are United. When we play at home, it is very difficult to beat us. We will try to do our best to win the game again. Of course we are confident. We should be confident every time we play at home. Even when we play away. The most important thing is at home, we have to believe we are going to win most of the games.'

Nevertheless, for the first time since August 2007, the Reds went into a derby trailing their neighbours, and Sir Alex Ferguson admitted: 'I think City are doing fantastically well. If they hadn't thrown away a two-goal lead at Fulham they'd have a one hundred percent record. It could be quite a game on Sunday and I'm looking forward to it.'

The manager also played down the significance of the meeting, given its early timing in the campaign, claiming: 'You can only judge it at the end of the season, in terms of the bearing on the title race. Whichever team wins, it will make a difference. But it's still early doors and we can recover from that, no doubt about that.'

Prophetic words, indeed.

Barclays Premier League

23 October 2011 | Old Trafford | Kick-off 13:30 |
Attendance: 75,487

Manchester United 1 (Fletcher 81)
Manchester City 6 (Balotelli 22, 60, Aguero 69,
Dzeko 90, 90, Silva 90)

The Theatre of Dreams has lived up to its name on countless occasions since its construction in 1910 but, for one unforgettably dark afternoon, it hosted United's worst nightmare.

Sir Alex Ferguson's side trailed by a single Mario Balotelli goal at half time, despite giving as good as they got during an evenly contested first period. Within two minutes of the restart, however, the dismissal of Jonny Evans gave City an extra man, which, to their credit, they exploited emphatically.

The Reds conceded twice more before reducing the arrears through Darren Fletcher's strike, and the Scot's effort merely ignited United's inherent need to chase lost causes, an instinct mercilessly exploited by Roberto Mancini's side, who scored three goals in the final four minutes of the game.

Even before the first whistle, United's attacking intent was apparent. Wayne Rooney, Anderson and Nani all returned after sitting out the Reds' draw at Anfield, while a ring-rusty Nemanja Vidic was omitted in favour of Evans. From the off, Sir Alex's bold approach looked destined for success.

United dominated the early possession, with Nani and Ashley Young lively on the flanks, and Rooney dropping deep to dictate the play. City remained impenetrable in defence, however, and looked to break at speed whenever they could. They did so in devastating fashion on 22 minutes, as the elusive David Silva found James Milner, whose pull-back was steered into the far corner of David De Gea's goal by Balotelli.

Buoyed, the visitors pressed on and began to look more threatening in attack. Initially shaken from their stride, United gradually recovered and ended the half in the ascendancy. Young curled an effort just wide, while Anderson and Rooney both fired at Joe Hart in quick succession, but the hosts' only clear opening of the half fell to Evans, who missed his kick from close range after being found in space by Rooney.

Matters worsened within two minutes of the second period when Evans halted Balotelli's run on goal, giving referee Mark Clattenburg little option but to brandish his red card. Nevertheless, United's commitment to pushing forward remained total, with Danny Welbeck outstanding as the target man in a rejigged formation.

Young had an effort deflected narrowly wide and Rooney fired straight at Hart from distance, before City's patient approach began to create holes in the Reds' depleted ranks. Twice in quick succession, the visitors manufactured tap-ins by exploiting space and failure to track down United's left flank, as Milner crossed for Balotelli and Micah Richards squared for Sergio Aguero.

Punch-drunk, United continued to commit men forward despite City's dominance. The on-song Silva and substitute Edin Dzeko both spurned chances to widen the gap between the two sides, before Fletcher narrowed it by curling a sublime finish into Hart's top left-hand corner from just outside the area.

Heartened by finally making a breakthrough, the Reds kept expending energy in pursuit of the impossible. This approach yielded disaster in injury time as lackadaisical defending from a corner allowed Dzeko to turn home Joleon Lescott's pull-back, then Silva broke clear to nutmeg De Gea and Dzeko strode into space before firing home City's sixth and completing United's nightmare afternoon.

The Teams

Manchester United: De Gea; Smalling, Evans, Ferdinand, Evra; Nani (Hernandez 65), Fletcher, Anderson (Jones 66), Young; Rooney, Welbeck

Subs not used: Lindegaard, Berbatov, Park, Fabio, Valencia
Booked: Evra, Smalling, Anderson, Welbeck
Sent off: Evans

Manchester City: Hart; Richards, Kompany, Lescott, Clichy; Milner
(Kolarov 89), Barry, Y.Toure, Silva; Aguero (Nasri 75), Balotelli
(Dzeko 70)
Subs not used: Pantilimon, Zabaleta, K.Toure, De Jong
Booked: Richards, Kompany, Balotelli

'It was just silence all around,' recalls Danny Welbeck, of the Reds'
dressing room. 'Everyone was just stunned and gutted. I imagine
there were a few broken hearts in there. It wasn't just the players in
there, we let down the whole club and the fans too. It wasn't a good
day at all for the Red side of Manchester.

'Obviously it's a Manchester derby, everyone's looking forward to
it, the city's buzzing and you're going into the game wanting to do
your best and get the right result. Things just went down the drain
that day and City came out on top. It was just not like Manchester
United and everyone was bitterly disappointed. It was a moment you
don't ever want to get into again and all the players will remember
that time and know they've got to use it as a positive. Once it's over
and done with, you can't take much out of it other than the positives.
You've just got to remember it and make sure you never feel that way
again.

'I've been brought up in Manchester and mainly all my people
are Reds, but I know a few Blues and they had their fair share of
banter that day. There's not much you can do about it afterwards,
except recover from it, and we showed the Manchester United spirit,
that we'll never die.'

At the time, however, there was no immediate sense of vengeance
or glances to the future. Even Sir Alex Ferguson appeared numbed
when he emerged for his post-match interview. 'For the first ten
minutes, we absolutely dominated the game and played some

brilliant football, so it was hard to believe when we went one-nil down,' he reflected. 'But that was retrievable. The sending-off was a killer blow to us.

'The player didn't control the ball, but the fact Jonny tugged his jersey gave the referee plenty of reason to send him off. It was a killer, a really bad blow to us because City are so strong defensively. We just kept attacking. It's all right playing with the history books, but common sense has to come in at times. With the experience we had at the back, we should have realised that and settled for what we had when it went to four-one. At times our full-backs were almost our wingers and we were playing almost two versus three at the back. That was suicide and crazy.'

Nevertheless, despite also declaring himself 'shattered', the manager still drew upon his wealth of experience to declare: 'You have to recover. In the history of Manchester United, it is another day and we'll recover from this, there's no question about that.'

Crushing defeats had occurred before and would undoubtedly rear their ugly heads again, but past experience had shown that the best course of action was to get straight back into action. Fortunately, the Reds' Carling Cup trip to Aldershot came just two days after the derby debacle.

'It's obviously going to be a massive game for Aldershot with Manchester United coming into town,' explained Michael Owen, so often a starter – and scorer – on Carling Cup nights. 'I'm sure it'll be a full house and we're treating it as an important game as well.

'There are players who weren't involved against City, me being one of them, and a lot of the lads need games so it'll be quite a strong Manchester United playing against them. It's a competition we want to do well in. We've done quite well in the Carling Cup over the years and we want to progress and win a trophy. That's the end game.'

While one predatory striker looked to the short term, another looked further forward. Mexican hotshot Javier Hernandez provided a welcome dose of uplifting news by penning a new five-year contract to ensure his future lay at Old Trafford until at least the end of the 2015-16 season.

'The last player I remember making an impact as big and as quickly as Javier is Ole Gunnar Solskjaer and he reminds me of Ole a lot,' admitted Sir Alex. 'His talent for creating space in the box and his finishing ability mark him out as a natural goalscorer. Off the pitch, he is a pleasure to manage. He works very hard and is a popular member of the squad.'

Chicharito would not be required as the Reds travelled to the Recreation Ground, looking to quickly return to winning ways.

Carling Cup fourth round

25 October 2011 | Recreation Ground | Kick-off 19:45 | Attendance: 7,044

Aldershot 0
Manchester United 3 (Berbatov 15, Owen 41, Valencia 48)

A completely changed United side began the gradual process of healing its post-derby wounds with a routine Carling Cup progress at the expense of Aldershot. Dimitar Berbatov and Michael Owen made the most of rare starts with goals in the first half, before Antonio Valencia's outstanding long-range drive soon after the restart ended the match as a contest and secured the Reds' smooth passage to the fifth round.

Sir Alex Ferguson started with an entirely different side to that which was humbled by Manchester City two days earlier, but the Reds quickly slipped into gear. Tom Cleverley, making his first appearance since suffering an ankle injury at Bolton in September, fired the game's first attempt just over the bar, but United were ahead inside the first quarter-hour.

Ji-sung Park played an incisive one-two with Cleverley and the South Korean nudged an instant pass to Berbatov, who took one touch before swivelling to sweep a finish past Aldershot goalkeeper Ross Worner.

Berbatov should have been awarded a penalty when he was clearly felled by Luke Guttridge inside the box before Fabio's shot was deflected wide, but the hosts showed willing to trade blows with their guests when top scorer Danny Hylton forced Ben Amos into a low save. That was Aldershot's last sniff of parity, however, as Owen timed his run perfectly to drill Berbatov's tee-up underneath Worner.

There would be no blame attached to the Shots goalkeeper for United's third goal, however, as Valencia collected a Cleverley pass and hit a stunning drive with whip and bend that crashed high into the net from 30 yards.

The remainder of the game was primarily a fitness exercise for some under-utilised players, with Berbatov particularly in the mood, before youngsters Ravel Morrison, Paul Pogba and debutant Michael Keane – who had taken great strides in the Reds' Reserves – were introduced for senior cameos.

Park fired off target, Worner pushed away a Berbatov free-kick and Valencia blazed an inviting opportunity over after bursting through on goal in the closing stages, but United had long since assured themselves of a step down the road to recovery.

The Teams

Aldershot: Worner; Herd, Jones, Morris, Straker; McGlashan, Guttridge, Vicenti (Collins 73), Rodman (Bubb 46); Hylton, Rankine (Smith 82)
Subs not used: Young, Brown, Pulis, Panther

Manchester United: Amos; Fabio, Vidic, Jones, Fryers (M.Keane 70); Valencia, Cleverley (Pogba 60), Park, Diouf (Morrison 70); Berbatov, Owen
Subs not used: De Gea, Vermijl, W.Keane, Cole
Booked: Vidic

'There was a little bit of pressure after the City result,' admitted Michael Owen, scorer of his third Carling Cup goal in two ties. 'Although no one started at the weekend, we still had the Manchester United reputation to look after in many ways. No matter what side we put out tonight, we wanted to bounce back and thankfully we got the win.

'As you can imagine really, the usual laughs and jokes at training quietened down a little bit after Sunday and it focused our minds. Sometimes you need a kick in the teeth to get up and going again and to concentrate on the basics. It was a big kick in the teeth and we were eager to bounce back.

'We played some good stuff in the first half. It was quite similar to the last tie at Leeds, as again we went three-nil up and then took our foot off the gas a little bit. It was a bit more even in the second half, and, to their credit, Aldershot never let their heads drop. We're thankful we're through to the next round of the Carling Cup. Roll on Everton now.'

The Reds had traditionally made light work of the short trip to Goodison Park, taking maximum points in 13 of their first 16 Premier League visits. Two points from the most recent trio of trips, however, indicated the growing difficulties posed by David Moyes' obdurate Toffees.

Nemanja Vidic, scorer of the Reds' last winner at Goodison in 2007, was ready to rejoin the champions' title defence after completing 90 minutes at Aldershot, and he was determined to help his side bounce back from their chastening derby day.

'When you lose a derby, especially by that scoreline, it's difficult to take, but the players have shown character this week,' said the Serbian. 'We haven't come to training with our heads down. We have come in and worked harder because we want to play better and improve. This is the right mentality to have to try and get over bad results. They are the positive things that have come from this week.

'When you lose games you can always look at the things that you did wrong and what you can improve. Losing that game was difficult for all the players, but it's important to focus on the next match and look forward. Even when you win you can't spend time celebrating, you have to focus on the next game. Hopefully we can prove that the derby was just one bad day and show how good we are on Saturday.

'We are preparing for a physical game on Saturday and if we challenge for every ball and compete with them, we will have a big chance to win. We have quality in our team, we have pace and players that can score goals. Mentally and physically we'll be ready and hopefully with a bit of luck we can win the game.'

Vidic prepared for the trip to Merseyside with the announcement that he was retiring from international football; another boon for Sir Alex Ferguson, who would have one more key player at Carrington during the forthcoming lulls in the club calendar. The boss's immediate focus was on the near future, however, which ruled out getting ahead of himself and, more pertinently, not dwelling on the derby.

'We can analyse it as much as you want, but it won't do us any good,' he told his pre-Everton press conference. 'My attitude is to completely forget it – it never happened. It won't do us any good looking back on that game. What we can do at Everton is show Manchester United in its proper light. We didn't do that last week. We can do that tomorrow.

'We've done that pretty well over the years. We lost five-nil to Newcastle [in 1996-97] and won the league by ten points or something like that. We have the experience of being able to recover many, many times. That's what you have to do when you're at a club like United. There's no other way.

'Expectation lives with us every minute of our lives. We get used to that. Saturday is no different to when we've lost games in the past – we have to recover. It's only October. The league will be decided at the beginning of May. It could go to the wire this season. It's a long way off, but I would expect us to be there at the end.'

The first steps on that long road would be of critical importance.

Barclays Premier League

29 October 2011 | Goodison Park | Kick-off 12:00 |
Attendance: 35,494

Everton 0
Manchester United 1 (Hernandez 19)

After succumbing to a succession of sucker punches against Manchester City, United used the traditionally taxing visit to Goodison Park to get back to basics: defending doggedly and showing the spirit of champions. Though far less compelling than the annihilation of Arsenal and the swashbuckling defeat of Chelsea earlier in the season, the importance of making an immediate return to winning ways in defence of the Barclays Premier League title could not be understated.

Goodison Park is never a hospitable venue for visitors, and the partisan home support were baying in time-honoured fashion inside the first minute when Seamus Coleman burst forward and fired off-target. United's response was a neat move that led to Danny Welbeck's cross being nudged goalwards by Ji-sung Park, only for Tim Howard to make a smart save.

When a goal did arrive, it was no more than United deserved for dictating matters, as Tom Cleverley, one of five changes from the City defeat, and Welbeck worked the ball to Patrice Evra on the left and the Frenchman's cross was touched home by the ever-alert Javier Hernandez.

Any thoughts that United would continue to dominate were soon dismissed as Leon Osman latched onto a Marouane Fellaini header to work David De Gea, and the Spanish stopper was grateful to see Jack Rodwell lash wide after finding space on the edge of the box. De Gea needed the aid of his bar to keep out Leighton Baines' free-kick in the 40th minute, watching anxiously as the shot smacked against the woodwork, but that was as close as the Toffees would come to restoring parity.

Despite showing spirit to mount more pressure after the interval, David Moyes' side, visibly drained by a gruelling Carling Cup tie against Chelsea three days earlier, rarely seemed capable of extending De Gea. The former Atlético Madrid keeper blocked a Rodwell drive with his face after a rare lapse by Jonny Evans gifted the ball to Coleman, but would not be called upon again.

An injury to Cleverley upset United's momentum and necessitated a restructuring of the midfield when Nani replaced him, but Wayne Rooney continued to work hard in a deeper role aimed at beefing up the Reds' core. Rooney managed to outmuscle highly rated Toffees youngster Ross Barkley to launch a rare raid that led to Hernandez picking out Welbeck, and the young forward forced Howard to push a left-foot drive over the bar, but, in truth, the former United keeper was a spectator for much of the half.

With the clock ticking down, hopeful home appeals for a penalty were rightly waved away by referee Mark Halsey when Evra stood his ground against substitute Magaye Gueye. Returning skipper Nemanja Vidic organised his troops to keep the door closed on the hosts for a lengthy period of stoppage time and the final whistle represented a major step away from the previous weekend's disappointment.

Sir Alex's choice of personnel and tactical plan had paid off. After the despair, came discipline.

The Teams

Everton: Howard; Hibbert, Heitinga, Jagielka, Baines; Coleman, Fellaini, Rodwell, Osman (Vellios 76), Bilyaletdinov (Barkley 46); Saha (Gueye 84)
Subs not used: Mucha, Mustafi, Stracqualursi, McFadden
Booked: Rodwell, Coleman, Fellaini

Manchester United: De Gea; Jones, Vidic, Evans, Evra; Park, Cleverley (Nani 57), Fletcher; Rooney, Welbeck (Valencia 73); Hernandez (Berbatov 67)
Subs not used: Lindegaard, Ferdinand, Owen, Fabio

Hardly back with a bang – more returning with a rumble – but victory at an unwelcoming venue with the concession of few chances represented a hugely satisfying day for the reigning champions.

'Everyone showed today what Manchester United are about,' stressed Phil Jones. 'It was a bad day at the office last week, but we've shown fantastic team spirit in training, got our heads up and picked ourselves up quickly. This is a massive win for us today and we're delighted in the changing room.

'It was tough and we expected it from Everton because of previous years of coming here. It was mad [at the end] and we had to defend it, but we did that and, thankfully, got the three points. It's very nice as a defender [to keep a clean sheet]. Defensively as a unit, I thought eleven players defended and not just four. Eleven players defended terrifically well. They were throwing the kitchen sink at us today and I thought we stood strong as a unit and held together.'

'It was a hard game,' added Sir Alex Ferguson. 'We expect a hard game every time we come to Everton, in fairness. The crowd get behind them and they show great enthusiasm. In the first half in particular, we played very, very well. Second half, we defended well and that was the pleasing aspect for me. Winning one-nil – I'll take half a dozen of those any time, because that's championship form when you get those kind of results.

'We had probably the best chances in the game. All their attempts were crosses and we managed to get most of them away. Really David [De Gea] has not had anything to do in terms of saves. I thought we just battled in the second half and got the result we wanted. Everyone's telling us the stats about chances made against us. We have to reduce that; if we're going to win the league we have to reduce those types of statistics against us. Today we were very solid.'

The United manager also had to break the news that Chris Smalling had missed the game – and would most likely sit out the next month – with a small fracture to his foot, while Ashley Young's persistent toe injury would require further weeks of rest. Though the initial prognosis of Tom Cleverley's injury was 'nothing serious', he would be out of action until the following February.

Looking back on aggravating the ankle injury he initially suffered under Kevin Davies' lunging challenge, Cleverley confirms: 'I didn't feel it "go", as such, I just knew it wasn't right. I thought I'd played quite well at Everton, but it just wasn't right. We then made the decision to get it one hundred percent right, so I had a couple of weeks just basically resting and staying off my feet. That helped massively. Then I got back into the gym and started working massively hard.'

For Cleverley and his colleagues, graft would prove to be key over the coming weeks and months.

5

November – A Knight to Remember

Amid the frenzy of another hectic season – and particularly the post-derby hubbub – an enormous landmark had stalked matters: the 25th anniversary of Sir Alex Ferguson's appointment as United manager.

In November 1986, Ron Atkinson was relieved of his duties, with the Reds struggling in the lower reaches of the First Division table. The discussion as to who might replace him was only brief. 'There might have been a few names mentioned – probably just whoever was popular at the time – but none of them was seriously considered,' recalls then-chairman Martin Edwards. 'It was a unanimous decision from the board to go for Alex Ferguson. He was absolutely the preferred choice of all of us.

'We'd first met him when we signed Gordon Strachan from Aberdeen. Gordon had already signed a contract with Cologne and we really wanted to extricate him from that deal, so that's when Alex came in. He was batting on Manchester United's side, probably because he wanted him to come to United, but also because the move would get Aberdeen more money if he did. So he was very helpful to us and that's when I first got to know him.

'We knew how well he'd done in overtaking Glasgow Rangers and Celtic and he'd won the Cup-Winners' Cup in 1983 against the mighty Real Madrid, so his pedigree was there. When we actually met him and realised what a firebrand he was and saw the way he conducted himself, that really just confirmed how impressive he was.'

United's kingmakers nevertheless had to tread carefully, with no guarantee that their target would leave Pittodrie in the midst of such spectacular and sustained success, so director Michael Edelson rang the Dons' switchboard pretending to be Gordon Strachan's accountant, and was swiftly put through to Ferguson.

'Alex came on the phone, Mike told him I would like a word with him and he put me through,' continues Edwards. 'We arranged to see him that evening – Bonfire Night – up in Scotland and it was the usual cloak-and-dagger thing: myself, Mike, Bobby [Charlton] and Maurice [Watkins] met him at a petrol station, he drove us round to his sister-in-law's house and we all met him. It just confirmed that he was the one that we wanted.

'But really what we wanted to know from him was if his chairman, Dick Donald, would allow him to leave. Alex made it quite plain that he wanted to join us, and he also said that he had an agreement with his chairman that he could leave if United came in. Alex had actually said that he wanted something in his contract that he could join a big team, and Dick Donald had said: "You're only leaving if Manchester United come in." That wasn't difficult really. So I rang Dick Donald the next day and he agreed to see me.'

A quarter of a century (and 37 trophies) on, the board's choice had been emphatically ratified. The man himself, however, would continue to eye up new challenges, and the bid to guide his new-look side onwards and upwards in the Champions League faced a must-win game against Romania's finest at Old Trafford.

Otelul Galati had been comfortably, if not clinically, despatched in Bucharest, and another three points would represent a sizeable step towards the knockout stages, with two games still to play. The Reds' first European outing of the season at Old Trafford had resulted in the dramatic procurement of a point against Basel, having surrendered a position of comfort, and Ji-sung Park was insistent that there would be no repeat against Galati.

'We have that experience now, so we know what happens when we lose concentration, and if we are United we have to do a proper job against Galati,' said the South Korean. 'In the first couple of matches, we couldn't get the results we wanted, but now we have five points. We need to win if we want to get through the group stage in first position. Galati's not an easy game. Away in Romania we won two-nil, but it was a tough game for us. Old Trafford is a different situation and we have to show them that.'

UEFA Champions League Group C

2 November 2011 | Old Trafford | Kick-off 19:45 |
Attendance: 74,847

Manchester United 2 (Valencia 8, Sarghi 87 (og))
Otelul Galati 0

United grasped a position of power atop Group C, after another unspectacular but imperative victory over Otelul Galati at Old Trafford. Antonio Valencia's eighth-minute tap-in gave the Reds an early lead, but Sir Alex Ferguson's side postured for much of the game before landing the killer blow three minutes from time, when Wayne Rooney's long-range effort found the Stretford End goal, via a sizeable deflection.

The United striker influenced proceedings from a central midfield role, quietly dictating the game's tempo, just as he had at Goodison Park five days earlier. Rooney looked bright from the first whistle and played a part in the Reds' opening goal, spreading the ball to Dimitar Berbatov, who held the ball up briefly before releasing Phil Jones on the overlap. His ball to the near post just eluded Michael Owen's stretch, but waiting behind was Valencia, who completed the formalities.

United's joy was tempered almost immediately when Owen limped from the field, having sustained an injury in the build-up to Valencia's goal. Chicharito entered the fray as his replacement, but it was Phil Jones who came closest to emphasising the Reds' half-time dominance, as his curling, left-footed effort was headed wide by Sergiu Costin.

Galati almost stunned Old Trafford just before the break, as Ionut Neagu pounced on Anderson's loose pass and advanced on goal. His shot nicked off Rio Ferdinand and forced David De Gea into a smart reflex save. After the interval, the Spaniard's evening continued to be busier than he might have hoped, as he clutched Costin's header to his chest.

The Galati defender remained a central figure when he raced to clear Anderson's effort off the line, before Berbatov poked off-target from a promising position with 15 minutes remaining. Before nerves could fully grip Old Trafford, however, Rooney ensured the three points with a long-range effort, which Cristian Sarghi unnecessarily attempted to clear, but only diverted past his own goalkeeper.

Job done, three more points in the bag for the Reds and top spot in Group C. Now only a pair of points shy of the annual ten-point target Sir Alex sets his side to ensure qualification, the outcome far outweighed a forgettable display.

The Teams

Manchester United: De Gea; Jones, Ferdinand, Evans (Fryers 89), Fabio; Valencia, Rooney, Anderson (Park 80), Nani; Berbatov, Owen (Hernandez 11)
Subs not used: Lindegaard, Evra, Welbeck, Pogba
Booked: Evans

Otelul Galati: Grahovac; Rapa, Costin, Sarghi, Salageanu; Neagu, Filip, Giurgiu (Paraschiv 81), Antal (Iorga 61), Pena; Ilie (Frunza 52)
Subs not used: Branet, Skubic, Benga, Punosevac
Booked: Costin

'It's down to us,' shrugged Sir Alex. 'The winning was important tonight. Our opponents were aggressive, defended very well, pressed the ball everywhere on the pitch, put some energy into their game and made it difficult for us. If we beat Benfica, we've won the group – simply that. It's a good incentive for us, being at home on a big night. Manchester United and Benfica . . . the history between the two clubs is fantastic, so hopefully it will be a very, very good night.'

The United manager singled out his moonlighting midfielder, Wayne Rooney, for special praise, admitting: 'I thought he was fantastic in central midfield, I really did. His awareness of people around him, his choice of passing was very, very good. He did really well for us. It's difficult to say how Wayne would play in another Champions League game, but I'd be confident playing him there. We're just trying to organise our midfield a little bit. We've had injuries in that department. Michael Carrick's still injured, Tom Cleverley's still injured and we're spacing out Darren Fletcher's games.'

Having dictated the tempo of a victory in a must-win Champions League game, Rooney was in predictably confident mood, post-match, agreeing with his manager's assertion that he was cut out for auxiliary duties in the middle of the park if required.

'I've said it before, I'm a good enough footballer to play anywhere on the pitch,' he said. 'That's not being big-headed. I feel I'm capable of doing that. If the manager wants me to play there, I've no problem doing that. I played there a lot when I was younger. You get a lot of the ball there. If the manager asks me to do it, I'm happy to do it. I don't know if it's long term, that's down to the manager, so we'll see what he decides.'

As well as deciding his approach for the looming visit of Sunderland, Sir Alex also had to acknowledge his incredible landmark. As well as other, more intimate shindigs with close associates, the manager was the subject of a star-studded bash at Lancashire County Cricket Club, 24 hours after the win over Galati. The guest list featured United players past and present, opposing managers and all manner of celebrities, all of whom were intent only on paying tribute to one man.

'It was such a good night,' reveals Danny Welbeck. 'Just to go there, where everyone's gracing the manager's twenty-five years in charge at one of the biggest clubs in the world, was incredible. It's a massive achievement and everyone wanted to pay their respects and show how happy they were for him. To go there and meet so many ex-players, the whole squad was there, it was a great time for the club. You see different people from around the club who you haven't seen for a while, and there were just people coming out from everywhere!

'It was really good, the entertainment was good. I actually like Mumford and Sons after their little set! Wazza [Wayne Rooney] is always listening to them in the changing room and now I'm a fan too. It was a great evening and everyone really enjoyed themselves. We were all really pleased for the manager and to see him be given that occasion. We got to see him in his traditional kilt as well, which was a first! We made a few jokes about it, but it was all good fun.'

'It was a really nice night, obviously seeing all the players who've been involved with the manager over the years, all coming together into one big room,' adds Jonny Evans. 'It was great entertainment and obviously we couldn't stay too long and enjoy ourselves, because we had a game at the weekend, but it was a great night and really nice to be a part of. There were a lot of players there, past and present, and we all managed to get in a big photograph together so that's definitely one I'm going to keep.'

Both Evans and Welbeck had benefited from previous loan deals with Sunderland, and were relishing the chance to get re-acquainted with the Black Cats at Old Trafford. Though they were enjoying a so-so season under Steve Bruce, the Wearsiders would be granted great respect as the Reds looked to extend their winning run.

'Sunderland have had a bit of a slow start this season, but I think Steve Bruce has bought a lot of new players and it's taken some of them a while to gel,' admitted Evans. 'They'll be coming here wanting to put in a big performance. Steve Bruce's teams always seem to do well in the Premier League and he's a good manager. I've got a lot of fond memories from my time at Sunderland, but I'll be looking to do a job on Saturday and get three points before the international break.'

'I know quite a few of the players, so it'll be good to see them again, but when it comes down to it, I'll be ruthless,' Welbeck added. 'I just want to win the game. There are no friends out on the pitch. It was a great club to go to, a massive club and I really enjoyed my time there. The fans were great and I can't thank them enough.'

With the champions lagging league leaders Manchester City by five points, Evans conceded that the Reds merely had to hold onto the Blues' coat-tails and wait for their blistering pace to ease up, as it inevitably would.

'We've played quite a lot of the big teams around us,' he explained. 'I don't think City have done that yet. Obviously, they could go on and win all those games – we don't know that yet – but we need to keep our run going and hope City slip up. I think we've defended quite well. The most disappointing thing was that we were giving away chances but, again, that was probably down to the attacking football we were playing. It's a case of finding the right balance and we want to learn from our mistakes and come up with the complete package.'

If they could manage that against Sunderland, it would be the perfect present for the man of the hour.

Barclays Premier League

5 November 2011 | Old Trafford | Kick-off 15:00 |
Attendance: 75,570

Manchester United 1 (Brown 45 (og))
Sunderland 0

A United veteran ensured that Sir Alex Ferguson could celebrate his 25th anniversary at the Old Trafford helm with a victory. Unfortunately for Sunderland, it was Black Cats defender Wes Brown, back in M16 for the first time as an opponent, who scored the decisive goal.

The United youth product, who spent 13 years in the club's senior set-up, diverted Nani's corner into his own net in first-half injury time to secure the outcome on a day where the outstanding moment was provided by the revelation that the North Stand had been renamed the Sir Alex Ferguson Stand.

Announced before kick-off, the gesture was a complete shock to Sir Alex, who was predictably not among the handful of people who knew of the club's plans. There were other tributes, of course, with a giant banner hung the length of the Stretford End and commemorative tribute magazines handed out to supporters, while both teams formed a guard of honour.

The game itself was never likely to be on a par with the pre-match razzmatazz, and it was bitty from the very first minute, when Sunderland striker Conor Wickham injured himself with a sharp change of direction and had to be replaced by Ji Dong-Won.

It was another Black Cats forward, Nicklas Bendtner, who forced the first save of the game with a low shot which his countryman, Anders Lindegaard, needed two attempts to gather. Conversely, United lacked true menace for much of the first period.

Wayne Rooney blasted a shot straight at Keiren Westwood in the Sunderland goal and Phil Jones volleyed narrowly over the bar from the edge of the area, before Nani came to the fore in decisive fashion. The Portuguese forced Westwood into an alert, low save before aiming the subsequent corner towards Danny Welbeck. The former Sunderland loanee rose to head the ball, challenged by Brown, and the ball ricocheted off the ex-Reds defender and beat Westwood to give United the edge going into the break.

If the lead was scarcely deserved until that point, the Reds did their best to justify it after the interval. Nani blasted a 30-yard free-kick just wide of the post and Chicharito's effort was headed off the line by another Old Trafford graduate, Kieran Richardson, who turned in an impressive display on the left side of the visitors' defence.

Then came late controversy. Sebastian Larsson whipped a cross towards Ji, who rose with Rio Ferdinand and Nemanja Vidic. The ball clearly struck an outstretched arm, and referee Lee Mason awarded a penalty to the visitors. United's players quickly vented their ire, while Mason consulted his assistant on the touchline and, after a brief discussion, the pair correctly concluded that the Sunderland striker had committed the offence.

But for the heroics of Westwood in the Sunderland goal, United would have been out of sight almost immediately. Having flung himself to his right to parry Rooney's powerful shot, the Manchester-born stopper somehow arched and contorted himself to tip Patrice Evra's follow-up over the bar. That proved to be the final noteworthy act on an afternoon that won't live long in the memory, but nevertheless provided a fitting outcome for a knight to remember.

The Teams

Manchester United: Lindegaard; Jones, Ferdinand, Vidic, Evra; Nani, Fletcher (Fabio 89), Rooney, Park (Carrick 83); Welbeck (Berbatov 73), Hernandez
Subs not used: De Gea, Evans, Valencia, Diouf

Sunderland: Westwood; Bardsley, Brown, Turner, Richardson; Larsson, Cattermole, Colback (Elmohamady 76), Sessegnon (Meyler 76); Bendtner, Wickham (Ji 5)
Subs not used: Carson, Gardner, McClean, Egan
Booked: Larsson, Ji

'It was an anxious day for the players,' admitted the manager. 'I think they showed that. They wanted to do well for me. These occasions can be a wee bit like that. I remember the fiftieth anniversary of the Munich air disaster and we lost two-one to Manchester City. It got to the players that day. Maybe it happened a little bit today. That last fifteen minutes was torture. I'd have been quite happy if the whistle had gone at half time when we were one-nil up. Sunderland threw everything at us and played very well in that last fifteen minutes.'

That the Black Cats failed to carve a route back into the game owed much to the defensive work of Nemanja Vidic and Rio Ferdinand, starting just their third game of the season together. Having established one of the most functional central defensive partnerships in the club's history, the duo made life simple for goalkeeper Anders Lindegaard.

'Obviously Vida and Rio know each other well and they complement each other very well,' said the Dane. 'The two of them were amazing today. It was very enjoyable being a goalkeeper behind them. I thought we did very well defensively. We didn't give Sunderland any real chances all game. It was maybe the best defensive game from us this season. But there's still room for improvement.'

Lindegaard also marvelled at the club's gesture of renaming the North Stand after the manager, quipping: 'One of the biggest stands in the world is now named Sir Alex Ferguson. I'd be thrilled if I could just have one seat out there called the Anders Lindegaard seat!'

The Dane was among a dozen players who clocked up the air miles over the coming days, jetting around the globe in the season's latest international break. For once, the timing suited United, with so many players struggling with injury, and the body count continued to swell as Michael Owen was ruled out for at least six weeks by the thigh injury he had sustained against Otelul Galati. 'It's a tragedy for the lad,' admitted Sir Alex. 'I really feel for him; he's a really good player.'

While the ex-Liverpool striker came to terms with the setback, it was a current member of the Anfield playing staff who would grab all the headlines, as Luis Suarez was charged by the Football Association for his alleged racial abuse of Patrice Evra. The Uruguayan striker quickly pledged to clear his name as soon as he returned from international duty.

United, meanwhile, declined to comment on the situation, a silence that would last for the duration of what would prove to be a lengthy case. The focus was only on short-term matters, with players gradually filtering back to Carrington largely free of injury, the exception being Danny Welbeck, who had suffered a muscle strain during training with England.

That meant the striker was out of the Reds' trip to Swansea, whom United had never beaten on home soil. With Brendan Rodgers' side catching the eye as they popped passes with abandon, midfielder Darren Fletcher conceded that a stern test awaited the champions.

'It's a new experience for us all,' said the Scot. 'They're the first Welsh team in the Premier League and going there will be a great experience. Swansea have been applauded for the football they've played this season. When I was on international duty, I spoke to a couple of my Scotland team-mates who have played against them and they told me how well Swansea keep the ball.

'They play football in the right way and have been a breath of fresh air since coming into the Premier League. It's going to be a real challenge for us on Saturday. I'm sure this is the sort of fixture Swansea and their fans have been dreaming about for years. Welsh fans are always passionate and I'm sure the stadium will be packed out, so it should be a fantastic atmosphere.'

Barclays Premier League

19 November 2011 | Liberty Stadium | Kick-off 17:30 |
Attendance: 20,295

Swansea City 0
Manchester United 1 (Hernandez 11)

United kept Premier League leaders Manchester City within reach, as Chicharito's early strike gave the Reds their first-ever win at Swansea City, and also inflicted the Swans' first home defeat of the season.

Chances were at a premium in a skilfully conducted game where both sides displayed their nous in possession, but defences ultimately enjoyed the upper hand over attack. It was the only defensive slip of the day, from Angel Rangel, which gave Chicharito the opening goal.

As the hosts struggled to deal with United's high pressing game early on, the Spaniard dithered on the ball at the back and his attempted pass was easily cut out by Ryan Giggs. The midfielder powered into the area before sliding a low cross into the path of Hernandez, who aimed his downward finish past Michel Vorm.

Though United always looked dangerous and were clearly in the mood, the hosts should have drawn level within minutes. Just after Patrice Evra had seen a low drive well held by Vorm, Wayne Routledge's cross hit Michael Carrick and fell perfectly for Scott Sinclair, who somehow missed the ball in front of a gaping goal. Having survived that scare, United remained in control thereafter and might have doubled their lead when Giggs flashed a free-kick just wide nine minutes before the break.

It was the Swans who had the first sight of goal after the restart, as De Gea did well to parry Sinclair's powerful effort, but still United looked the likelier side to find the net, despite the hosts' comfort in possession. The visitors' game-plan increasingly became one of looking to cause damage on the break, and the pace of Chicharito always threatened to do so, even if it was the Mexican's team-mates who chanced their arm.

Vorm handled a long-range Rooney blockbuster with aplomb, then brilliantly tipped Phil Jones' shot onto the post after a trademark surge from the youngster. Nani curled just wide from the edge of the box as the Reds sought to emphasise their victory, but ultimately Chicharito's early strike proved enough to secure a fifth consecutive victory in all competitions.

Having fallen eight points behind the league leaders before kick-off, quickly clawing back three points at an increasingly danger-fraught venue for visitors sent out a timely reminder that the champions had no intention of relinquishing their crown without a fight.

The Teams

Swansea City: Vorm; Rangel, Monk, Williams, Taylor; Gower (Dobbie 79), Britton, Dyer, Routledge (Allen 46); Sinclair, Graham
Subs not used: Tremmel, Lita, Moore, Allen, Moras

Manchester United: De Gea; Jones, Ferdinand, Vidic, Evra (Fabio 51); Nani, Carrick, Giggs (Fletcher 76), Park; Rooney, Hernandez (Valencia 84)
Subs not used: Lindegaard, Evans, Berbatov, Young
Booked: Evra

Despite helping achieve a quietly impressive victory, and registering his own first league win in the country of his birth, Ryan Giggs was still critical of the Reds' display at the Liberty Stadium.

'We scored an early goal and then we sat back,' said the Welshman. 'We shouldn't have done that really. Sometimes it can happen that way, though. It's a tough place to come, their record this season shows that. They were unbeaten here until today, so we knew it would be tough.'

The veteran winger conceded that United's rhythm had been disrupted by ongoing injury concerns and the recent international break, but refused to peddle excuses for an unspectacular outing.

'You have different players at different fitness levels,' he said. 'Some of our players hadn't had a game for two or three weeks and some, like Phil Jones and Nani, had two tough games. But that's not an excuse. We probably need to play better if we're going to get more positive results.'

Sir Alex Ferguson described Michael Carrick's display as 'outstanding', and the midfielder was in upbeat mood after his first Premier League start of the season, admitting: 'I want to play in every game, like everyone else. But I understand the situation, it is a long season and I've been here before when I haven't played too much at the start and ended up having a good season. It can be frustrating but I am patient and I have just got to be ready. I enjoyed it.

'We always want to score more goals, of course, but I don't think it's a concern. It's about winning games and it's a good sign that we can win games like that. We haven't been at our best, but there'll be a point in the season when everything will come easily. We'll score some more goals because of the talent in our team. We believe we can do that, but at this time it is about grafting, sticking together and showing a lot of character.

'We are happy; we weren't at our best but three points is nice. The football wasn't as fluent or easy on the eye as it could have been, but one-nil is a win and we'll take that. At this stage of the season, it is about picking up points and wins – judge where we are by Christmas and we'll kick on from there.'

With the champions' Premier League title defence chugging along nicely, it was time to try to secure progress to the knockout stages of the Champions League. Though the Reds topped Group C on goal difference from Benfica, who would next face United at Old Trafford, Sir Alex was well aware of the precarious position his side would be in if they failed to overcome their visitors.

'We showed a bit of carelessness against Basel, but we are joint top with Benfica,' the manager said. 'Basel have got five points, though, so it's still not over; if you look at all of the different scenarios, we can still beat Benfica and go out. As stupid as it may seem, if Basel were to go and wallop Otelul Galati and then beat us, they'd be on the same points as us and could knock us out on goal difference, unless Benfica can score enough goals against Galati in their last game. If they do then we are out, so it is interesting.'

The battling nature of United's group-opening draw at the

Estadio da Luz had underlined the menace posed by Jorge Jesus' side, and Portuguese winger Nani (now a Ballon d'Or nominee along with Wayne Rooney) informed the Reds' pre-match press conference of exactly where he thought Benfica's danger lay.

'I think their strongest point is their midfield,' he said. 'If we are able to control the midfield, then I am sure we have a good chance to have a positive result. I'm sure Benfica will play some good football, but with a lot of care as well because they know they are playing away at our ground. We will do our best to get the positive result that we aim for.'

United's chances would be further hindered by niggling injuries which forced the absence of Wayne Rooney (training knocks) and Jonny Evans (tight hamstring), while Anderson (knee) missed out for the second game in succession and Chris Smalling was unlikely to be fit enough to start after returning from a fractured foot. Nevertheless, Sir Alex conceded: 'The squad I've got now is very strong and I can make changes.'

UEFA Champions League Group C

22 November 2011 | Old Trafford | Kick-off 19:45 |
Attendance: 74,853

Manchester United 2 (Berbatov 30, Fletcher 59)
Benfica 2 (Jones 3 (og), Aimar 61)

The unforgiving nature of the Champions League was spelled out to United's youngsters in emphatic – if entertaining – style as the Reds left their group-stage qualification in a perilous position with a surprise draw against Benfica. United recovered from Phil Jones' early own-goal and overturned the scoreline through goals from Dimitar Berbatov and Darren Fletcher, only to immediately allow the visitors to draw level again through Pablo Aimar.

A point all but ended the Reds' hopes of topping Group C, sitting behind Benfica on goal difference but also holding an inferior head-to-head record with the Portuguese side, while Basel's win at Otelul Galati gave them renewed hope of overtaking United.

The Reds' evening began in nightmare fashion when highly rated winger Nicolas Gaitan motored down the right flank and thumped in a cross, which Jones inadvertently shinned past the helpless David De Gea.

Commendably, however, the hosts were unflustered. Benfica goalkeeper Artur was forced into action by Nani's free-kick and a shot from Ashley Young, and the United wingers combined to haul their side level on the half-hour. Young and Patrice Evra worked the ball to Nani, who swung in a left-wing cross which Berbatov clinically headed wide of Artur and into the net to bag his first Champions League goal since hitting a brace against Celtic in 2008.

The goal sparked a frantic spell, with Young firing a one-on-one opportunity against Artur's legs after linking well with Berbatov, and Aimar bringing a smart stop out of De Gea seconds later. The lively Young then teed up Berbatov, only for the Bulgarian's effort to be deflected over by Ezequiel Garay's desperate block.

An enthralling first half was matched for excitement by the second period. Fabio spurned a glorious chance when Jones put him in the clear with just Artur to beat, only for the visiting stopper to thwart the Brazilian's attempted chip. Within minutes, however, Fletcher edged his team in front, as Evra's superb ball into the box allowed the Scot to prod home, even though Artur had half-saved the midfielder's initial shot.

United's lead and apparent passage to the knockout stages was short-lived, however, as De Gea's misplaced clearance gifted possession to the visitors. Bruno Cesar's cross hit Rio Ferdinand and fell kindly for Aimar, who gratefully smashed home from close range to haul Benfica level in the untidiest of circumstances.

Still United looked to hit back – Berbatov had a goal questionably chalked off for an offside call against Young, then volleyed wastefully over the bar from Fabio's teasing cross – but shoddy defending and careless finishing has never reaped rewards in the Champions League. The Reds had one more game to show that they had learned their lessons and deserved a spot in the knockout stages.

The Teams

Manchester United: De Gea; Fabio (Smalling 82), Jones, Ferdinand, Evra; Valencia (Hernandez 80), Carrick, Fletcher, Nani; Young; Berbatov
Subs not used: Lindegaard, Giggs, Park, Rafael, Gibson
Booked: Fletcher, Carrick

Benfica: Artur; Pereira, Luisao (Vitor 58), Garay, Emerson; Garcia, Cesar; Gaitan (Matic 68), Witsel, Aimar (Amorim 83); Rodrigo
Subs not used: Eduardo, Cardozo, Nolito, Oliveira
Booked: Garay, Pereira, Artur

'The goals we conceded were very disappointing – they were a bit freaky to be honest,' lamented Sir Alex Ferguson. 'One was an own goal and the other was a bad kick out from David De Gea. The back pass could have been a little bit better, it wasn't a bad back pass but David couldn't really play it into the stands.

'But we played so well tonight, we made a lot of great chances and played some really good football. I have no problems with my players at all. But that's the game, it's a cruel one at times and it was cruel for us tonight. We had to get into our rhythm and tempo. We had a bad start by losing a goal after three or four minutes, which takes the steam out of you and the wind from of your sails. But once we got into the game, we played really well and should have been two or three up by half time.

'We kept on playing and creating chances in the second half and I think we were very unfortunate not to win the game. We were missing a few players like Tom Cleverley; Chris Smalling has only just come back and Nemanja Vidic was suspended, but the squad we've got is good enough. We've no complaints. That's why we've got this squad and they proved themselves tonight and did really well.'

For all the positives in the performance, however, the fact remained that United now had to go to Switzerland and take at least a point from Basel; an increasing uncertainty in an unpredictable Champions League campaign to date, especially without Michael Carrick, the recipient of a harsh late booking which ruled him out of the Group C finale.

'We're disappointed as topping the group looks like it's going to be difficult now,' said Darren Fletcher. 'It's still in our hands to go to Basel and get a positive result and go through. We've lost goals at bad times and they were bad goals, but these things happen. We lose goals as a team and we created enough chances to win the match by a few goals. Unfortunately we didn't take them and suffered because of that. We'll go to Basel to win our match with a faint hope of topping the group, but the most important thing is to get into the next round.'

It quickly became apparent that midfield would prove a problematic area for the Basel trip, with Carrick suspended and Anderson confirmed as a long-term absentee alongside Tom Cleverley, who had already been ruled out until Christmas, as all parties sought to allow the youngster's ankle ample time to fully heal.

'It's in the midfield area where we've still got issues with Tom Cleverley and Anderson,' revealed the manager. 'It's not good news about Anderson; we don't think he'll be fit until February. He's got this knee injury and we've sent him back to Portugal to see the specialist who operated on his knee last time. That's a bit of a blow; we didn't expect that one. So that's the two midfield players who are going to be missing for a spell now.'

While the Basel tie would present personnel problems due to Carrick's absence, Sir Alex maintained that he still had sufficient resources in central areas to avoid delving into the transfer market – despite ongoing press speculation that the Reds' season would hinge on making a big-money signing in the middle of the park.

'We're not as bad as people think we are in midfield,' he stressed. 'Ryan Giggs gives you experience of course, Michael Carrick's form in the last two games has been outstanding. He had a little bit of a problem with his Achilles earlier on in the season, but he's got over that now and the grounds are softer now, of course, which helps. Darren Fletcher, given the right preparation, is always a very, very good player for us. Getting Tom Cleverley back would be a bonus, if we can get him back around Christmas time. It would be a bonus to get him back because he's such a clever footballer. I think we're okay, we've got a strong squad.

'It's dead easy to say you'll go out and buy players. But it's not easy to buy players who are good enough for Manchester United, especially in January. I could choose two or three players who you'd like to have at this club who are not available. So there's no point in even going there.'

The Reds' depleted ranks faced a tricky test in their next outing: the Premier League visit of Newcastle United. The Magpies had suffered only their first league defeat of the season a week earlier, at a rampant Manchester City, and Sir Alex was full of admiration for the job conducted – on a tight budget – by Alan Pardew.

'He is very meticulous in training, he's grasped the nettle at Newcastle very well and he's showing he's determined to succeed,' he said. 'They're all working like Trojans up there. Newcastle aren't doing much wrong at the moment and the quality of the league is improving – you can throw a net over the top five or six.'

'Newcastle have had a really good start,' added Newcastle-born midfielder, Michael Carrick. 'Not a lot of people would have put them up there if you had asked a few months back. But credit to them, they have stuck together and they are certainly enjoying being up there. They are my hometown club and the team I watched as a boy, so it is great to see them at the top. I am glad they are doing well, but obviously come Saturday, it will be different for me.'

Barclays Premier League

26 November 2011 | Old Trafford | Kick-off 15:00 |
Attendance: 75,594

Manchester United 1 (Hernandez 49)
Newcastle United 1 (Ba 64 (pen))

The frustration of an afternoon in which a succession of United chances went begging was heightened by a stunningly controversial equaliser that somehow gave Newcastle a point. Alan Pardew's side were pummelled from start to finish but, though they defended heroically, they were inexplicably handed a point when Rio Ferdinand's fair challenge on Hatem Ben Arfa resulted in a penalty, converted by Demba Ba, to cancel out Chicharito's earlier opener.

A strong United side started slowly, but soon began to gather momentum as they realised the level of application required to break down the well-drilled visitors. Chicharito looked the Reds' liveliest attacker, and chanced his arm frequently, without severely testing goalkeeper Tim Krul.

The Dutch stopper did well to scoop away Fabio's menacing cross, but Krul's outstanding involvement would come after the break as United mounted a siege. That never seemed on the cards when the champions forged ahead within five minutes of the restart, when Steven Taylor's clearance rebounded in off Chicharito, amid a mêlée prompted by Wayne Rooney's close-range free-kick.

Fabio then fired off-target and Ashley Young drilled just wide as the Reds pushed for more, but there would be a twist in the tale. David De Gea produced a stunning save to turn away Fabricio Coloccini's powerful effort in a rare forward foray from the visitors, shortly before Ferdinand executed a fine tackle on Ben Arfa at the apparent cost of a corner.

United's players and supporters were irate, however, when referee Mike Jones instead awarded a penalty. After lengthy protests, Ba coolly slid home his finish to give the visitors undeserved parity. The prevalent sense of injustice prompted unyielding United pressure. Rooney fired wide, Young somehow slid past an open goal under the close attentions of Steven Taylor, Krul made a breathtaking reflex save from Nemanja Vidic's close-range header and then Young crashed a low shot against the inside of the post.

Amid that flurry of activity, Jonas Gutierrez picked up his second booking of the game to reduce the visitors to ten men. The decision had almost no impact on the play, with Newcastle defending heroically and United committing everything to the pursuit of victory. Former Red Danny Simpson made an unbelievable goal-line block to stop a Hernandez header, substitute Kiko Macheda could only nod a Giggs centre wide and Vidic was unable to scramble home a mis-hit shot by Ferdinand.

Then, in injury time, United appeared to have snatched victory as Hernandez slid home Giggs' cross, only for the effort to be correctly disallowed for a marginal offside. Late winners make such afternoons bearable, but taking a solitary point from such a one-sided affair was beyond harsh on United.

The Teams

Manchester United: De Gea; Fabio (Smalling 89), Vidic, Ferdinand, Evra (Macheda 88); Nani, Carrick, Giggs, Young; Rooney, Hernandez
Subs not used: Lindegaard, Evans, Park, Valencia, Gibson
Booked: Fabio

Newcastle United: Krul; Simpson, S.Taylor, Coloccini, R.Taylor; Obertan (Sammy Ameobi 65), Cabaye, Guthrie (Perch 74), Gutierrez, Ben Arfa (Lovenkrands 80); Ba
Subs not used: Elliott, Santon, Gosling, Shola Ameobi
Booked: Ben Arfa, Cabaye, Guthrie
Sent off: Gutierrez

'I think we deserved the win,' said Patrice Evra, with a wry grin. 'It's a draw, but you have to take the positives and I think the team has not played that way for a long time and created so many chances. If you want to win the league, you have to score more goals. Against Arsenal [in August], we created eight chances and scored eight. Today, we had maybe seven chances and only one goal. Sometimes, that's football – it's very strange. It's frustrating but it's a positive game for Manchester United.

'At the start of the season, we did very well – scored a lot of goals and conceded a lot of goals. After the big accidents against City, when they scored six goals, we decided to defend better and we know, if we have a strong defence, we're going to win games. It's why we looked like the old United when winning one-nil every time and winning the league in the end.

'Today, we looked more like we played at the beginning of the season and I know we're going to score more than one goal per game. There's big frustration, as I definitely wanted to finish that game being just two points behind City, but the league is a marathon not a sprint. There's a long way to go and I'm confident if the team keeps playing that well, I'm convinced we're going to win the league.'

Newcastle's highly dubious penalty award was an inevitable post-match topic, and Sir Alex Ferguson conceded: 'I think it was everyone's view [that it was a fair tackle], including the referee, as he thought Rio won the ball because he gave the corner kick. He let the assistant referee over-rule him.

'We had a situation a few weeks ago when the linesman gave a penalty kick to Sunderland for handball. The referee that day was put in a terrible quandary in between what to do, as he knew full well it wasn't a penalty and over-ruled his linesman. It's what the referee should have done today.'

Like Evra, the manager could clutch at some overriding positives from the performance as a whole, adding: 'Alan Pardew said Newcastle were the better team in the first half – I don't know what game he was at! Chicharito had four clear chances and we played some great football. The second half was just an onslaught and to not get three points from that is just a travesty.

'I'm not concerned if we're playing like that. Most of the time, we'd score three or four goals in that game. Their goalkeeper made some fantastic saves, there were shots blocked, cleared off the line and we had one or two bad misses. So it's just an incredible result. They had a few blocks and put their bodies on the line all the time. Give credit to Newcastle, but we absolutely slaughtered them and we just couldn't get the result. It's disappointing in that respect but, if we play like that every week, I'll be very happy.'

The disappointment at United's dropped points quickly made way for a sense of shock which gripped British football when, the next day, the news broke that Wales manager Gary Speed had been found hanged, aged just 42.

For Ryan Giggs in particular, as a former international team-mate of the popular Speed, the news came as a huge blow. 'I am totally devastated,' Giggs admitted in a statement. 'Gary Speed was one of the nicest men in football and someone I am honoured to call a team-mate and friend. Words cannot begin to describe how sad I feel at hearing this awful news. It goes without saying my thoughts are with his family at this tremendously sad time.'

Speaking in his capacity as a Sky Sports pundit, former Reds captain Gary Neville also paid tribute to the midfielder, just hours after the news emerged. 'It's absolutely devastating,' said a visibly stunned Neville. 'Our careers crossed paths often and I played against him many times. He was a fantastic professional, a winner with a great reputation. We sometimes think of football being important, but it's not.'

It was quickly agreed that a minute's applause would provide a tribute to Speed ahead of United's next outing – their third home game in a week – against Crystal Palace in the quarter-final of the Carling Cup.

Sir Alex Ferguson had continued his time-honoured tradition of blooding youngsters in the early rounds of the competition, and he planned to do so again in the last-eight tie against Dougie Freedman's Championship side. Watching his youngsters blending with the senior players in training was a welcome sight for the United manager.

'Paul Pogba, Ravel Morrison, Jesse Lingard, Zeki Fryers, Larnell Cole and Michael Keane . . . they're all training with the first team,' he said. 'That allows me to see how they cope playing against seasoned professionals, it lets me judge their temperament. It allows me to get a far better picture of how they're progressing. And, while this is going on, you hope they're playing well for the Reserves and displaying the right attitude and enthusiasm.

'They enjoy the challenge and it's an opportunity for us to see what they're like in these sessions, how they cope with the older players. It's how they handle the likes of Rio Ferdinand and Nemanja Vidic if they give them a bit of stick . . . It's a good part of a young player's progress when they can be involved with the big boys.'

There were cautionary words, however, from Patrice Evra, who was aware of the youngsters' undoubted potential from his glimpses of them on the Carrington proving grounds. The Frenchman said: 'This is a big chance for them, but they have to be careful because Sir Alex gives you an opportunity and if you let him down, it's difficult to get another one.

'This is the United way: if you play well, you'll get another chance, but if you play only an average game, the boss will put you on the bench. There's always someone ready to come in and try to do better than you. That's why players must be ready to grasp the chance. Before the game they must think to themselves how lucky they are to be playing with the first team already.'

Alas, those warnings would seemingly go unheeded by squad members young and old on a night to forget at Old Trafford.

Carling Cup quarter-final

30 November 2011 | Old Trafford | Kick-off 20:00 |
Attendance: 52,624

Manchester United 1 (Macheda 69 (pen))
Crystal Palace 2 (Ambrose 65, Murray 98)

A trying week took a turn for the worse for United, when Crystal Palace dumped the Reds out of the Carling Cup in embarrassing fashion at Old Trafford. Dougie Freedman's side put in a display of composure and commitment that was never matched by the hosts, moving Sir Alex Ferguson to apologise to United supporters after the visitors' extra-time triumph.

Palace had moved ahead midway through the second period after Darren Ambrose's unbelievable long-range effort, only for Kiko Macheda to quickly draw United level from the penalty spot. Rather than move with that momentum, however, the Reds never looked like progressing, and were undone by Glenn Murray's extra-time header.

On a night when Sir Alex Ferguson lost Fabio, Rafael and Dimitar Berbatov to injuries, the fact that Murray's winner had been scored from an offside position almost paled into insignificance.

Eight of United's starting side were either current or retired senior internationals, yet the visitors looked brighter from the first whistle. Wilfred Zaha and Jermaine Easter both caused scares inside the opening ten minutes without testing Ben Amos, and it took United until the 45th minute to muster a noteworthy effort, when Mame Biram Diouf rounded off a speedy counter-attack by sending an acrobatic effort just over the crossbar.

The first period was most noteworthy for the loss of Fabio and Palace's Sean Scannell (both to hamstring injuries), and Berbatov (ankle). In the second period, Rafael (ankle again) also fell victim in the game. Though Berbatov's replacement, Ravel Morrison, injected unpredictability into the United attack, the game remained an uneventful encounter.

Morrison stung Lewis Price's palms from distance and Antonio Valencia slid wide after defensive uncertainty from the visitors, but when the first goal came, the deadlock was obliterated, never mind broken.

Veteran midfielder Ambrose, on as a substitute, collected the ball 40 yards from goal before advancing briefly and firing an unstoppable effort into the top corner of the Stretford End goal. Though shock gripped Old Trafford, a smattering of applause betrayed the goal's brilliance.

Within three minutes, however, the Reds were level. Macheda slotted home from the penalty spot after being tugged to the ground by Patrick McCarthy, who clearly had a handful of the Italian's shirt. There would be no late charge from either side, though. Extra time beckoned, and again it was Palace who struck first, again through a substitute. Murray was clearly ahead of play when Ambrose's free-kick was whipped in, but his header stood and United would again have to fight back.

Despite bossing possession and applying plentiful pressure, however, there would be no trademark late recovery from the Reds, and instead it was Palace who marched into a semi-final date with Cardiff City.

The Teams

Manchester United: Amos; Rafael (Pogba 64), Evans, Smalling, Fabio (Fryers 37); Valencia, Gibson, Park, Diouf; Berbatov (Morrison 46), Macheda
Subs not used: Lindegaard, W.Keane, Cole, Lingard
Booked: Gibson, Fabio

Crystal Palace: Price; Clyne, McCarthy, Gardner, Wright; O'Keefe, Dikgacoi, Moxey (Ambrose 46), Scannell (Parr 45), Zaha; Easter (Murray 74)
Subs not used: Speroni, Iversen, Jedinak, Ramage

'I don't know where to start to be honest,' said a shell-shocked Sir Alex Ferguson. 'My apologies go to our fans tonight, because that was not a Manchester United performance. I don't want to take anything away from Crystal Palace – I wish them every success and I hope they get to the final. It was a fantastic, mammoth effort from all of them. Every one of their players worked their socks off to get to the semi-finals.

'We maybe played too many short passes, but I'm not going to dwell on it and go into the ins and outs of it all. When it went to extra time I thought we must win it, but it wasn't to be. Their second goal was offside from what I've seen on the cameras, but I can't take it away from Crystal Palace, they fought hard to get the result and they deserve it. It's a very disappointing night for Manchester United.'

Though the chance to reach a third final in four years had been spectacularly passed up by the 2009 and 2010 winners, skipper-for-the-night Jonny Evans urged all involved to move on as quickly as possible; a manageable feat given the hectic demands looming in December's packed fixture list.

'Before the game I was delighted to be given the armband, but I'd happily take that away to have the victory instead,' said the defender. 'We're very disappointed not to be in the semi-finals. I thought we would go on after we scored. And going into the first period of extra time, playing towards the Stretford End, I thought we'd have a chance of getting a goal and seal it from there. But they went down the other end and scored against the run of play, really. We had a lot of possession but we couldn't break them down. The games are coming thick and fast, and the manager will need his squad. So we need to pick ourselves up and hopefully win on Saturday [at Aston Villa].'

The trip to Villa Park would be one of seven vital games in December. Despite the looming congestion and ongoing issues with injuries, Sir Alex was keeping calm and aiming merely to stay in the hunt for honours.

'I don't think we are looking over our shoulders or up above us at this time, as it is so early on in the season,' the manager declared. 'The important thing is for us to do our jobs right. December is a hectic month, you have the Boxing Day and New Year fixtures and it's a congested programme. That's why you have to utilise your squad to navigate your way through all of that. By 31 December, we'll hopefully be in the right position.

'To me, that is always a good indicator about how your chances are and who your dangers are. I always use that barometer at that time of the year. I'll be happy with top – I'll be happy with second as long as we are within a point or two – that will do me fine.'

6

December – The Rough
with the Smooth

United staggered into the final month of 2011, disappointed at the nature of the Carling Cup exit to Crystal Palace and carrying an ever-growing number of casualties. In the game against the Eagles alone, Rafael, Fabio and Dimitar Berbatov had all sustained knocks or strains that ruled them out of the early-December trip to Aston Villa.

'We've been getting a few injuries, but it happens,' shrugged Sir Alex Ferguson. 'Every club gets them. At the moment, we're going through a spell where we're getting a few a week, but we have a strong squad and we just have to get on with it.'

Villa Park has traditionally been a hospitable venue for the Reds in both league and cup games, but there was no guarantee of the reception Ashley Young would face on his return to his former club, just five months after leaving for Old Trafford.

'I'm excited about going back,' he said. 'I have very happy memories of my time there and hopefully I'll get a warm reception. But I'm just concentrating on going there and doing well. I've still got friends there who I speak to pretty much every week, so it will be nice to go back there and see them. It will be even nicer if we come back winning. If we apply ourselves in the right way, I'm sure we'll get the three points.'

Manchester City's incessant winning run had maintained their five-point lead at the head of the table – and extended it to eight shortly before the Reds' early evening kick-off – but Young maintained that there was still plenty of mileage in the title race.

'I don't think you can talk about who's going to win the league just yet,' he insisted. 'There are still plenty of games to play, plenty of points to pick up. If we go about our job in the way we have done since the start of the season, then we'll keep picking up points and I'm sure the title will be coming back here.'

Barclays Premier League

3 December 2011 | Villa Park | Kick-off 17:30 |
Attendance: 40,053

Aston Villa 0
Manchester United 1 (Jones 20)

Phil Jones scored his first goal in senior football as United ground out a narrow but comfortable win at Villa Park. Operating in central midfield once again, the youngster embossed another eye-catching display with the winning goal after 20 minutes, racing onto Nani's left-wing cross to clinically side-foot home a volley on the run.

The visitors were rarely troubled by the shot-shy hosts, who applied any meaningful pressure only late on. United were equal to their efforts, however, and registered another valuable clean sheet without Anders Lindegaard being called into noteworthy action.

A slow-burning start to the game was further doused early on when Javier Hernandez twisted his ankle after a sudden change of direction, adding himself to the Reds' growing list of casualties. United recovered from that setback, which prompted the introduction of Antonio Valencia in the Mexican's place, and moved into the lead with the game's first sustained attack of menace. Patrice Evra swiftly found Nani on the left flank, and the winger's measured delivery was expertly placed past Shay Given by the rampaging Jones, whose goal prompted a blend of delight and mirth on the United bench.

The visitors took the goal as their cue to surge forward. Given pushed away Nani's close-range header and Valencia rocketed a shot narrowly over the bar, before the game again ground to a halt when Given was taken off with a hamstring injury and replaced by Brad Guzan.

United were unable to thoroughly test the American, however: in part due to poor decision-making in the final third, but also because of last-ditch blocks from Stephen Warnock and James Collins on Wayne Rooney and Jones respectively.

After Jermaine Jenas had also succumbed to injury, Villa finally carved out some openings themselves, as substitute Emile Heskey was unable to convert a Richard Dunne flick-on and Collins' header was tipped over by Lindegaard.

Ashley Young, on his return to Villa Park, aimed a tame shot straight at Guzan and Rooney flashed a volley over the bar, before substitute Danny Welbeck, on for Young, had a goal correctly disallowed for offside. Heskey miscued in the dying stages of the game as United comfortably saw out another narrow but vital victory.

The Teams

Aston Villa: Given (Guzan 38); Hutton, Collins, Dunne, Warnock; Albrighton, Jenas (Heskey 64), Herd (Petrov 59), Bannan; Bent, Agbonlahor
Subs not used: Delph, Ireland, Clark, Cuellar

Manchester United: Lindegaard; Smalling, Vidic, Ferdinand (Giggs 64), Evra; Nani, Carrick, Jones, Young (Welbeck 79); Rooney, Hernandez (Valencia 12)
Subs not used: De Gea, Evans, Park, Fletcher

'I'm delighted to score but it wasn't about the goal,' grinned match-winner Phil Jones. 'It was about three points and I thought the lads did exceptionally well. We knew it was going to be a hard-fought game as Villa are a tough team to beat at home, but we played terrifically well. After last week, when I stuck one in the back of my own net [against Benfica], I was delighted to score and get off the mark. I signalled to Rene [Meulensteen, first team coach] as he was giving me a bit of stick for not scoring. It's just a coincidence that I scored today so I gave him a point of the finger!'

'We'd kept winding him up and saying: "We paid sixteen million pounds for you and we can't even get a shot off you!"' added Sir Alex Ferguson. 'The staff have been giving him stick so he was very, very pleased.'

But while Jones took a substantial share of the plaudits for his decisive strike, the growing contribution of United's defensive nous was also noticeable. Having conceded just one goal in five Premier League games since the Manchester derby, the Reds' miserly streak had returned to bolster the champions' title defence.

'Clean sheets are like goals for goalkeepers,' said Anders Lindegaard. 'In ten games, nobody will remember how many fantastic saves were made – they will remember how many clean sheets were kept. For my sake, I would rather win one-nil than ten-one, because I am a goalkeeper and I want a clean sheet.

'It was a very important win. We were under a lot of pressure because of the other results, so I think we did very well and played brilliantly in defence. It was top class and very enjoyable. It's not easy – if it looks easy, then it's a big compliment to the goalkeeper. One of the biggest compliments you can get as a keeper is if you make difficult things look easy. You have to be one hundred per cent focused all the way. I think, personally, one of my best attributes is my ability to focus and stay focused. I don't find it very difficult.'

The alternation of Lindegaard with David De Gea was breeding a healthy competition for a solitary spot in the team, and the Danish international welcomed the challenge. 'It's very good,' he explained. 'It keeps us both sharp. I enjoy working with him very much. He is a great lad and always comes in with a smile and a good attitude. It's very enjoyable and it makes us both better.'

While armed with a surfeit of talent when choosing his goalkeeper, Sir Alex was increasingly short of options in other areas, and his striking department was looking relatively threadbare after the freak injury to Chicharito. With the Mexican expected to miss four weeks with ankle ligament damage, Dimitar Berbatov struggling with his own ankle problems, Michael Owen out long-term and Danny Welbeck feeling his way back to fitness, the manager had key decisions to make ahead of the make-or-break Champions League trip to Basel.

The suspension of Michael Carrick, allied to injuries for Anderson and Tom Cleverley, made matters harder, yet Sir Alex was still in upbeat mood as his side touched down in Switzerland. 'Our form away from home in Europe over the last three or four years has been fantastic,' he explained. 'We've really done well and it needs to be that kind of performance on Wednesday.

'The only advantage is they do need to win and they have to try to beat us. We've always kept good possession of the ball and made that a dominating factor of our game. It can take the temperature out of the game. We went to Besiktas and Bursaspor and the noise was incredible, but you can kill that with good possession of the ball and the concentration levels have been really terrific. You need that in these games.'

The boss did concede, however, that his newest iteration of United was learning on the job in European football, and had already sustained some lasting lessons. 'Europe represents a different challenge,' he said. 'Maybe we have to bring our game up a bit and maybe don't under-estimate the group stages. Perhaps our casualness in that game [against Basel] at Old Trafford could cost us, you know. But we've got the players to get us through, there's no question about that. We've got to perform – it won't be an easy game and we're not expecting it to be easy either.'

Were any added motivation required for such an important game, Darren Fletcher and his more experienced colleagues could draw on the embarrassment of United's previous group stage exit. Ominously, it had come exactly six years before the clash with Basel, as the Reds slipped to a 2-1 defeat at Benfica.

'We have experience of it not going right when it comes down to the last game, so we'll try to draw from that match and make sure it doesn't happen again,' said the Scot. 'There are a few of us still in the squad who experienced the disappointment of that night. We'll reiterate that feeling to the rest of the lads.'

Unfortunately, the entire travelling party would soon be able to relate to the elders' past experiences.

UEFA Champions League Group C

7 December 2011 | St Jakob-Park | Kick-off 19:45 |
Attendance: 36,894

FC Basel 2 (Streller 9, A.Frei 84)
Manchester United 1 (Jones 89)

United's stuttering Champions League campaign ground to a halt in shocking circumstances, as Basel deservedly overcame the Reds on a bleak night in Switzerland.

Marco Streller put the hosts into an early lead and whipped up a red-hot atmosphere in the freezing arena of St Jakob-Park, and even though an equaliser would have ensured the Reds' progression, Alexander Frei headed a late second to book Basel's place in the second round.

Phil Jones scored his second goal in as many games to give the Reds a flicker of hope, but it was too little, too late on an evening in which a demotion to Europa League football offered scant consolation for

Sir Alex Ferguson's side, while a serious knee injury to Nemanja Vidic compounded the Reds' misery.

Basel opened the scoring with their first attack, as a defensive mix-up by Vidic and Chris Smalling allowed Xherdan Shaqiri to advance and drill in a low cross. David De Gea used his feet to clear the danger, but only teed up Streller to volley home from close range.

United's response was initially defiant, and led by an impressive display on the wing by Nani. Shortly after the Portuguese had fired off-target, his perfect right-wing cross was somehow miskicked by Wayne Rooney when it appeared easier to tap home.

More Nani trickery gave Ashley Young a headed opportunity, which was directed off target, before Rooney shot straight at Yann Sommer. United's dominance looked like it would surely reap dividends, only for the visitors to be dealt a damaging blow before the interval, as Vidic bore the full weight of Basel skipper Streller on his right knee, which buckled under the strain.

The second period was an altogether more even affair. Rooney bent a shot off target after a fine through-ball by Ryan Giggs and Nani forced a diving save out of Sommer, but Basel almost doubled their lead when De Gea then produced a flying save to keep out Alexander Frei's free-kick.

On the hour, only the woodwork denied the Reds as Markus Steinhofer inexplicably hammered a Nani cross against the underside of his own bar, lending further evidence that this was not to be United's evening. Young and Rooney both then missed the target as time started to run out, before Shaqiri's fine cross was allowed to reach Alexander Frei, who nodded home from close range to send the home support wild.

Jones offered the Reds a late lifeline, as Sommer failed to keep out his header after substitutes Danny Welbeck and Kiko Macheda had been denied by the goalkeeper and the crossbar respectively, but no time remained for the unlikeliest of salvage jobs. Instead, United could only reflect on dropping points in four of six group games, and a humbling descent into the Europa League for the first time since 1995.

The Teams

FC Basel: Sommer; Park, Dragovic, Abraham; Shaqiri (Stocker 89),
F.Frei, Cabral, Steinhofer, G.Xhaka (Chipperfield 83); Streller,
A.Frei (Kusunga 89)
Subs not used: Colomba, Kovac, Zoua, Ryong-Pak
Booked: G.Xhaka, F.Frei

Manchester United: De Gea; Smalling, Ferdinand, Vidic (Evans 44),
Evra; Nani, Jones, Park (Macheda 82), Giggs, Young (Welbeck 64);
Rooney
Subs not used: Lindegaard, Fletcher, Valencia, Gibson
Booked: Evra, Young

'It's a big disappointment,' conceded a shell-shocked Patrice Evra. 'Since I played with Monaco, I've never been out in the first round. It's catastrophic and we feel very sad, but we deserved to go out. It's not about tonight but throughout the competition – we threw away qualification. We created a lot of chances tonight and they get only two chances but they win – and deserved to win. From the beginning, we never played well in the Champions League.'

Yet, as ever, the Frenchman remained the sultan of the soundbite, quickly doing his best to rouse the Reds' dejected ranks. 'If you play for Manchester United, you have to be strong,' he urged. 'I think the gaffer knows the players will get back, because they've got a strong mentality. For six years, as I said, I've never been out in the first round, so it's a new experience for us. We have got to get back and get focused on the Premier League as that's the target – to win the Premier League.

'It will be more difficult for us [with Europa League commitments], but we deserved it with the way we played. We deserve to play on Thursday and Sunday. But we are Manchester United. Today is a really bad day for everyone – the fans, staff and players. We must make sure we don't throw the season away. We still have things to win and must make sure we play with heart.'

Another experienced defender, Rio Ferdinand, also provided a voice of reason and defiance, insisting that the Reds would have to deal with the situation. 'We're in the Europa League now and I've always said that whatever competition we're in, we don't enter it to come second or to get knocked out in the early stages,' he said. 'We're always in it to win it and this is no different.

'We'll learn from this, dust ourselves down and move to the next game. We won't dwell on this, although we're massively disappointed at the moment. But we've got massive games coming up and we need to make sure we're in the right frame of mind to win those games.'

While the rest of the dejected party made their way back to Manchester, Wayne Rooney remained in Nyon to attend a UEFA disciplinary hearing regarding his dismissal for England against Montenegro. The striker received a timely morale boost with the news that he would serve only a two-game suspension instead of three.

That minor boost was offset by a huge loss for the Reds, as Sir Alex Ferguson confirmed to his Friday morning press conference that Nemanja Vidic had ruptured his cruciate knee ligaments in Switzerland.

'We thought it was a bad one,' said the manager. 'He's out for the season. It's not unexpected but it's still bad news. He'll see a specialist on Monday to work out the progress of when he has the operation. It won't be immediate as we have to let the swelling come down.

'We'll now have to choose between Jonny Evans, Phil Jones and Chris Smalling. I thought Rio had his best game of season on Wednesday. His experience will be vital. It is a loss and we missed him in the early part of the season for five weeks with his calf injury against West Brom. He's such a dominant character, particularly his defending in the penalty box. That's always a strong feature of his game.'

The boss was speaking ahead of the visit of Mick McCarthy's Wolverhampton Wanderers, and found himself defending his young players after their inexperience had been so emphatically punished in Basel.

'When the likes of [Ryan] Giggs and the other young lads came in to the side, they came in for criticism early on,' he said. 'We've experienced that many times over the years. But the Wes Browns and John O'Sheas and Darren Fletchers all became the foundation of the club and that's what will happen with these young players.

'They've achieved many great things so far. Chris Smalling, Phil Jones and Danny Welbeck have played for their country – they will be the foundation of the club in a few years' time, there's no question about that. They had a nasty experience on Wednesday, but they know they have the trust of me and my coaches, and they will not be hounded because of one bad performance. Time will prove us right.

'We're not the only club in the world that can have a bad result. Everyone gets them. How you recover from them is important and it's good for our young players, in particular.'

Unfortunately for Wolves, the Reds – young and old – would heed their manager's words.

Barclays Premier League

**10 December 2011 | Old Trafford | Kick-off 15:00 |
Attendance: 75,627**

Manchester United 4 (Nani 17, 56, Rooney 27, 62)
Wolverhampton Wanderers 1 (Fletcher 47)

United mustered an ideal response to their Champions League humbling, with an entertaining dismantlement of Mick McCarthy's Wolves at Old Trafford. Nani and Wayne Rooney both bagged braces, flanking a header from Steven Fletcher that briefly set nerves jangling among the home supporters, only for the hosts to turn on the afterburners and complete a swaggering victory.

It was the manner of the Reds' display which was most pleasing, coming so soon after a costly, out-of-sorts display in Switzerland, and Sir Alex Ferguson's side were on the front foot from the off, with Nani and Antonio Valencia in unplayable form.

A cross from the Ecuador international was headed just over the top by a diving Michael Carrick, before Rooney forced Wayne Hennessey into a pair of decent stops, but the dam broke just after the quarter-hour mark, as Valencia fed Nani and the Portuguese winger meandered infield and drilled a low shot past Hennessey from 20 yards.

A second goal wasn't long coming. Chris Smalling, Carrick and Nani were all involved in the build-up that led to Rooney's sharply taken strike catching Hennessey out and beating the keeper's despairing dive. Still the chances flowed, as Rooney, Nani and Danny Welbeck all came close.

It was the visitors, however, who mustered the first opening – and goal – of the second half. Matt Jarvis did well down the left wing and his deep cross was met by Fletcher, who outjumped Patrice Evra and looped his header into the far corner to halve the arrears.

Mettle suitably under scrutiny, United responded in style. The outstanding Valencia collected a pass from Phil Jones and drove into the visitors' area before firing in a low cross that was touched home by the alert Nani.

The Ecuadorian was soon at it again, notching his third assist of the game with a perfectly weighted cross for Rooney, who showed textbook technique to superbly volley a difficult opportunity past Hennessey.

David De Gea was called into action as the game drifted towards its conclusion, fending away efforts from Fletcher, Jarvis and Jamie O'Hara, but United were equally prolific in their chance creation. Rooney, Welbeck and substitute Kiko Macheda all came close to adding gloss to the scoreline, but it was the emphatic nature of United's performance that gave most festive cheer.

The Teams

Manchester United: De Gea; Smalling, Jones, Ferdinand, Evra (Fryers 67); Valencia, Carrick, Jones, Nani (Young 77); Rooney, Welbeck (Macheda 74)
Subs not used: Lindegaard, Giggs, Park, Gibson
Booked: Ferdinand

Wolverhampton Wanderers: Hennessey; Zubar, Johnson, Berra, Ward; Doyle, Edwards (Milijas 32), Henry, O'Hara (Hunt 71), Jarvis; Fletcher (Ebanks-Blake 77)
Subs not used: De Vries, Elokobi, Stearman, Hammill

After scoring a brace to help quickly banish the ghosts of Basel, Nani was in predictably upbeat mood, post-match. 'I think we had a fantastic performance,' enthused the winger. 'Everyone played well and I think everyone wanted to win this game. It's the way we normally play, who we are and, of course, it was a fantastic afternoon with a lot of goals. Everyone is happy with the game.

'It's been tough. We know we always go the final stages of the Champions League and we're used to qualifying easily through the groups, so this time it's disappointing. We did not expect to go to the Europa League, but we are still alive and still have the opportunity to play like today. We just have to do our best to win the competitions we are in. Of course, the last game was a bad moment, but I think we responded very well with this game today and I hope we keep doing the same until the finish of the season.'

Like Nani, Wayne Rooney had capped an impressive personal display with a pair of goals, ending a run of five barren games. Sir Alex was hopeful to see his main striker off and running again as a vital part of the season approached, saying: 'We hope he goes on a spurt now. With Wayne in particular, he tends to score in spurts – for instance, early this season he scored eleven in the early part of the campaign. Now we're heading towards an important part of the season and if we get that sort of goal ratio from Wayne again that will put us in good fettle.'

The Reds' festive mood was spurred on by Manchester City's first defeat of the Premier League season: a 2-1 reverse at Chelsea that left the champions only two points off the head of the table. With European football off the agenda and such a menacing position in the league, the scene was set for Carrington's annual Christmas panto, a club tradition in which the club's Academy players perform in the canteen in front of the facility's entire workforce. Organised by masseur Rod Thornley, the show is invariably a smash hit with everyone.

'This year's was really good; one of the best yet,' grins Danny Welbeck. 'Obviously, I've been there before, so I know how nerve-wracking it is to step up in front of all of Carrington. This year Rod didn't have much time to organise everything, because not all the youngsters were around, so he only had a couple of days to get it sorted, but he came up with a really good plot and it was one of the funniest yet.

'Charni [Ekangamene] was really good, mimicking a member of staff at Carrington, and he might have done Ando as well. Someone did Zeki [Fryers] against Crystal Palace, where he was tackled by a ghost, and just the usual ones got it as well. It's all friendly banter and never goes too far, so everyone always enjoys it and looks forward to it.'

In the spirit of Christmas and team bonding, every player who partakes gives their all, regardless of what Thornley requires them to do. 'I had a wig on, a skirt . . . it had to be one of the saddest days of my life,' laughs Welbeck. 'Though I have to add I didn't wear a skirt for rehearsals! I didn't look too bad though: I've got the long legs for it! Another year I was Trevor McDonald reporting live from Carrington. I stepped up in those plays; anyone around Carrington would give me props for that. The first year I was really scared, but once you get into it you just go along with it. If you do it without any enthusiasm, it's just rubbish, so you've just got to see it as a laugh.'

Welbeck isn't the only senior squad member to have been through the panto proving ground. 'They're good fun,' admits Jonny Evans. 'I took part when I was in the youth team, and all I'm saying is that I had to wear fake boobs, a wig and some wonky teeth, and a pair of pleats. And a mini-skirt!'

Though the panto injected a welcome dose of merriment to life at Carrington, there were also far more serious matters to consider, most notably with the shock announcement that Darren Fletcher would be taking an indefinite break from football in order to battle ulcerative colitis, a chronic inflammatory bowel condition. The midfielder's previous sporadic absences had been attributed to a viral infection, but the club revealed in a statement that this had been a mistruth in order to protect the Scottish international's right to medical confidentiality.

'The medical people have made the right decision,' stressed Sir Alex. 'They regarded Darren's health as the more important issue and we as a club agree completely with that. He's not been in training – he was in hospital for a few days, and he'll rest now.

'Darren is a loss – he's such a great professional and it's not easy to replace that, but we'll have to think about that. Hopefully he'll make a full recovery. It's obviously going to take a bit of time and rest is the most important thing at the moment. It'll be the medical people who make all the decisions and we're quite happy with that. I can't put a timescale on it.

'It's an accurate assessment by the medical people and also Darren knowing his own situation and how he was feeling. There was no persuasion needed at all. He's disappointed, but you have to deal with these things; but he can do that because he has a strong character. It's easier now it's out in the open. That was the big decision he had to make. We were trying to address the confidentiality part of it in a different way by talking about a virus, but that was down to protecting Darren. He got to the position, particularly in Scotland, where there was more delving into why we kept talking about a virus, and I think he felt a bit uncomfortable about it. So he decided to make it public.'

With the January transfer window looming large, the possibility of recruiting a replacement for Fletcher was mooted by the media, but the manager quickly batted back talk of panic buying.

'Not necessarily,' he replied. 'I don't know why people keep going on about that. It's never been a route we've taken consistently, unless a player that we've been interested in appears, but there is no sign of that at the moment. So therefore it's not always suitable to us.

'If you look at the options we have: Jones has played a few games [in midfield], Ryan obviously can play there too and Ji is capable of playing there too. There are maybe one or two other options – Darron Gibson is an option. He had an early-season injury, but he has the experience needed to play in central midfield. The options are not too bad. Young [Paul] Pogba is an option. He's progressing very well. It's one of these situations – unless there is a player we've been interested in for a while appears and you can get him, then there isn't much point in bringing an individual in because it gives you another player. Pogba is a possibility. He's a big strong lad, a good athlete. He's improving and developing well.'

There were, however, question marks over the French midfielder's future, as negotiations over a contract extension continued to rumble on, and international media speculated that he might be a transfer target for several Italian clubs.

'You hope he gets the right advice,' said the boss. 'All young players who remain here always do well, particularly the ones with talent. It is down to the individual, also. Matt Busby summed it up perfectly when he said you don't need to chase money at a club like Manchester United. He said it will eventually find you; if you are a good enough player, you will earn money. You become rich playing for Manchester United.

'Players can chase their money early in their career, but at the end of it it's not the same as if they'd stayed here. You wouldn't think you'd need to consider what he has here too long, because he just needs to look around about him to realise that. A player has to take the decision himself as to what they think their best future will be. Most of the players who stay here have a good future.'

For United, the immediate future promised a return to Loftus Road for a first league meeting with Queens Park Rangers since 1996, and the chance to take top spot in the Premier League, albeit temporarily, with Manchester City hosting Arsenal later in the day.

'City have obviously had that psychological edge over us over the last few weeks in terms of being top. If we can go above them, it will put a lot of pressure on them when they play a couple of hours later,' claimed Chris Smalling.

'It would be a good psychological boost to get back to top spot. City have maybe got a little comfy in terms of being on top, but if we can get that back then we'll be hard to knock off, because we're only going to get stronger as the season goes on.'

Barclays Premier League

18 December 2011 | Loftus Road | Kick-off 12:00 |
Attendance: 18,033

Queens Park Rangers 0
Manchester United 2 (Rooney 1, Carrick 56)

United turned in a devastating display of incisive attacking football, which might have yielded a resounding win over Queens Park Rangers, but still secured an impressive victory through goals from Wayne Rooney and Michael Carrick.

Rooney headed home the opening goal inside a minute at Loftus Road and Carrick added a fine solo goal early in the second period, and only the woodwork and some inspired goal-keeping from Radek Cerny prevented the Reds from running up an eye-catching scoreline.

Rooney and Antonio Valencia had returned to form against Wolves in superb fashion, and the pair combined after just 52 seconds at Loftus Road to give United a dream start. Having nicked possession, Valencia redirected the ball to Rooney and raced onto the striker's headed return pass before arcing a magnificent cross into the path of the onrushing Rooney. Though the striker had to contend with the attentions of Rangers defender Matthew Connolly, he managed to fling himself and redirect the ball inside Cerny's post.

The visitors' red-hot start almost yielded further reward before three minutes were up. Nani pounced on a loose ball, exchanged passes with Rooney and fed Danny Welbeck, whose scuffed effort was blocked by Cerny. The pair then combined again for Welbeck to finish neatly, though it was contentiously deemed offside, before the Reds enjoyed a spell of pressure around the half-hour that should have killed the contest.

First, after Welbeck had beaten Cerny to Nani's corner, Jonny Evans nodded onto the top of the crossbar from inside the six-yard box. Phil Jones was then thwarted in a one-on-one encounter with Cerny, who then heroically flung up an arm to deny Valencia from close range. From the subsequent corner, Evans' header was hoofed off the line by Alejandro Faurlin.

The danger of creating and spurning such a procession of chances was that QPR remained in the game, so the second goal, when it came, was vital. It was Carrick's first strike of the campaign. Pouncing on an errant pass from Joey Barton, the midfielder surged into a yawning gap in the hosts' half and slotted a low finish past Cerny.

Soon enough, Cerny was in action again with a spectacular save to fend away Welbeck's curling effort. Rooney then jabbed over as he tried to redirect Evans' stabbed effort, before Jones curled a superb low shot against the base of Cerny's post.

In a bid to improve his side's fortunes, Neil Warnock introduced Adel Taarabt and DJ Campbell from the bench, and the latter wastefully spooned the former's superb cross over the bar from close range almost immediately.

That was the only occasion in which the hosts managed to pierce United's imperious backline, providing further evidence of the Reds' miserly defensive work after a cavalier opening to the season. Allied to that familiar attacking swagger – and a run of six wins and a draw in seven league games – United's momentum was building ominously.

The Teams

Queens Park Rangers: Cerny; Young, Connolly, Gabbidon, Traore; Wright-Phillips (Taarabt 65), Barton, Faurlin, Mackie; Helguson (Campbell 66), Bothroyd (Hill 75)
Subs not used: Kenny, Orr, Derry, Smith
Booked: Gabbidon

Manchester United: De Gea; Smalling, Ferdinand, Evans, Evra; Valencia, Carrick, Jones, Nani (Young 88); Rooney (Giggs 79), Welbeck (Hernandez 63)
Subs not used: Lindegaard, Berbatov, Park, Fryers
Booked: Ferdinand, Jones

'The last time I scored a goal from inside my own half was probably when I was playing Under-12s,' smiled Michael Carrick, scorer of the all-important second goal. 'It just seemed to open up for me and I kept on going and going and thought: "Why not?" It was great to see it go in. We had so many chances in the game, so many opportunities to get a shot on target . . . I was starting to wonder if it was going to be one of those days. So I was delighted to see it go in, though, even if the run [of two years without a league goal] seemed to take forever.'

Sir Alex Ferguson saw the funny side of his midfielder's rare strike, quipping: 'He's supposed to sit in the middle of the pitch. I'll maybe have to fine him!'

The manager added: 'We could have scored a lot of goals. The one good thing that comes out of it is that Queens Park Rangers in their home games have been a real problem to a lot of teams, but we kept them quiet for most of the game and we played some terrific football at times. We're top of the league for a while at least, but the important thing is to be there on New Year's Day. If you're involved right in the top part then, then you know the second half of the season, we'll relish that.'

The Reds barely had time to arrive back from London before they were due back in the capital, this time for an increasingly tricky trip to Fulham. Before they could head to Craven Cottage, however, the long-awaited outcome of the Suarez–Evra case was announced, with the Football Association banning the Uruguayan for eight games and fining him £40,000 after finding him guilty of racially abusing the United defender.

Evra was among a travelling party looking to end a run of poor away results against the Cottagers, who had established themselves as a bogey side for United in previous seasons and had lost only twice at home in 2011-12. Michael Carrick, however, insisted the champions would be ready for Martin Jol's side.

'Fulham have had an up-and-down time this season, but they beat QPR six-nil at their place and have had some other good results,' he said. 'We know they're a strong team: they're well organised and Craven Cottage is a tough place to visit, but it's a good, old-fashioned football ground and we look forward to going there.'

'The players always look forward to this time of year, with plenty of games,' added Chris Smalling, procured from the Cottagers in 2010. 'We're used to the demands and it's a big opportunity to pick up a lot of points – we want to get maximum points. Christmas can be a hindrance for some and can sometimes make or break you in terms of kicking on, but this is a period where we really need to kick on and show everybody we mean business.'

Fulham would get the message, loud and clear.

Barclays Premier League

21 December 2011 | Craven Cottage | Kick-off 20:00 |
Attendance: 25,700

Fulham 0
Manchester United 5 (Welbeck 5, Nani 28, Giggs 43, Rooney 88, Berbatov 90)

A run of three winless trips to Craven Cottage was obliterated as United romped to victory over Martin Jol's Cottagers.

For the third game in succession, the Reds reaped the rewards of a bright start as Danny Welbeck swept home Nani's left-wing cross inside the first five minutes, before the Portuguese winger and Ryan Giggs ensured a three-goal lead at the break. Fulham hit back and missed a succession of chances, before impressive but contrasting late strikes from Wayne Rooney and Dimitar Berbatov secured an emphatic degree of victory.

The Reds' evening began badly, with Phil Jones sustaining a stray elbow to the face from Clint Dempsey, a knock that would prompt his substitution midway through the opening period. By that point, Welbeck had clinically turned in a left-footed finish after Nani had been allowed to rampage down the left flank.

Shaken, the hosts were clearly second best for the remainder of the opening half. Giggs headed Jones' cross just wide, before he, Nani and Rooney all tested Cottagers goalkeeper David Stockdale. Ashley Young replaced Jones, moving Nani to the right wing with Valencia at right-back, and the latter pair were involved as United doubled their advantage.

Giggs and Valencia swapped passes from a short corner before the veteran curled an inviting cross into the area, which Nani glanced into the far corner for a rare headed goal – his first for the club.

United had victory all but sealed two minutes before the break, though, as Giggs ensured he kept up his phenomenal record of having found the net in 22 consecutive seasons in the top flight, albeit via a sizeable deflection. Nani weaved his way into the area before pulling the ball back to the Welshman, whose goal-bound shot hit Philippe Senderos and looped over the helpless Stockdale.

Fulham rallied after the break, and brought smart saves from Anders Lindegaard through Dempsey's header from a corner and Andy Johnson, repeatedly. United's cause was hindered when substitute Young suffered a knee injury and was replaced by Ji-sung Park. Johnson dragged wide after a defensive mêlée in the United area, and with that miss went Fulham's hopes of a comeback.

United summoned a barnstorming end to the game, as Rooney swerved a stunning 30-yard drive past Stockdale, before substitute Berbatov dismissively back-heeled Valencia's cross into the far corner to cap an impressive night's work for the Reds.

The Teams

Fulham: Stockdale; Baird (Kelly 74), Senderos, Hangeland, Riise; Dembele, Etuhu, Murphy, Ruiz; Dempsey (Zamora 85), Johnson
Subs not used: Etheridge, Gecov, Duff, Hughes, Frei
Booked: Baird

Manchester United: Lindegaard; Jones (Young 20 (Park 59)), Evans, Smalling, Evra; Valencia, Carrick, Giggs, Nani; Rooney, Welbeck (Berbatov 77)
Subs not used: De Gea, Hernandez, Rafael, Fryers

'You saw what we're capable of,' smiled Ryan Giggs, 'and that's the standard we set ourselves. It was a similar story at Queens Park Rangers. There, we just didn't finish the chances off. Today, we managed to score the goals. To come to a place like Craven Cottage and have that sort of movement and interplay was first-class.

'For myself and Michael Carrick in midfield, the movement in front of us was brilliant. Obviously, the defending was good as well.

But when you have so many options on the ball – people running in behind, people dropping in the hole – we're a very difficult team to play. The performance was really pleasing.'

Again, however, the Reds' joy was tempered by concern for injury victims. While a few bodies had filtered back into the squad ahead of the trips to Loftus Road and Craven Cottage, Phil Jones' potentially serious jaw injury and a heavy blow to Ashley Young's ankle took the edge off the evening for Sir Alex Ferguson.

'We'll send Phil for an X-ray tomorrow,' said the manager. 'He had an elbow to his jaw. It was an elbow by Dempsey, but I don't think it was deliberate. But Fulham were very aggressive and Ashley Young has paid the price for that. He'll be out for two or three weeks. We had to make some changes before the match and then Phil picked up his injury. So it says a lot for the players. They stood up to a really difficult game. The games against Fulham over the last three years tell you how difficult it is to come here; we'd only won one point from nine.'

Jones' precautionary trip to hospital wouldn't be his last of the week. Soon after receiving the welcome news that he had sustained only heavy bruising, the England international and his United colleagues were partaking in another Christmas tradition at the club: a festive visit to dispense gifts at the Royal Manchester Children's Hospital.

While an invariably heart-wrenching affair, the Reds are well aware of the joy they are spreading with their presence, as well as their presents.

'We've been doing it as long as I can remember and it's kind of not a nice thing to have to go into a hospital at that time of year,' admits Jonny Evans. 'You don't want to trespass on people's privacy, but on the other hand you can see the joy on some of the kids' faces. Obviously, a lot of them are going through big illnesses and major problems, so especially at a time like Christmas it is hard seeing them like that, but you've just got to look on the other side of it and see the happiness that you can bring.

'It is humbling and for me, maybe because I am still young, you find it hard to realise how much of an influence Manchester United players can have on people, especially little kids. I suppose if I look back on when I was a kid, if I'd been ill and a United player had come to see me I'd be over the moon. Going to the hospital makes you really humble and it's great the club do that.'

Through the Manchester United Foundation, hospital visits take place year-round, and midfielder Tom Cleverley – for whom they carry special significance – is proud of the non-stop efforts of the club.

'I think it's massively important,' he says. 'I went to The Christie this year with Wazza, Ji and some of the others, and it's very important to the team and personally important to me. I've done a lot of work for The Christie. My mum's just recovered from cancer, so it's something that's very close to me and I'm more than happy to do it.

'It's a big dose of reality to see the patients. They love to see us. I think it just brings everyone together, like Wazza's just sat there having a game of FIFA with one of the patients. It's just like chilling out with the boys. Even though we would like to do it more often, we have such a busy game schedule that it's hard. It's great for everyone to get together; they all do such a fantastic job.'

As is customary, the players even had to report to Carrington for training on Christmas Day, with Wigan Athletic due at Old Trafford the next day. As the turn of the year loomed, Sir Alex was keen for his players to keep building on their impressive run of league form – though he warned that Roberto Martinez's side would be no pushovers.

'I watched Wigan versus Chelsea the other day and I thought Wigan were terrific,' said the manager. 'It says a lot for Roberto – he continues to play good football irrespective of what position they're in. We have a good record against Wigan, but we won't take anything for granted. We need to keep our foot on the pedal.'

Barclays Premier League

26 December 2011 | Old Trafford | Kick-off 15:00 |
Attendance: 75,183

Manchester United 5 (Park 8, Berbatov 41, 58, 78 (pen), Valencia 75)
Wigan Athletic 0

A clinical hat-trick from Dimitar Berbatov and well-taken finishes from Ji-sung Park and Antonio Valencia gave United a second successive five-goal victory and moved the Reds level on points with Manchester City at the head of the Barclays Premier League table.

Park opened the scoring inside ten minutes and Berbatov added a double either side of the interval, before Valencia blasted home against his former club and Park won a penalty for Berbatov to confidently convert with ten minutes remaining. Elsewhere, City's unexpected stalemate at West Bromwich Albion left only goal difference between the two title rivals.

A much-changed Reds side coped comfortably with extensive reshuffling, though their cause was aided by the harsh dismissal of Wigan striker Conor Sammon for a perceived elbow on Michael Carrick, who deputised in defence.

Once again, United's 90 minutes began brightly and soon yielded tangible reward. Patrice Evra ended some patient possession play by bursting into the Wigan area, bypassing challenges from Victor Moses and Antolin Alcaraz and sliding a ball across the area for Park, who stabbed a neat finish around Maynor Figueroa and past the unsighted Ali Al-Habsi.

The hosts poured forward and a second goal seemed inevitable. Steven Caldwell escaped embarrassment as his pressured clearance ricocheted against Al-Habsi, while Darron Gibson's effort from 25 yards was deflected wide by Ronnie Stam and Nani's free-kick from similar range curled a yard off-target.

Stam then flung a superb ball across Anders Lindegaard's area, only for the Latics' lack of attacking numbers to undo its excellence. Then, just as the visitors were growing in confidence, they were dealt a crippling double blow, as they lost a player and a second goal in the space of two minutes. Referee Dowd judged that Sammon deserved a red card for catching Carrick with a stray arm, but the apparent lack of intent in the striker's flailing prompted irate protests from his colleagues.

Their fury was compounded soon afterwards, as Gibson's curled cross found its way to Berbatov on the edge of the six-yard box. Though the Bulgarian's first touch, for once, sent the ball looping out of control, he admirably held off Alcaraz and clinically tucked a left-footed finish underneath the onrushing Al-Habsi.

As the visitors commendably reshuffled into a 3-4-2 formation for the second half, United merely eased away from them. Park and Berbatov came close, before the latter controlled Valencia's ball with his right instep and spun to face the goal in one motion, then toe-poked a fabulous finish high into Al-Habsi's net.

The Omani international provided a superb close-range save from Javier Hernandez and turned away Kiko Macheda's cross-shot, before Valencia heaped further misery on his former employers with a cracking strike which he thundered across a packed area and into the far corner.

United were making substantial inroads into the goal-difference deficit City had built up during the opening months of the campaign, and notched up another when Alcaraz felled Park on the cusp of the area. Berbatov duly stroked home the penalty to complete his treble.

The joyous feel around Old Trafford was further heightened by news of City's stalemate at West Brom: an unexpected festive fillip for the champions.

The Teams

Manchester United: Lindegaard; Valencia, Evans (Fryers 46), Carrick, Evra; Park, Gibson, Giggs (Macheda 64), Nani (Rooney 64); Berbatov, Hernandez

Subs not used: De Gea, Welbeck, Rafael, Diouf
Booked: Evans, Giggs

Wigan Athletic: Al-Habsi; Alcaraz, Caldwell, Figueroa; Stam, McCarthy, Gomez (McArthur 71), Diame (Di Santo 46), Jones; Moses (Rodallega 80), Sammon
Subs not used: Pollitt, Gohouri, Crusat, Watson
Booked: Jones
Sent off: Sammon

'As I said some weeks ago, somebody was going to suffer,' said Sir Alex. 'We're really hitting good form now and there's a real goal threat about us from all departments. If we're top of the league or joint top with City by New Year's Day I'll be happy.'

The manager also paid tribute to Dimitar Berbatov, after his fourth goal in under a week, saying: 'It was the right game for him. I needed his height for set-pieces against us and he's weighed in with a hat-trick. We're really pleased for him and it helps with confidence. Dimitar hasn't had the best of starts to the season in terms of selection, given the options I have with Welbeck, Rooney and Hernandez, so I'm really happy for him.'

For Patrice Evra, it was the Reds' collective oneness that most caught the eye. After deputising at centre-back alongside Michael Carrick in the second period, the Frenchman opined that such selflessness is a priceless commodity in the Premier League title race.

'This is the United spirit: you can play everywhere,' he said. 'If you want to win, you have to accept it. You can see Antonio Valencia playing right-back as well. Only because United play like a team. The team is the star, not only one player. That's why you can put me and Michael Carrick at centre-back; we're going to win because it's the team effort and team spirit. That's why I'm confident. I've said that from the beginning – in six years playing here – the Man United spirit . . . no one team has got that spirit. This is United. This is why I'm so proud to play here.'

The Boxing Day win marked an eighth league victory in nine games for the Reds, and a fourth successive win since the Champions League defeat at Basel; a defeat that Evra viewed as a potential watershed moment in United's season.

'I think it was a big disappointment when we went out early in the Champions League,' he said. 'But I think it was a wake-up call, because maybe everyone looked at themselves in the mirror and said: "We can do much better." What the fans expect of every player, we are doing now. That's why I'm very pleased. Nothing is easy; it's because we're working hard. If we stopped working hard and think only with the United name, everything is going to be wrong.

'That's why we have to keep going with this momentum and trust each other, because it's a big squad and everyone wants to show they deserve to play. If we win and score goals and keep many clean sheets, like we did tonight, we're going to be at the top of the league at the end of the season.'

At the other end of the table lay Blackburn Rovers, the Reds' next opponents, who were due at Old Trafford for the game on Sir Alex Ferguson's 70th birthday. Rovers manager Steve Kean had been the subject of intense personal abuse from some of the club's supporters for much of the opening half of the season, as well as incessant media speculation that he would be removed from his job. The Scot, however, had an ally at Old Trafford.

'I have never seen anything as bad,' said Sir Alex, of the abuse Kean suffered during his side's home defeat to Bolton, two games before their Old Trafford trip. 'For goodness' sake, give the lad a break. It doesn't say a lot for society. I feel for the lad. I tried to phone him, but he probably quite rightly had his phone switched off.'

One of Kean's former players, Phil Jones, was in line to face his boyhood club after overcoming a badly bruised jaw, and he conceded that it would be a bizarre experience to face Rovers while clad in red and white.

'I'm still a massive fan,' admitted the defender. 'As soon as we come off the pitch I always look to see how Blackburn have got on.

I still have a lot of friends at the club. I'm sure they'll kick on and things will improve. They're a lot better than their league position shows. Unfortunately, for whatever reason, they're at the bottom of the table now. We won't find it easy, though. It's going to be tough. I know what sort of squad Blackburn have and there are some cracking players there. We can't take them lightly.'

The youngster's words would prove oracular, as the most unforeseen circumstances unfolded.

Barclays Premier League

31 December 2011 | Old Trafford | Kick-off 12:45 |
Attendance: 75,146

Manchester United 2 (Berbatov 52, 62)
Blackburn Rovers 3 (Yakubu 16 (pen), 51, Hanley 80)

United were on the receiving end of the shock result of the season, as rock-bottom Blackburn Rovers stunned Old Trafford with a 3-2 victory to spoil Sir Alex Ferguson's 70th birthday celebrations.

Dimitar Berbatov's second-half brace had hauled the Reds level, after Yakubu had put the visitors two goals clear. But, rather than complete the comeback, United were hit by a late sucker punch as Grant Hanley nodded home an untidy winner to shock the champions.

United's injury problems led to Rafael and Ji-sung Park forming a makeshift central midfield partnership with Michael Carrick continuing in defence, while Rovers had problems of their own, with David Dunn and Junior Hoilett heading the list of absentees.

A subdued atmosphere suited a lacklustre start from both sides. United had little to show for their early endeavours, bar a left-footed effort from Nani that passed Mark Bunn's post with room to spare. Then, in their initial real forward foray, the visitors landed the first blow when Berbatov hauled down Chris Samba inside the United area and referee Mike Dean awarded the spot-kick, which Yakubu clinically converted.

United's response was muted. There was a shout for another penalty when Patrice Evra was sent flying by Radosav Petrovic and man-mountain Samba got his head in the way of a Danny Welbeck drive, but the Reds were some way short of the side that had strung together an impressive domestic run.

The champions finally started to build a head of steam as half time approached. Nani, the likeliest source of inspiration, finally extended Bunn with a snap-shot after controlling an Evra cross, and the keeper also thwarted Javier Hernandez at his near post as the pressure grew.

The Mexican made way at the interval as Anderson was introduced, but it was Rovers who unexpectedly struck the game's next goal. Yakubu steamrollered through a static central pairing of Carrick and Phil Jones, before lashing a fierce drive under David De Gea. Suitably stung, United responded properly. Straight from the kick-off, Rafael drove into the box and fired across goal for Berbatov to steer in a diving header. Game on.

Within minutes, with Valencia now dominating the right flank, the Reds levelled. The Ecuadorian, revelling in a return to his familiar right-wing role, sped past a couple of defenders to tee up a firm finish by Berbatov for his sixth goal in three games.

Only one winner, it seemed. Blackburn defended frantically but effectively, and Bunn had to be alert to turn away Ryan Lowe's errant clearance as the pressure built, before inexplicably subsiding. As the atmosphere and application drooped in tandem, United struggled to maintain any rhythm, and Rovers somehow summoned the reserves to push forward once again.

With ten minutes remaining, they found the winner their desire had deserved. Hanley pressurised De Gea, as the Spaniard attempted to punch a corner clear and, as the ball looped up, the young defender nodded home from close range.

Now Old Trafford was completely deflated, and desperation took over as the Reds sought to wrest anything from the game. Berbatov headed over from Carrick's cross, before Will Keane entered the fray for his debut. Though the youngster looked lively, his telling contribution came when he inadvertently blocked Jones' goal-bound drive in injury time, confirming the unlikeliest of wins for the beleaguered visitors.

The Teams

Manchester United: De Gea; Valencia, Carrick, Jones, Evra; Nani, Rafael (W.Keane 86), Park, Welbeck; Berbatov, Hernandez (Anderson 46)
Subs not used: Lindegaard, Diouf, Pogba, Fryers, Cole
Booked: Nani, Carrick

Blackburn Rovers: Bunn; Henley, Hanley, Samba, Lowe; Formica (Goodwillie 85), Petrovic, Nzonzi, Rochina (Morris 55), Pedersen; Yakubu (Slew 89)
Subs not used: Kean, Blackman, Vukcevic, Linganzi
Booked: Petrovic, Lowe

'It's a disappointment,' rued Sir Alex. 'We never expected that. We've lost two terrible goals and you can't do that in games like this. You can expect Blackburn to put up that sort of fight, though. They were resilient, they defended well, blocked shots on the line. They did that all day. But if you lose goals like that it gives them a big opportunity to hang on. But in the second half we rallied and got back to two-two. I thought at that point we were a certainty to win it.'

'I think that was our downfall,' reasoned Phil Jones. 'Coming back too soon. I think we thought we'd won it. We got one back, got two back and probably thought we'd won it. We eased off and they punished us. I knew it'd be a tough game – they came here and full credit to them. They thoroughly deserved the win as we weren't at the races today.'

With Chris Smalling ruled out by a bout of tonsillitis – not glandular fever, as reported by some media outlets – and Jonny Evans unfit after sustaining a knock against Wigan, United's injury woes showed no signs of abating. The shock omission of Wayne Rooney, Sir Alex explained, stemmed not from yet another injury, however, more a lack of sharpness on the training ground. 'Wayne hasn't trained well this week,' said the manager. 'He's missed a few days and we're hoping that he trains today, tomorrow and, by Wednesday [when United were due to travel to Newcastle], he should be okay. It's little strains here and there.'

Though Manchester City afforded the Reds a let-off when they slipped to an injury-time defeat at Sunderland in their game in hand, United prepared to visit the North-East in the knowledge that a stern test awaited them, with Alan Pardew's side still riding high in the top half of the table.

Despite ending 2011 on a down note, the year's undulating nature suggested that plenty more ups and downs lay in store in 2012.

7

January – New Beginnings

A New Year hangover is hardly a rarity, but United began 2012 still stunned by their shock home defeat to Blackburn Rovers. The media was awash with stories linking the Reds with a host of new signings – especially central midfielders – but Sir Alex Ferguson quickly sought to play down talk of an active transfer window, not just at United but across the Premier League.

'The reason there may not be many big signings in January is because the players clubs want are not available,' he explained. 'To be honest with you, who would want to sell their best player in January? I don't see it happening. There are cases of players whose contracts are running out in the summer, but they won't get the same money anyway. It'll be well reduced.'

There was sharp movement away from Carrington, however, as Kiko Macheda joined Queens Park Rangers until the end of the season. The Italian revealed that he had consulted Rio Ferdinand, brother of Rangers defender Anton, before agreeing to move to Loftus Road.

'I spoke with Rio and he told me that QPR is a very good club and that if I did come here it would be good for me and would help me develop as a player,' said the 20-year-old. 'There is a lot of competition at Manchester United. There are some very good strikers there, but I am still young and I need to get more experience in the Premier League.'

Though bereft of Macheda for the rest of the campaign, Sir Alex's striking ranks were swollen for the trip to Newcastle by the availability of Wayne Rooney, who had been left out of the defeat to Blackburn after sitting out some of the Reds' preparations.

'Wayne Rooney will be available, of course,' confirmed the manager. 'We had a few training sessions which he missed. You've got to be fit to play in this league; you can't miss training sessions. We're trying hard to get Rio Ferdinand for Wednesday, and Ryan Giggs, which would make a good difference to us. Anderson should be better; he had forty-five minutes on Saturday after months out. There are no other ones to come back immediately.'

After suffering only a second league defeat of the season in such unforeseen circumstances against Blackburn, the Reds travelled to a Newcastle United side seemingly punching above their weight in the top half of the table. But for Dimitar Berbatov, one of the few players to come out of the New Year's Eve defeat with any credit, the Magpies were perched where they belonged. With Manchester City three points clear after crushing Liverpool, the Bulgarian warned that the Reds would face a stern challenge to keep pace at the Sports Direct Arena.

'I think Newcastle have a really good team and good players,' said the Bulgarian. 'I don't think anybody should be surprised by their position. If you're high in the table then you deserve to be there.'

Any remaining doubt over the Magpies' strength would be blown away during the course of a harrowing evening for the Reds.

Barclays Premier League

4 January 2012 | Sports Direct Arena | Kick-off 20:00 |
Attendance: 52,299

Newcastle United 3 (Ba 33, Cabaye 47, Jones 90 (og))
Manchester United 0

United suffered back-to-back Premier League defeats for the first time in ten months, as Newcastle turned in an impressive perform-ance to emphatically exploit a lacklustre Reds showing at the Sports Direct Arena.

Despite the return of Rio Ferdinand, Ryan Giggs and Wayne Rooney, the Reds were comfortably second best from the moment Demba Ba hooked home a superb opening goal. Yohan Cabaye gave the champions a mountain to climb with a fabulous free-kick right after half time, before Phil Jones' injury-time own-goal summed up a miserable evening for the visitors.

There was no repeat of November's Old Trafford draw, in which Newcastle's defiant defending and United's profligate finishing con-spired in maddening circumstances. Instead, the Magpies were first out of the blocks, and Anders Lindegaard was tested early on when Cabaye and Cheik Tioté both tried their luck from distance.

The Reds' best period came midway through the first half, as Tim Krul parried away Nani's effort and Dimitar Berbatov headed Patrice Evra's cross against the base of the hosts' post. Rooney narrowly failed to connect with an attempted flick at Giggs' beautiful through-ball, before the hosts began to move out of sight.

Not long after Ferdinand had fortunately escaped the punish-ment of a penalty for a tangle with Ba, the Senegalese striker exacted quick revenge when he stylishly hooked Shola Ameobi's flick-on into the far corner of Lindegaard's net – the Dane's first Premier League concession.

Ba continued to prove problematic, winning a free-kick which Ryan Taylor sent narrowly over and then forcing Lindegaard into another solid save. The striker then won another set-piece in the opening moments of the second period, and marvelled with every-one else as Cabaye curled an unstoppable effort over United's wall and into the net, via the underside of the crossbar.

United briefly rallied, and came close to pulling a goal back when substitute Danny Welbeck flicked Nani's cross towards Rooney, whose volley beat Krul but was blocked on the line by former Reds defender Danny Simpson. Another substitute, Chicharito, almost reached a long punt ahead of Krul, but the Mexican was ultimately left frustrated as the Dutchman just nabbed possession first.

Krul ended the game with an inadvertent assist, as his hefty punt was allowed to bounce and, as he sought to keep out substitute Leon Best, Jones accidentally nudged the ball past Lindegaard and into the untended goal to sum up a night of frustration on Tyneside for the champions.

The Teams

Newcastle United: Krul; Simpson, Coloccini, Williamson, Santon; Gutierrez, Tioté, Cabaye (Perch 78), R.Taylor; Ba (Obertan 89), Shola Ameobi (Best 75)
Subs not used: Harper, Ben Arfa, Sammy Ameobi, Vuckic
Booked: Tioté

Manchester United: Lindegaard; Valencia, Ferdinand, Jones, Evra; Nani, Carrick, Giggs, Park (Hernandez 66); Berbatov (Welbeck 57), Rooney (Anderson 75)
Subs not used: De Gea, Rafael, Pogba, Lingard
Booked: Valencia, Jones

'We started reasonably well,' reflected Sir Alex Ferguson. 'We had a good chance when Wayne Rooney was through and the ball ran under his foot. That was a great opportunity and if we'd taken it, we could have gone on to win the game. Newcastle scored not long after that. It was a fantastic goal and it really got their fans up. They became aggressive; they got stuck right into us and made it difficult for us.

'It was a great hit on the volley and the second one just after half time – a marvellous free-kick, you have to give the boy credit – was a killer for us. That really put them in the driving position. They were very difficult to beat after that. We didn't make enough of our possession with the ball. You've got to take your chances away from home. We didn't play well enough to win the game. The own goal just summed up the whole night to be honest. But take nothing away from Newcastle, they fought hard and deserved their victory, no question.'

Though disappointed, the manager was far from downbeat, preferring to look forward. With an FA Cup third round trip to Manchester City next up, it wasn't hard to be focused on the future. 'It's not a time to panic,' he said. 'We've got the patience and experience to cope. But we need to get the show on the road for the run-in, particularly March and April. The plus is that we had two or three players back and hopefully we have one or two on the road back; that will make a difference.'

Both Jonny Evans and Chris Smalling were rated unlikely to return from a calf injury and tonsillitis respectively in time for the derby, but retained an outside hope of making the short trip across Manchester. Tom Cleverley, Ashley Young and Michael Owen remained entrenched in their respective recoveries, while back-to-back defeats merely reinforced City's status as favourites to progress at United's expense.

However, the galvanising effect of being underdogs with the odds stacked against them had worked in United's favour before, and Michael Carrick was relishing the chance to get cracking at the Etihad Stadium.

'We've just got to get on with it,' said the midfielder. 'We tend to overcome setbacks pretty well here and hopefully we can do the same. Sunday's game is a massive game – against our biggest rivals – and we're looking forward to it. We want to be playing in the big games, when there's real pressure and a whole lot at stake. These are the games in which we really test ourselves and in the past, we've been really good at finding a way to win. That's what we'll be focusing on.'

Much hype abounded around the game – the latest in a succession of derbies to attract blanket press coverage – but, with the transfer window open, silly season was also underway. The days prior to the game had United linked with a shock swoop for Frank Lampard, and one report even suggested that Wayne Rooney would be leaving Old Trafford some time that month.

The club and player quickly issued a joint statement repudiating the story as 'complete nonsense', while Sir Alex Ferguson also addressed the Lampard stories. 'You're not going to tell me that Chelsea would sell to Manchester United in January,' he chuckled at his pre-match press conference. 'Do you really believe that? There's no foundation to that story simply because Chelsea are like us: they want to do something. The second half of the season is going to be important to them. If they want to try to win the league, they're going to have all their best players. That's the name of the game.'

In any case, the manager had already secured the services of one of the game's finest midfielders. Weeks earlier, Paul Scholes had broached the topic of reversing his retirement, a suggestion that met with elation from the manager. The 37-year-old had retained his fitness and sharpness in his daily role training with Warren Joyce's Reserves, and he quietly stepped up his endurance work as both player and manager kept the decision secret from the entire squad. Well, almost.

'Obviously I knew before the City game,' grins Ryan Giggs. 'I'd spoken to him a few days before that, so I knew it was in the pipeline. It wasn't that he wasn't enjoying coaching; it was just that he was still training with the Reserves and missed playing. I'd ask the lads in the Reserves how he was doing and they'd just say: "Man of the match again." He'd kept his fitness up, but also his quality – which has never been in doubt. It was a surprise, of course, because it's a tough decision to make halfway through a season, but obviously it was the right one.

'It was funny that all the lads had no idea until we were in the changing room. At the time it was a bit of a laugh and a joke and a surprise for everyone. It was a clever move in that it was such a big game, a massive game, that the focus was partly on Scholesy, but as a player you're still mainly focusing on the game, and it gave everyone a real lift.'

'I missed it more than I thought,' revealed the 37-year-old. 'At the end of last season, I thought it was the right time to finish. But after coming in to Carrington for a few months and still seeing people and still doing a bit of training with the Reserves, I was missing it more than I thought I would. Ask any player who has finished; they will all miss it for a period of time. I missed it and decided to give it another go. I went to see the manager and said that I wanted to come back playing. I didn't know what he would say. I didn't know what his reaction would be. Thankfully, it was a positive one.'

The new boy immediately took a place on the visitors' bench at the Etihad Stadium, as United looked to redress all talk of a power shift across the city and book a place in the fourth round of the FA Cup.

FA Cup third round

8 January 2012 | Etihad Stadium | Kick-off 13:00 |
Attendance: 46,808

Manchester City 2 (Kolarov 48, Aguero 65)
Manchester United 3 (Rooney 10, 40, Welbeck 30)

United edged into the fourth round of the FA Cup after an enthralling, draining victory over holders Manchester City at the Etihad Stadium. The Reds bossed a thrilling first half in which City skipper Vincent Kompany was contentiously dismissed, and had a three-goal lead at the interval through Wayne Rooney's brace and Danny Welbeck's acrobatic volley.

To their credit, City rallied after the break and pulled goals back through Aleksander Kolarov and Sergio Aguero, and almost snatched an injury-time leveller when Anders Lindegaard had to fist away a Kolarov free-kick.

The pre-match build-up was overshadowed by the shock announcement that Paul Scholes had reversed his retirement, signing a deal to return until the end of the season and immediately taking a place on the United bench. Amid the furore, the news that Chris Smalling and Jonny Evans had returned from injury was almost lost. The former was fit enough to start at centre-back, with Phil Jones moving over to right-back, while Evans took a place on the bench.

Nevertheless, City began the game on the front foot, herding United back and coursing with confidence on their fruitful home turf. The Reds were happy, however, to sit back and wait for the opportunity for counter-attacks to arise, and one duly did to spawn the game's first goal.

Rooney dropped between City's lines to collect the ball before spreading it wide to Antonio Valencia. The Ecuadorian swung the ball towards the far post, where Rooney bulldozed between Nani and Micah Richards to power a header against the underside of the cross-bar and into the net.

The deafening din from the away end had barely subsided two minutes later when City skipper Kompany was dismissed in controversial fashion. The Belgian launched into a two-footed challenge to rob Nani of possession, but won the ball cleanly. Referee Chris Foy paused before brandishing his red card, whipping the Etihad Stadium into a storm of fury.

City's initial response was one of defiance. Aguero forced a magnificent full-stretch save from Lindegaard with a curling effort from the edge of the area, but United soon made the extra man tell.

Nani fed Patrice Evra down the left flank and, though the Frenchman's cross was half-cleared, Welbeck pounced on the loose, looping ball and hooked an unstoppable volley into Constel Pantilimon's bottom corner from 12 yards. The game's only Mancunian starter revelled in the moment, kissing his United badge as he wheeled away in delight.

Welbeck was involved again ten minutes later as United established a three-goal lead. The 21-year-old was needlessly scythed down by Kolarov inside the City area, prompting the award of a clear penalty by referee Foy. Pantilimon superbly parried out Rooney's penalty, only for the United striker to calmly nod the rebound into the unguarded goal.

Seeing his side overrun, Roberto Mancini reshuffled at half time and sent out his side to sit back in a 3-5-1 formation in the second period. Attacking was merely an afterthought, but it almost reaped rewards. Kolarov arrowed home a spectacular free-kick from almost 30 yards within two minutes of the restart and, though United had all the ball and dominated territorially, the Blues' sporadic forward raids were a menace.

Sir Alex sought to shore up his side's midfield with the introduction of his new signing. Sporting number 22 for the first time since the 1996 FA Cup final, Scholes trotted onto the field in place of Nani, who was carrying a booking.

Shortly after United had been denied what appeared another clear penalty, as Kolarov felled Valencia without censure, City struck again as James Milner crossed for Aguero and, when his initial shot was spilled by Lindegaard, the little striker pounced to send the home fans wild.

Hearts were in mouths for all of a Red persuasion when Kolarov lined up a free-kick just outside the area in injury time, but Lindegaard palmed the ball to safety and United held on for a draining victory.

The Teams

Manchester City: Pantilimon; Richards, Kompany, Lescott, Kolarov; Milner, de Jong; Johnson (Zabaleta 46), Nasri (Hargreaves 82), Silva (Savic 46); Aguero
Subs not used: Hart, Clichy, Suarez, Razak
Sent off: Kompany

Manchester United: Lindegaard; Smalling, Ferdinand, Jones, Evra; Valencia, Carrick, Giggs, Nani (Scholes 59); Rooney, Welbeck (Anderson 75)
Subs not used: De Gea, Evans, Park, Hernandez, Rafael
Booked: Nani, Evra, Ferdinand, Welbeck

Despite having overcome United's sternest title challengers, dumping them out of the FA Cup and ending their year-long unbeaten home run, Sir Alex Ferguson was less than impressed at full time.

'I don't think it does us any good at all today,' he said. 'It was a careless performance in the second half, and we should have been home and dry. We had a clear scoreline but we were too careless and that's the area where, if we keep doing that, we will make mistakes. I think we made them look better than they were. We just had a carelessness in the second half. The problem was, we were three-nil up at half time and we thought we were through and took our foot off the pedal.'

While relief outweighed triumphalism at the final whistle, the game underlined a marked difference in how both United and City reacted to losing a man amid a Manchester derby. The Reds had shipped five goals in just over 40 minutes at Old Trafford, but the Blues – perversely benefiting from losing Kompany so early – had fought back to almost salvage a replay.

Looking back, Danny Welbeck opines: 'It's a plus if you do get a half-time break after you've had someone sent off, because you can regroup and everybody knows exactly what the tactics are with the manager for the rest of the game. When City beat us at Old Trafford, we lost Jonny straight after half time and it was really tough. Losing a centre-back that early in the half is never good, but the manager and the coaches can't get their instructions across as well as if it had happened before half time. But I still think that day at City was ours anyway, even if they'd had eleven men. We started really well and had our tactics one hundred percent correct.'

Welbeck's fellow Etihad goalscorer, Wayne Rooney, sought to use his post-match interview to scotch all talk of a transfer away from

Old Trafford. 'I think everything which has been in the press of late has been a load of nonsense, really,' said the striker. 'Because it's me, because it's Manchester United, it's blown up out of context. There's no problem with me at this club and I want to be at the club for a long time.'

Sir Alex backed Rooney's assertion, but warned his star man that the media's spotlight would remain trained on him, saying: 'We must explain this about Rooney – he's a headline-maker, whether it's good or bad. The press don't mind. It's a situation we experienced many years ago with Paul Gascoigne. This is the new Paul Gascoigne: a head-line-maker, and we're better seeing him like that today, when it's good stuff. Any flaws in Wayne will be absolutely annihilated by the press because that's what they're like. That's the animal we're dealing with.'

Once the dust had settled on an eventful few days, the shock sub-plot of Paul Scholes' return became the main feature. 'We just thought he was coming along for the game,' laughed Rooney. 'But we saw him getting changed and somebody asked him what he was doing. And then we saw the number twenty-two Scholes shirt, which was a bit weird seeing him with that number. But it's great as he is a well-liked lad around the dressing room.'

'It was a massive boost for all of us,' added Chris Smalling. 'I was really disappointed when he called it a day last year. I spoke to Danny Welbeck before the City game; we were really excited that he's back and it gave the whole squad a boost.'

Rooney was quickly en route to Zurich, joined by Sir Alex and Nemanja Vidic, to attend the FIFA Ballon d'Or gala, where he was nominated for the FIFA Puskas award, handed to the scorer of the best goal of the previous year. The striker's overhead kick against Manchester City was pipped to the prize, however, by Neymar's stun-ning solo goal for Santos against Flamengo, though he was offered the consolation of a spot in the FIFA/FIFpro team of the year, alongside Vidic. Sir Alex ensured there would also be silverware on the flight home, picking up the ceremony's Presidential Award in recognition of his 25th year at United, and the club's record-breaking 19th title.

The travelling party returned to Carrington to find that Darron Gibson had completed a permanent transfer to Everton – 'He has terrific ability but has to get on with his career,' said the manager – while the remainder of the first-team squad had sustained further injury setbacks. Anderson had picked up an ankle knock, while Chris Smalling and Phil Jones continued to carry the scars of a bruising derby win. That meant the trio were either doubtful or out of the visit of Bolton, who remained mired in the Premier League's relegation zone.

'So we've got a reasonable squad for the game,' said Sir Alex. 'And we need a good performance against a team that will battle for everything. Any team near the bottom of the table will do that, as we experienced at home to Blackburn. We went into the Blackburn game with respect for them, but it wasn't a great performance. We have to address Bolton's challenge properly. It's a local derby too, which adds something to it.'

Among those fit and available was Paul Scholes. Despite having played just half an hour of competitive football in the previous eight months, the veteran midfielder was being considered for inclusion.

'He's one of the best passers in the game,' Sir Alex said. 'He's always had that great talent, and he'll probably be able to do that when he's fifty! For Scholes, I think all the players idolise him anyway, so it was an easy decision to make. He's been training quite intensively for two or three weeks, and he's looking very good,' said the boss. 'I wouldn't be against playing him because that's the quality he brings to your team. You can't ignore that.'

Barclays Premier League

14 January 2012 | Old Trafford | Kick-off 15:00 |
Attendance: 75,444

Manchester United 3 (Scholes 45, Welbeck 74, Carrick 83)
Bolton Wanderers 0

Paul Scholes' decision to reverse his retirement began to look like a shrewd move, as the veteran midfielder scored on his Old Trafford return to set the Reds en route to a timely resumption to winning ways against struggling Bolton. The 37-year-old swept home Wayne Rooney's cross in first-half injury time, ensuring the Reds had an interval lead after Rooney's earlier penalty miss, before Danny Welbeck and Michael Carrick killed off the game in the second period.

Owen Coyle's relegation-threatened side were on the back foot from the first whistle, as Nani blasted a shot wide inside the opening minute, before Trotters stopper Adam Bogdan was forced to field a close-range Welbeck effort. Sam Ricketts then blocked Rooney's effort and Mark Davies cleared the striker's looping header off the line, before Bogdan took centre stage.

Zat Knight was fortunate to escape a red card for clumsily hauling down Welbeck deep inside the Bolton area, but Bogdan superbly flung himself to his right to turn away Rooney's spot-kick and, in doing so, flattened the Old Trafford atmosphere.

It was boosted again just before the break, as Rooney turned provider with an expert ball across the Trotters' six-yard box, where the unmarked Scholes was lurking to score on his United bow for the second time, having bagged a brace on his original debut over 17 years earlier.

Neither manager made changes at the break, although Bolton emerged more adventurous in spirit. When Davies pounced on a stray pass in the United defence and surged into the penalty area, he teed up David Ngog, only for the former Liverpool striker to blaze over from close range. Rafael then needed to be brave to fling himself in the way of Martin Petrov's volley and alert to clear Gretar Steinsson's header off the line.

The Reds had always retained a threat in possession, however, and the double introduction of Ryan Giggs and Ji-sung Park, at the expense of Scholes and Nani, coincided with the game's decisive second goal. Rooney squeezed the ball through the visitors' clustered defence, allowing Welbeck to slide in and roll the ball past the exposed Bogdan.

Welbeck clashed with the Hungarian in scoring the goal and needed to be replaced by Chicharito, but it was midfielder Carrick who had the final say. Taking advantage of lax closing down by the flagging visitors, the 30-year-old strode towards goal and curled a pin-point left-footed finish into Bogdan's bottom corner from 25 yards.

The Teams

Manchester United: Lindegaard; Rafael, Ferdinand, Evans, Evra; Valencia, Carrick, Scholes (Giggs 69), Nani (Park 70); Rooney, Welbeck (Hernandez 78)
Subs not used: De Gea, Berbatov, Fabio, Pogba

Bolton Wanderers: Bogdan; Steinsson, Knight, Wheater, Ricketts; Eagles (Riley 69), Muamba (Pratley 81), Reo-Coker, M.Davies, Petrov (Tuncay 88); Ngog
Subs not used: Lynch, K.Davies, Klasnic, Boyata
Booked: Knight

'We still have some injuries, but I think when everyone is back fit, it will give us the strength to win the title,' said a typically bold Patrice Evra, having captained the Reds to a first Premier League win since Boxing Day. 'We have to keep talking about Manchester United. The most important thing was winning. After that, it doesn't matter if they [City] win, lose or draw.

'We just need to have a rest and focus on the next game. I think people talk a lot about City, but we just need to be focused on what we do and how we play, and I think we're going to win the league. It was a good afternoon for us. It was an important game, after the win against City, to show we are really confident and we are back. It was really important to win today.'

The three points owed much to the midfield exploits of Messrs

Scholes and Carrick, and the latter was keen to praise the former after his goalscoring return to Old Trafford. 'It was great to see him score and it's great to have him back for the quality that he brings, not just on the pitch, but from the way he carries himself around the place and for his attitude towards the game,' said Carrick.

'It's great for the younger players who have come in this season; they can train with him and learn a lot from him, just as we have in the past. He's such a world-class player and I've learnt so much off him, as well as other players. Being in my position, I've watched him a lot and learned off him and tried to add his attributes to my game. It's great to have him back and it's given everyone a lift. I'm sure he's delighted to come back, the reception he got from the fans was fantastic and I'm sure he'll look back on it as a special day.'

The good news would keep coming for Sir Alex and his squad. Phil Jones and Chris Smalling were swiftly passed fit for the invariably taxing trip to face fifth-placed Arsenal at the Emirates Stadium, while the manager also confirmed that Ashley Young and Tom Cleverley were making good progress in training.

For Cleverley, the season had been derailed by his September injury at Bolton, subsequently aggravated the following month at Everton. A collective decision had been taken to allow the youngster to recuperate fully, which meant a long, arduous road back to availability. Looking back, however, Cleverley reveals that the break allowed him to develop his all-round game.

'The first couple of weeks was just basically resting and staying off my feet,' he says. 'That helped massively. Then I got back into the gym from then for about two months and worked massively hard with Neil Hough, Rob Swire, the doc [Doctor Steve McNally] and the hard work paid off. I definitely filled out a bit. When you're not on the pitch you can work on other areas. I did work with video analysis, I worked hard with [strength and conditioning coach] Gary Walker in the gym on my upper body, and I did vision work too. It's a fantastic training ground, because you can work hard on all aspects of your game when you're injured. Everything I could work on, I worked on. I've improved in other areas that you can work on when you're injured, so I've done everything I can while I've been out.'

Cleverley would return from injury to find that, while Darron Gibson had left, Paul Scholes had returned. More competition, of course, but the Bradford-born playmaker could only see positives in the veteran's comeback.

'He's a great player; he's someone I can learn off,' says Cleverley. 'At a club like United, you're always going to have world-class players competing for the same positions, so it's something that, if I'm here for many years to come, I'm going to have to deal with. Mainly I just thought it was great to have a world-class player back to learn from, even though it's more competition for me!'

Though players were vying for involvement throughout Sir Alex Ferguson's squad, arguably the first name on his teamsheet at the time was Antonio Valencia, whose scintillating displays from early December had played a major part in the Reds' post-Basel revival.

'Valencia is back to his best form now,' stated the boss. 'It took him a bit of time to get over his injury. Really he's had two injuries with us and this one took him a bit of time to come back from. Also, because Nani's form was so good at the time, I was playing him right-back in some of the games and he had to cope with that. Maybe he was thinking: "Am I going to get in my normal position again?" His form has got better and better.

'Ashley Young got injured and I moved Nani to the left-hand side and you've seen Antonio come right back to his best form. That's pleasing as he's a good boy, a tremendous professional, who works very hard at his game. He tries to go past his man most of the time, but he's clever enough to come inside and can pass a ball. He's a good passer, actually. He's got a lot going for him. Last week, against Bolton, obviously that was him starting to show his real top form. He's been threatening it and we've seen him gradually getting to that point where he's in really good form now.'

Arsenal would soon be able to vouch for the Ecuadorian's unstoppable force.

Barclays Premier League

22 January 2012 | Emirates Stadium | Kick-off 16:00 |
Attendance: 60,093

Arsenal 1 (Van Persie 71)
Manchester United 2 (Valencia 45, Welbeck 81)

Danny Welbeck struck a priceless late winner over Arsenal, as United survived another taxing trip to the Emirates Stadium to stay firmly in the hunt for the Barclays Premier League title.

The Reds deservedly led at the interval, as Antonio Valencia headed home Ryan Giggs' excellent cross in first-half injury time, but the Gunners rallied after the break and looked set to take a share of the spoils when Robin van Persie squeezed home a leveller with 19 minutes remaining. United hit back, however, and re-took the lead when Valencia capped a storming individual run by setting up Welbeck to power home a finish and keep the champions right on Manchester City's coat-tails at the head of the table.

City's last-gasp victory over Tottenham ramped up the pressure on the champions ahead of kick-off, while the loss of Phil Jones to a twisted ankle after 15 minutes provided a further setback, yet the introduction of his replacement, Rafael, coincided with United's growing control of proceedings.

Patrice Evra and Nani were an increasingly potent threat down the left flank, and they combined to force Wojciech Szczesny into action for the first time, the Portuguese drawing a smart, near-post stop after good approach work from the Frenchman.

The visitors knocked on the hosts' door with increasing regularity and impatience. Wayne Rooney did well to cushion Giggs' clipped pass inside the Gunners' area before tumbling under pressure from Alex Song. Referee Mike Dean declined to award a penalty, and Rooney's ire was hardly soothed when, moments later, Nani wastefully slid the ball well off-target instead of looking to pick out his unmarked number ten.

In first-half injury time, Giggs made the fullest use of United's next opening. The veteran Welshman exploited Johann Djourou's reluctance to pressure him by curling in a magnificent cross. At the far post, Valencia stole in behind Thomas Vermaelen to power a header across Szczesny and into the bottom corner.

The Gunners almost drew level within five minutes of the restart, albeit by accident rather than design. Smalling slipped in possession midway inside his own half, giving Tomas Rosicky a clear route to goal. The Czech midfielder squared for van Persie, who shimmied away from the covering challenge of Evans before inexplicably and uncharacteristically blazing wide.

Per Mertesacker dramatically slid the ball off his own line after Welbeck had lifted a deft shot over the onrushing Szczesny, but it was increasingly the hosts in control of the second period, and a quick counterattack brought them level when Alex Oxlade-Chamberlain's slide-rule pass gave van Persie an opening, and he fired through Jonny Evans' legs and past Lindegaard, via the inside of the Dane's post.

Alex Ferguson introduced Paul Scholes and Ji-sung Park for Nani and Rafael, and sent Valencia to right-back. The move didn't curb the Ecuadorian's attacking intent, however, and he played a key role as United regained the lead, bypassing three players before swapping passes with Park, then teeing up Welbeck for an emphatic finish past Szczesny.

A victorious start to a taxing run of high-profile fixtures for the Reds sent out a clear message of defiance from the champions, regardless of Manchester City's breathtaking pace in the title race.

The Teams

Arsenal: Szczesny; Djourou (Yennaris 46), Mertesacker, Koscielny, Vermaelen; Walcott, Rosicky, Ramsey (Park 84), Song, Oxlade-Chamberlain (Arshavin 74); van Persie

Subs not used: Almunia, Squillaci, Benayoun, Miquel
Booked: Ramsey, Song, Rosicky, van Persie, Koscielny

Manchester United: Lindegaard; Jones (Rafael 17 (Park 77)), Smalling, Evans, Evra; Valencia, Carrick, Giggs, Nani (Scholes 75); Rooney, Welbeck
Subs not used: De Gea, Berbatov, Hernandez, Fabio
Booked: Rafael, Evra

'It was right at the start of a tough run of games,' recalls Danny Welbeck, United's match-winner. 'We had to make sure we started that run with a win, and the workrate throughout the team that day was top-notch; we worked really hard for each other. We knew the right way to play against them and we created several opportunities. Maybe we should have stuck a few more away, but I was buzzing to score the winner.'

With an FA Cup jaunt to Liverpool next up, followed by a make-or-break run of league games against Stoke, Chelsea, Liverpool, Norwich and Tottenham, as well as a Europa League tie with Ajax, the cost of that winning start at the Emirates seemed high.

'It's not good news for us,' lamented Sir Alex Ferguson. 'I think Jones will be out for a few weeks – it's ankle ligaments. Carrick was feeling his hamstring in the second half and he just had to sit in the middle of the pitch.' With Wayne Rooney also limping and Nani hobbling off after a cynical challenge from Laurent Koscielny, the Reds were struggling to piece together a squad for the trip to Anfield – even if everybody wanted to play.

'You always want to be involved in big games like this, because anything can happen,' admitted Ryan Giggs. 'You feel so much better when you come out on top in a game like this, and vice-versa it's so much worse if you lose one of them. You know what's at stake and you can't wait for it. Tackles will be flying in, and there's always a massive rivalry between the two clubs. It's one of the games that you're going to miss when you finish your playing career.'

Though such a prestigious fixture with a cup-tie edge would have been enough to have fans of both sides – and neutrals – salivating at the prospect, the first return of Patrice Evra to Anfield since October's incident with Luis Suarez hogged the headlines in the run-up to the game. Naturally, Sir Alex looked to deflect the focus back to the football.

'There is a responsibility on the players to behave properly,' said the manager. 'That is what I expect my players to do, and also the fans. Both sets of fans have got to make sure we are talking about the game and nothing else. It can be that way because there are a lot of good players on the pitch. It is a big game and at the end of the day we want to talk about a game of football. Both sets of players have to be aware of that. I'm confident there won't be problems.'

The manager's most persistent problem was selecting his side, with question marks hanging over the availability of several players even as the game loomed large. 'It's not the best situation for us,' he shrugged. 'But we'll be up for it. It's a big FA Cup tie – there's no doubt about it. In my time there haven't been many cup-ties between the clubs. It's one to look forward to and I think the players will follow that. I always think home draws make you favourite, but it's a massive game for both clubs.'

FA Cup fourth round

28 January 2012 | Anfield | Kick-off 12:45 |
Attendance: 43,952

Liverpool 2 (Agger 21, Kuyt 88)

Manchester United 1 (Park 39)

United's long wait for FA Cup success was extended by another season as the Reds succumbed to a late Dirk Kuyt sucker punch at

Anfield. Despite bossing possession for much of the game, and always appearing the more likely winners, the Reds lost concentration with two minutes remaining, allowing the Dutch striker to ram home the winner to knock United out of the competition.

The Reds had earlier negated Daniel Agger's opener with a well-worked leveller from Ji-sung Park, but were left to rue an inability to translate their dominance into chances in the second period.

Plenty of pre-match focus was on Patrice Evra, returning to Anfield for the first time since his altercation with Luis Suarez, and the Frenchman was roundly booed by the home support for his role as the victim in the unseemly saga.

Evra began the afternoon in fine form, linking well with Ryan Giggs, whose 20-yard volley forced Pepe Reina into a routine save in the game's first effort. The second, however, left Liverpool's Spanish keeper clutching at air, as Antonio Valencia darted inside off the right touchline, motored towards the penalty area and unleashed a rocket of an effort which bashed against the far post and out to safety.

The visitors' frustration was heightened just four minutes later when a Steven Gerrard corner dropped onto the head of Agger, who rose highest amid a packed six-yard box to head home.

Still, the Reds enjoyed long spells of possession in Liverpool's half before restoring parity just before the break. Rafael bombarded down the right flank and skipped past Jose Enrique's challenge before cutting the ball back from the goal-line for the onrushing Park, who drilled a low effort past Reina in front of the Kop.

In the second period, chances were at a premium. Chris Smalling escaped a half-hearted penalty shout when the ball brushed his hand, before Danny Welbeck nudged the ball past Reina, only for Martin Skrtel to swiftly snuff out the danger. United bossed possession but, shorn of the string-pulling influence and attacking power of Wayne Rooney, lacked a cutting edge in the final third.

The introduction of Chicharito for Paul Scholes sought to remedy that, but it was another substitute, Kuyt, who would have greater impact on proceedings, as he latched onto Andy Carroll's flick from a long Reina punt, before drilling a low shot past David De Gea to send Anfield wild.

Too little time remained for the Reds to pick their way through the already massed Liverpool ranks, and the hosts were able to comfortably close out their victory and leave the Reds with just the Premier League and Europa League to aim for.

The Teams

Liverpool: Reina; Kelly, Skrtel, Agger, Jose Enrique; Rodriguez (Kuyt 63), Gerrard (Bellamy 72), Carragher (Adam 63), Henderson, Downing; Carroll
Subs not used: Doni, Johnson, Coates, Shelvey

Manchester United: De Gea; Rafael, Smalling, Evans, Evra; Valencia, Carrick, Scholes (Hernandez 76), Giggs (Berbatov 89), Park; Welbeck
Subs not used: Lindegaard, Ferdinand, Fabio, M.Keane, Pogba
Booked: Rafael

'I don't know how we lost it,' lamented Sir Alex Ferguson. 'It was a really good performance from us. That can happen in the FA Cup though – you can have one bad break against you and you lose the game. It's a sudden-death situation which we've experienced many times over the years and anything can happen. It's a bad blow, though, because we didn't deserve that.

'I'm pleased with my players. They performed very well, dominated the game and played good football. They didn't deserve to be beaten at all. We maybe should have won the game – we were the better team. But that's FA Cup football, I'm afraid, and it's not the first time it's happened. To lose it is a devastating blow. It is hard to believe, really.'

Dominance offered no compensation in defeat, and Jonny Evans was quick to underline that United's players were well aware of the need to react positively to a galling setback.

'Every player at this club knows what's expected,' said the defender. 'When you're at Manchester United, you know defeats like that aren't acceptable. We don't need anybody else to tell us that. We know it deep down. We've responded really well after disappointing moments this season, like the six-one defeat against City and then the Blackburn and Newcastle defeats at the turn of the year. We went on a great run after the City game and then after the New Year games we beat both City and Arsenal away. That's what this team does.'

Evans and his cohorts wouldn't have to wait long for their opportunity to right the wrongs of Anfield. Three days on, the Reds would welcome Stoke City to Old Trafford. The Potters had taken a Premier League point off the champions for the first time in the sides' September meeting at the Britannia Stadium, and ever since had continued to battle their way through the season in trademark fashion.

'We've played really well against Stoke in the last few games, both at home and away,' continued Evans. 'We've beaten them comfortably over the last few seasons, but they're improving all the time and nobody ever looks forward to playing against Stoke. They have a different approach to the way most teams play.

'People have this preconception of them and think that because they're a big side they're a dirty side. But that's not the case at all. I think they're hard but fair, and Tony Pulis goes out of his way to make sure they don't cross that line.'

The Potters would face a United side still shorn of Wayne Rooney, while Anders Lindegaard had sustained an ankle injury in training that would require surgery. Sir Alex Ferguson opted to give David De Gea the night off, and instead prepared to promote Ben Amos for his Premier League debut.

There was also the small matter of the transfer window to consider, and the Reds did partake in a brief flurry of activity, as Mame Biram Diouf joined Hannover 96 on a permanent deal and highly rated Ravel Morrison was sold to West Ham United in the hope that the youngster could realise his brimming potential at Upton Park.

Inbound was Frederic Veseli, a 19-year-old Swiss defender, who made the short move from Manchester City, where he had featured in the Blues' pre-season tour without making the step up to sustained senior involvement.

While those moves ensured that Carrington's club staff would have a busy deadline day, the players were free to concentrate on extending a burgeoning run of Premier League form.

Barclays Premier League

31 January 2012 | Old Trafford | Kick-off 20:00 | Attendance: 74,719

Manchester United 2 (Hernandez 38 (pen), Berbatov 53 (pen))
Stoke City 0

Javier Hernandez, Dimitar Berbatov and Darron Gibson all scored crucial goals as United drew level with Manchester City at the head of the Barclays Premier League table. United's strike duo for the evening bagged a penalty apiece in an attritional but comfortable win over Stoke City, while ex-Red Gibson timed his first Everton goal to perfection: ramming home the only score against league leaders City at Goodison Park.

The Irish midfielder's strike provoked one of the biggest roars of a low-key evening at Old Trafford, where Stoke City's dogged resistance crucially faltered on two occasions, giving the Reds the opportunity to secure the points from the spot. Chances in open play were few and far between, but the first fell to Stoke's Jon Walters, who flashed a shot just wide from inside the area.

In between the posts for United was Ben Amos, making his Premier League debut, with Anders Lindegaard injured and David De Gea rested. That also meant a first senior involvement of the season for Tomasz Kuszczak, who took a place on the bench.

On-song Antonio Valencia provided the hosts' first noteworthy attempt, drilling in an angled drive, which Thomas Sorensen did well

165

to push to safety amid a forest of bodies. The Dane was soon beaten when Michael Carrick latched onto Berbatov's through-ball, but could only fire just past the far post.

The deadlock didn't last long, however, as Ji-sung Park was upended by Jermaine Pennant in the box, giving Chicharito the chance to bag his first Old Trafford goal since mid-November. The Mexican typically kept his head and tucked the spot-kick into the bottom left-hand corner with Sorensen diving in the other direction.

Shortly after the restart, United were given a second penalty when Walters wrestled with Valencia and clumsily halted the Ecuadorian's progress. Chicharito handed the opening to his strike partner, and Berbatov placed his shot under Sorensen's dive to secure victory for the champions.

Aside from Amos saving well from Cameron Jerome's header, the action was all in front of the Stretford End, which was baying for another penalty after Andy Wilkinson's rash challenge on Patrice Evra, but a third award never materialised. Paul Pogba impressed in a late substitute cameo, and was only denied a goal when Wilkinson blocked his shot, before Berbatov slotted wide in injury time from another cross by the unplayable Valencia.

The third, and arguably most important, goal of the evening had already been scored almost 40 miles away, as Darron Gibson helped out his former colleagues on an important night in the title race.

The Teams

Manchester United: Amos; Smalling, Ferdinand, Evans, Evra; Valencia, Scholes, Carrick, Park; Berbatov, Hernandez (Pogba 73)
Subs not used: Kuszczak, Giggs, Welbeck, Fabio, Rafael, W.Keane
Booked: Scholes

Stoke City: Sorensen; Wilkinson, Shawcross, Huth, Wilson; Pennant, Whitehead, Palacios (Delap 75), Walters (Fuller 75); Jones, Crouch (Jerome 57)

Subs not used: Begovic, Whelan, Etherington, Woodgate
Booked: Huth, Wilkinson, Walters

'There are a lot of players here who can take penalties,' grinned Chicharito. 'Sometimes it's Wazza, sometimes it's Ryan Giggs. Today it was me and Berbatov. I take them for Mexico and I'll be ready if [United] ask me again. If they want me to shoot one, I'll shoot. I just try to do my best and help my team with goals. I always say the most important thing is the points. It doesn't matter who scores. Against Stoke we did a great job against a very difficult team. It was a great night for Manchester United, with City dropping points and us winning against a very difficult team.'

'It's a good night for us, of course,' echoed Sir Alex Ferguson. 'But what I'm most pleased about is our own performance. I thought our football was terrific. We kept our composure, we were very patient. Okay, we won with two penalty kicks, but I think the manner in which we played our football was the most important thing.

'It's still early doors. It's only the last day in January. I always say that March is a very important month, as well as the beginning of April. We play Manchester City in April, for instance.'

With Premier League games against Chelsea, Liverpool and Norwich, plus the commencement of Europa League duties against Ajax to consider, February was also beginning to look like a potentially pivotal month in the race for honours.

8

February – Building Momentum

Though Darron Gibson's old-pals act had given United an unexpected boon in the race for the title, there was no mistaking the treacherous period through which the Reds needed to plot a careful course, and it began with a distinctly difficult trip to Chelsea.

It had been a decade since United had left Stamford Bridge with three Premier League points and, though Andre Villas-Boas' Blues reign had been fraught with setbacks and rumours of dressing-room discontent, those in Red knew they would be posed problems in West London. 'Chelsea have had a few ups and downs, a few poor results, but I don't think you can ever rule them out,' claimed Chris Smalling. 'They've won plenty of titles over the years and they have a strong squad.'

'When I play against Chelsea, I don't consider them as being out of the title race,' added Ji-sung Park. 'They are our rivals to win the title. I know the points gap between ourselves and Chelsea is quite a lot, but they won't give up until the end of the season. They will always try to fight.'

United's hopes were boosted by the return of Wayne Rooney and Ashley Young, while Nani and Tom Cleverley were also inching their way towards a recall. In goal, however, David De Gea was assured of involvement at Stamford Bridge and beyond, with Anders Lindegaard ruled out for at least six weeks with an ankle injury. Though he had rotated the two stoppers during the course of the season, and had rested the Spaniard in favour of using the relatively inexperienced Ben Amos against Stoke, Sir Alex Ferguson was unconcerned by turning to De Gea.

'The boy has got a great talent, there is no doubt about that,' said the manager. 'He has made two or three mistakes coming into the game at twenty years of age – he is twenty-one now – but in two or three years' time we won't be discussing that at all, because he will have matured. He will realise his potential then.

'At the moment, he has found it difficult coming into the English game. The first goal at Liverpool [in January's FA Cup defeat] was a case in point. He was crowded out. Our own players created a problem with so many players around him. They didn't give him any room to manoeuvre. He would never have experienced that in Spain, so that was difficult for him.

'It is highlighted when you make a mistake at United. It can be exaggerated a little bit. But there are mistakes and he wants to address it himself. He will do through maturity and the understanding of the English game. It is harder when you are replacing someone like Edwin van der Sar and Peter Schmeichel – they are probably two of the greatest goalkeepers in European football over the last forty years. We felt we should go for a young keeper who would develop and mature into the position because the potential is there.'

The Spaniard would validate his manager's faith in spectacular fashion in an absorbing clash at Stamford Bridge.

Barclays Premier League

5 February 2012 | Stamford Bridge | Kick-off 16:00 |
Attendance: 41,688

Chelsea 3 (Evans 36 (og), Mata 46, Luiz 51)
Manchester United 3 (Rooney 58 (pen), 70 (pen), Hernandez 84)

United roared back from three goals down to snatch a point in a breathless, enthralling draw with Chelsea at Stamford Bridge.

Jonny Evans' own-goal had given the Blues a scarcely deserved half-time lead, but strikes early in the second period from Juan Mata and David Luiz had seemingly condemned the Reds to a sizeable setback. However, Wayne Rooney clinically converted a pair of penalties midway through the second period, before the champions' trademark spirit yet again bore fruit as substitute Chicharito headed home a leveller with five minutes of normal time remaining.

A dramatic afternoon was spared a last-gasp twist thanks to David De Gea, who made two stunning injury-time saves to procure a valuable point for the Reds, who had seemed buried with half an hour remaining.

The Spaniard had been underemployed in a first half characterised by sloppy passing and few chances. The visitors were up in arms when Danny Welbeck was sent tumbling by Blues debutant Gary Cahill on the edge of the Chelsea area, only for referee Howard Webb to wave away the appeals.

Welbeck's frustration was exacerbated when Branislav Ivanovic slid in to clear Rooney's cross as it begged to be tapped home. At the other end, Welbeck's England Under-21 colleague Daniel Sturridge made the telling contribution of the first half when he picked his way to the United byline and jabbed a cross into a crowded six-yard box. At such close quarters, De Gea could only flick out a boot and divert the ball against the helpless Evans, off whom it ricocheted into the unguarded goal.

United's response was admirable, closing out the first half with efforts from Ashley Young, Welbeck and Rooney which all drew scurrying saves from Petr Cech. The early stages of the second half, however, looked likely to douse any embers of hope. Chelsea's first foray forward culminated in Mata lashing a brilliant volley into the roof of De Gea's net, and the Spanish playmaker soon crossed for Luiz to head home a third, via a sizeable deflection off Rio Ferdinand.

Undeterred, United continued to pick away at a Chelsea side still showing weaknesses. The visitors' advances were rewarded when Sturridge clumsily halted Patrice Evra's surge into the hosts' area. Rooney rifled the resultant penalty home. Half an hour to go.

Sir Alex promptly altered his side's shape, introducing Paul Scholes for Rafael and moving Antonio Valencia to right-back. Chicharito had replaced Young just before Rooney's penalty, and the narrower United were soon creating openings. Neat interplay on the edge of the Chelsea box ended with the ball reaching Welbeck, and Ivanovic sent the striker tumbling to the turf. Webb awarded another penalty and Rooney switched sides, planting his second effort to Cech's left and putting the game firmly back in the balance.

Chelsea missed the chance to end the contest when Fernando Torres dallied, deep inside the United area, and they were made to pay with five minutes remaining. Rooney's shot was parried away from goal by Cech but retrieved by Ryan Giggs, and the veteran winger was afforded time to pick out the unmarked Chicharito, who planted his header firmly past Cech to send the travelling fans wild.

Still, time remained for a winner from either side, but only De Gea's heroics prevented it. The youngster first produced a wonderful fingertip stop to claw Mata's top corner-bound free-kick around the post, then tipped Gary Cahill's scorching long-range effort over to preserve a vital point for the champions.

The Teams

Chelsea: Cech; Ivanovic, Luiz, Cahill, Bosingwa; Essien, Meireles, Mata; Sturridge (Romeu 70), Torres, Malouda
Subs not used: Turnbull, Ferreira, Hutchinson, Bertrand, Piazon, Lukaku
Booked: Ivanovic, Torres

Manchester United: De Gea; Rafael (Scholes 63), Evans, Ferdinand, Evra; Valencia, Carrick, Giggs, Young (Hernandez 53); Rooney, Welbeck (Park 86)
Subs not used: Amos, Fabio, Pogba, Berbatov
Booked: Evra

'I think it's two dropped points, because we played so well,' lamented Sir Alex Ferguson, clearly wrought with mixed emotions. 'Apart from a period of ten minutes after half time when we got off to a terrible start and lost two goals, I thought we were the far better team.

'It's not easy coming back from three-nil down and it was a massive effort from our players. It was a great game for the neutral watching. It was fantastic and Chelsea played a great part in it, too. Although I thought we were the better team, Chelsea made it an interesting game for anyone watching the match. And I was pleased with my players.'

In particular, he was impressed by the efforts of substitute Chicharito and goalkeeper David De Gea, both of whom made late contributions to procure United's point. 'To be honest, I maybe should have played Chicharito from the start,' he admitted. 'When he came on, he just had them on toast, really. He really put them under pressure with his movement and positional play. Danny Welbeck has been terrific and he's going to be a top player, but when Chicharito came on in the second half, it was a different game.

'David has played his part, no question. I think the save from the

[Mata] free-kick was unbelievable. It was going right in the top corner. He made two or three other saves, including a good one in the first half. I'm pleased, because we see the talent in the boy. We're going to trust that talent. The introduction to English football has been different for him. It's not what he's used to in Spain, but today he's shown he's prepared to get in among it, he's got in a couple of punches and he's done a great job.'

While Sir Alex was – like everyone – still shell-shocked by the chaotic nature of the afternoon, Ryan Giggs looks back on the six-goal thriller with a hint of regret at having failed to take all three points.

'Overall, we played well and we were surprised to be down, if I'm honest,' he reflects. 'Even at half time we felt we were in the game, but they scored two quick goals after the break. Obviously, we could have sat and felt sorry for ourselves, but I think they knew we were playing well and that we were still going to create chances. Chicha coming on was just a different problem for the Chelsea defenders. You know that he's going to be running in behind, always on the shoulder and as a winger and someone who wants to make goals, you know that if you put it in an area in which Chicha's going to be, he'll be there.'

Despite the fact that Manchester City had established a two-point lead with a routine victory over Fulham, Michael Carrick insisted the heroic, come-from-behind nature of events at Stamford Bridge could strike a blow to the Reds' title rivals.

'I think other teams who were watching that and seeing us go three-nil down, they would have been thinking what a good afternoon it has been for them,' smiled the midfielder. 'Then for us to come back in the manner we did might give them a little dent and a boost for us. It's a credit to the boys; we kept going, kept pushing and kept believing that we could get something out of the game, and in the end we did.'

A point procured from the precipice of a damaging defeat ensured that the players returned to Carrington with a spring in their step, and the collective cheer was further heightened by the news that Ryan Giggs – on the verge of reaching 900 appearances for the club – had signed a new, one-year contract extension.

'When I signed my first contract, I never thought I'd be able to play at United for twenty-two years, but I feel good and I know I can still contribute to keeping the team pushing for honours,' remarked the winger.

While Sir Alex added: 'In many ways, Ryan epitomises all my teams here at United: he has constantly re-invented himself, adapted to the changing nature of the game and retained that desire and hunger for success. In every training session and match, he is the example for others to follow. The young players in the dressing room have a great chance to learn from a player who will continue to break records that anyone in the game will find hard to beat.'

Records had provided a bone of contention between United and their next opponents, Liverpool, down the years. More recently, Luis Suarez's spat with Patrice Evra had added another dimension to an already feisty rivalry, and the Merseysiders' looming visit to Old Trafford was dominating the football media, with the two parties scheduled to shake hands as part of the Premier League's pre-match routine.

Looking back at the furore surrounding the build-up, however, Ryan Giggs insists the Reds were always at the eye of the hurricane. 'You know what, it's always the same with incidents like that,' says the veteran. 'Actually within the club and as a football player, you just concentrate on the game. The media and the fans try to make the most of it, but that's just the way it was. It was a massive incident, but as a player you just go out and play your game and worry about anything else after the game. You want to win any game against Liverpool, but obviously with the hype and the build-up to that particular game, and for the players involved, we really wanted to win as well.'

Barclays Premier League

11 February 2012 | Old Trafford | Kick-off 12:45 |
Attendance: 74,844

Manchester United 2 (Rooney 47, 50)
Liverpool 1 (Suarez 80)

The unwanted sideshow between Luis Suarez and Patrice Evra continued amid unpleasant scenes at Old Trafford, but it was Wayne Rooney's quickfire double that headlined a deserved and vital victory over Liverpool.

Rooney thundered home a close-range volley and tucked away a neat finish after Antonio Valencia had caught Jay Spearing in possession, bagging the decisive pair within five minutes of half time. The champions might have done more from promising positions in a one-sided second period, and were subjected to a nervy ending to the game when Suarez tucked away a late consolation strike for the visitors.

Much pre-match anticipation preceded the Uruguayan's involvement, and he started for Liverpool for the first time since receiving an eight-game ban for racially abusing Evra. While speculation had reigned over whether or not the Frenchman would shake hands with Suarez, events took an unexpected twist when the striker shunned the United skipper's hand.

The small matter of the match itself then took centre stage, though once again Evra and Suarez remained in the spotlight. Less than 30 seconds in, the pair were on collision course for a loose ball until Rio Ferdinand intervened, and felt the full force of Evra's totally committed challenge, which flipped him head over heels and prompted a lengthy stoppage for treatment. Once the game had restarted, it was the visitors who began the brighter, and might have forged ahead when Glen Johnson curled a left-footed effort just past David De Gea's post.

175

United were soon bossing matters, however, though it took a beautifully intricate passing move to give Paul Scholes a clear sight of goal after half an hour, only for the veteran midfielder to head his chance straight at Pepe Reina.

Liverpool were erroneously incensed when, on the stroke of half time, Suarez was denied a clear run on goal by an excellent Ferdinand challenge, and tunnel scuffles reportedly punctuated the half-time break. Whatever went on behind the scenes, it was the hosts who landed the first telling blow of the game, within two minutes of the restart.

Ryan Giggs' right-wing corner was inadvertently flicked on by Jordan Henderson as he jumped with Michael Carrick, and the ball fell perfectly for Rooney to thunder home a volley from six yards out.

Old Trafford erupted, and the primal roar had barely dipped before United's lead was doubled. Valencia's hustle provoked panic in the Liverpool ranks, and Spearing duly presented the ball to the Ecuadorian, who fed Rooney for a simple, left-footed finish between Reina's legs.

Rooney should have notched his treble before the hour-mark. Valencia again caused havoc on the right, and his ball inside was daintily ignored by Scholes, a fleeting piece of inspiration that foxed Rooney, who could only stab wide from close range.

Just as the Reds appeared to be routinely closing out the win, however, the visitors hit back. Substitute Charlie Adam whipped in a dangerous set-piece which dipped, hit Ferdinand and fell perfectly for Suarez to poke home a simple finish.

Though De Gea was forced to spectacularly fingertip a long-range effort from Johnson over the bar, United saw out a nervy ending in relative comfort. The Evra–Suarez spat was a consuming subplot, but in the bigger picture, United remained firmly in the hunt to retain the title.

The Teams

Manchester United: De Gea; Rafael, Ferdinand, Evans, Evra; Valencia, Carrick, Scholes, Giggs; Rooney, Welbeck
Subs not used: Amos, Fabio, Cleverley, Pogba, Park, Hernandez, Berbatov
Booked: Carrick

Liverpool: Reina; Johnson, Agger, Skrtel, Enrique; Kuyt (Adam 75), Henderson, Gerrard, Spearing (Carroll 61), Downing (Bellamy 61); Suarez
Subs not used: Doni, Kelly, Carragher, Shelvey
Booked: Downing

Try as everyone might, there was no escaping the pre-match handshake in the post-match analysis.

'I couldn't believe it. I just could not believe it,' said Sir Alex Ferguson. 'Patrice and I had a chat this morning and he said: "I'm going to shake his hand. I've got nothing to be ashamed of, I want to keep my dignity," and he [Suarez] refuses! He is a disgrace to Liverpool Football Club – that player should not be allowed to play for Liverpool Football Club again. The history that club's got, and he does that . . . in a situation like today he could have caused a riot. I was really disappointed in that guy; I thought it was terrible, what he did. It created a tension. You saw the referee: he didn't know what to do about it. It caught him off-guard and it was a terrible start to the game. A terrible atmosphere, it created.'

'I thought it was bad decision-making from their guy,' concurred Rio Ferdinand. 'It's a touchy subject at the minute and things could have been put to bed a little easier if the handshake had been done. After seeing what I saw, I decided not to shake his hand. He's not got the respect that he needs to have in these situations and acknowledge he's made a mistake and say sorry. There are a lot of things going on, both on and off the pitch. But the result was the most important thing: to win the game in an unbelievable atmosphere. I thought both sets of fans were good. That was pleasing. Hopefully we can talk more about the football.'

One of the hot topics post-match was of Ferdinand's inadvertent flip at the hands of Evra. Though the England defender's awkward landing had prompted fears of injury at first, his subsequent recovery rendered the incident fair game for dressing-room banter.

'We got in the changing room after the game and that was probably one of the funniest things of the day,' says Jonny Evans, looking back. 'Rio was fine about it afterwards – I think it sorted his back out for him: he hasn't been injured since!'

Danny Welbeck also continues to see the funny side of his colleagues' accidental clash: 'When it happened at the time I was so shocked, I made a little "oh" noise,' says the striker. 'You could just see it happening. You could see a fifty-fifty coming between Patrice and Suarez and you're just thinking: "I've got your back, Pat; whatever happens, I've got your back." Then you just see Rio coming in and you're like: "Noooo," and you just shy away from it. It could've been bad, but thankfully Rio was okay. It was funny afterwards when you could laugh about it!'

The following day, Liverpool issued a trio of apologetic statements representing the club, manager Kenny Dalglish and Luis Suarez himself and, once the dust had settled on the superfluous events at Old Trafford, the simple fact remained that United had deservedly taken the three points through Wayne Rooney's well-taken brace; a fact the striker revelled in afterwards, admitting: 'It's something that I had dreamed about as a young boy.'

Sir Alex was also delighted with the display, if not the scoreline. 'I thought it was a great performance by us,' he said. 'I'm disappointed it has ended up two-one, to be honest with you. Maybe we did tend to just try to play out the game and keep possession, and not really threaten the way we did before we got the goals.

'I think my heart's still out there! It was nervy in the sense that you're playing Liverpool, they've come back from two-nil down to two-one, and you know football: anything can happen. You only need a second to lose a goal or score a goal, so that was a worrying period, but we got through it. That's the only fault I can find in the players, because right the way through the team we played some fantastic football. Really, really good football.'

The manager's attentions quickly switched to his first tilt at the Europa League and, amid media suggestions that United would struggle to find motivation to compete in the second tier of European football, Sir Alex insisted: 'I'm definitely treating it seriously,' of his side's impending visit to face Ajax in Amsterdam. 'The great thing about Thursday is we don't have a game next Saturday, so I can play my strongest team and will play my strongest team.

'The thing is to look forward to it. It's still European football and still a good standard. It'll be a full house, too, with a great stadium and a great pitch. They're not having a great time at the moment, but I think, playing United, they will be well motivated for it and always play nice football too.

'I feel good about being in the Europa League. It's a tournament we're going to try to win and we have a responsibility to do better than we've done earlier in the season. Going out of the Champions League wasn't expected, but it happens. Being in this tournament should be great. We have so many young players who don't have much experience of Europe. But now there's a final in Romania: they want to be there, I want to be there and our fans want to be there.'

Only Patrice Evra, Ryan Giggs and Dimitar Berbatov sat out the short trip across the North Sea, while Tom Cleverley, Phil Jones, Nani, Chris Smalling and Ashley Young all rejoined the squad after injury. According to Wayne Rooney, everybody was keen to be involved in an intriguing tie.

'Ajax and Manchester United are two massive clubs,' said the striker. 'Who wouldn't want to play in this game? You look at the squad and there's motivation and desire in every training session. When you play in front of thousands of people, you want to win –

you want to do yourself proud and your team proud. We'll definitely be going out there trying to win.

'There are a lot of quality teams in the tournament and it's going to be a challenge. It's one we want to accept. We want to get to the final and win it, regardless of whether that's against Manchester City or a team from Italy, Holland or Spain. We want to win.'

UEFA Europa League

16 February 2012 | Amsterdam ArenA | Kick-off 18:00 | Attendance: 48,866

Ajax 0
Manchester United 2 (Young 59, Hernandez 85)

Second-half strikes from Ashley Young and Javier Hernandez gave the Reds a winning start to life in the Europa League, as Ajax were clinically overcome in Amsterdam. In a finely balanced encounter, the deadlock was broken just before the hour as Young fired through a crowd of players. Ajax continued to battle for a route back into the tie, however, and the victory was only assured when Chicharito capped a flowing counter-attack with five minutes remaining.

United's triumph owed much to an assured display from David De Gea, capped by a stunning fingertip save from Siem de Jong while the scoreline was blank. The game began at a pedestrian pace as both teams sized up each other, until de Jong arrowed a 25-yard effort towards the top corner, which the United goalkeeper brilliantly clawed around the post.

Ajax finished the half in the ascendancy as Dmitri Bulykin headed over and Christian Eriksen chanced his arm from range, before Rio Ferdinand escaped a strong penalty appeal when Miralem Sulejmani ran into him on the edge of the United box.

The interval prompted resurgence in the visitors, and Nani set the tone for the second period when he drew a fine save from Kenneth Vermeer within 90 seconds of the restart. The Ajax stopper then had to be alert to snatch the ball from Chicharito's feet and turn away Toby Alderweireld's errant header.

Vermeer was helpless, however, just before the hour-mark when Young collected Nani's low cross at the back post, wound his way towards the centre of the goal and fired a low shot through Vermeer's legs and past three defenders.

Briefly stunned but still unbowed, Ajax sought an equaliser. De Gea beat away Eriksen's powerful effort and a series of half-chances fizzled out in the United area. The visitors were a constant menace on the break, and punished the Eredivisie champions with a rapier breakaway in the 85th minute.

Michael Carrick released Antonio Valencia with a typically sublime through-ball, and the Ecuadorian's pass allowed Wayne Rooney to tee up Hernandez for a simple finish underneath Vermeer.

Valencia had to be replaced after suffering a hamstring injury during the build-up to the goal, but that was the only dark spot on an otherwise hugely satisfactory evening for the Reds in Amsterdam.

The Teams

Ajax: Vermeer; Alderweireld, Anita, Vertonghen, Koppers (Boilesen 63); De Jong, Aissati, Eriksen; Ozbiliz (Lukoki 80), Bulykin (Van Rhijn 60), Sulejmani
Subs not used: Cillessen, Blind, Lodeiro, Serero
Booked: De Jong, Alderweireld

Manchester United: De Gea; Jones, Ferdinand, Evans, Fabio; Nani, Carrick, Cleverley (Scholes 61), Young (Valencia 76 (Welbeck 86)); Rooney, Hernandez
Subs not used: Amos, Smalling, Park, Pogba
Booked: Fabio

'I'm delighted with the scoreline, but I think it was a very ordinary performance by us,' conceded Sir Alex Ferguson. 'We didn't reach any great heights in the game. We did improve in the second half and I thought we deserved to win it, but I didn't think we played well at all. There was no rhythm to our game. I know Ajax can make it difficult with their system and they pressed the ball really well, but we didn't get any tempo to our game. It gives us a good opportunity [to qualify], but we're taking nothing for granted, of course. We're at home at Old Trafford and we have a good opportunity to get through.'

The game was an invaluable taster of competitive action for a number of players making their return from injury, perhaps explaining the Reds' lacklustre tempo. Among them was Phil Jones, who was collectively satisfied on behalf of those who needed action. 'I've been out for three weeks, so I'm not going to get full match fitness straight away, but it's good to get ninety minutes under my belt and hopefully, if I'm selected, I can do well in the next game,' said the defender.

'I'm delighted for Tom Cleverley. He's a terrific talent. We missed him on the pitch while he was out. But I saw him every day in the gym, so I know his attitude's fantastic. He deserved to be out there tonight. Ashley's also terrific. He's come back from injury and done really well and I was pleased for him to get our first goal.'

On the flip side, Sir Alex had to confirm the bad news that Antonio Valencia looked likely to miss four weeks of action after sustaining a hamstring strain in setting up the Reds' second goal. 'It's a really big blow,' admitted Rio Ferdinand. 'Antonio's been a fantastic player for us this season. But when somebody gets injured or loses form at this club, the manager can always call upon another player to perform.'

The Reds returned to England with a rare weekend off to savour, as the FA Cup continued in their absence. That meant the return leg against Ajax a week later moved instantly into focus, and Jonny Evans was keen to stress that a two-goal advantage was by no means a decisive lead.

'I don't think anything is safe in Europe,' said the Northern Ireland international. 'Even in our home games, we probably didn't manage to get the right results, so we'll be looking to keep it tight at the back at Old Trafford and maybe stamp our authority on it a bit more.'

United would have to do so without Wayne Rooney, who had been struck down by a throat infection. In his absence, Chicharito would start for the second game in a row. The Mexican maintained, however, that he was happy just to be involved, and was enjoying his second season at Old Trafford, even if it presented different challenges to his maiden campaign in England.

'If I play one minute, ten minutes or ninety minutes, I try to play the same,' he said. 'My mind is always to do my best and help my team. There are some times in the game when we need to score and perhaps I have had a little bit of luck. I just want to help my team. I don't care if I'm on the bench. Last year, I was on the bench at the start and then I was in the team towards the end of the season. The gaffer has the answers.

'Every player in every team wants to play as many minutes as possible, but I don't care if I start or I'm a substitute. I just want to enjoy it. I am living a dream to play for Manchester United. The only thing I can do is ensure my attitude is positive so I can help my team. The most important thing is that Manchester United wins all the games.'

The Reds' victory in Amsterdam meant Ajax would arrive in Manchester chasing a shock victory, but Fabio da Silva insisted the Reds would be on the attack in time-honoured fashion. 'At Old Trafford always you have to press the other teams and try to score goals,' said the Brazilian. 'We are strong here and we always try to entertain the fans who have come to watch us. They have to come to Old Trafford to attack us and I think that will be hard for them.'

183

UEFA Europa League

23 February 2012 | Old Trafford | Kick-off 20:05 |
Attendance: 63,328

Manchester United 1 (Hernandez 6)
Ajax 2 (Ozbiliz 37, Alderweireld 87) (United win 3-2 on aggregate)

United edged into the last 16 of the Europa League by virtue of their clinical victory in Amsterdam, as Ajax earned a deserved second-leg victory at Old Trafford. Chicharito capped a swift United breakaway to open the scoring in the sixth minute, only for the visitors to hit back and level before the break through Aras Ozbiliz's 20-yard effort.

The visitors went for broke after the interval, and had United on the ropes for a ten-minute period in which David De Gea produced a wonderful, point-blank save to deny Siem de Jong.

Nerves were set jangling with three minutes remaining when the unmarked Toby Alderweireld powered home a header from Ozbiliz's free-kick, but the Reds withstood the visitors' late pressure to squeak into the next round and book a tie with Athletic Club.

United's starting line-up featured four changes to that which had won in Amsterdam a week earlier, but still made a bright start to the game. An interception from stand-in skipper Ji-sung Park redirected the ball to Dimitar Berbatov, who quickly released Chicharito. The Mexican shimmied away from Alderweireld and arrowed a left-footed finish past the helpless Kenneth Vermeer.

The state of the tie set the tone for the remainder of the night. Ajax pressed with abandon but, superbly marshalled by Jan Vertonghen, saw off United's repeated counter-raids. Then, with eight minutes of the first period remaining, a sustained period of Ajax pressure culminated in de Jong teeing up Ozbiliz just outside the area, and the Turk's shot rocketed past De Gea, via a slight deflection off Phil Jones.

Requiring two further goals, Frank de Boer rejigged his side's formation to a three-man defence, and the move worked wonderfully. De Jong was only prevented from giving the visitors the lead by a stunning reaction save from De Gea, and Sir Alex Ferguson introduced Paul Scholes and Jonny Evans for Tom Cleverley and Ashley Young in a bid to grab a foothold in the game.

It worked, and United might have secured a comfortable passage if Nani's long-range effort hadn't crashed against the top of Vermeer's crossbar. Instead, the next goal went to the visitors as Alderweireld rose, unmarked, to power home Ozbiliz's free-kick and send the travelling support wild.

Too little time remained for Ajax to cap their comeback, but their infliction of United's first-ever Europa League, UEFA Cup or Fairs Cup defeat at Old Trafford nevertheless provided another stark reminder of how unforgiving an arena European football can be.

The Teams

Manchester United: De Gea; Rafael, Smalling, Jones, Fabio; Nani, Park, Cleverley (Scholes 61), Young (Evans 61); Berbatov (Welbeck 72), Hernandez
Subs not used: Amos, Evra, Carrick, Giggs
Booked: Rafael, Evans

Ajax: Vermeer; Van Rhijn, Alderweireld, Vertonghen, Koppers (Klaassen 46); Anita, De Jong, Eriksen (Serero 61); Ozbiliz, Lodeiro (Blind 81), Sulejmani
Subs not used: Cillessen, Ebecilio, Ooijer, Aissati
Booked: De Jong

'It was very nervy at the end of the game,' puffed Sir Alex Ferguson. 'We didn't play well in the second half and they were by far the better team. I accept responsibility myself, because I picked a team with too many youngsters in the back four positions. They all have great potential, but on European nights you need experience in the back positions and it just made it a nervy night for us.

'You play Ajax and know that they can keep the ball all night. The problem is that they don't really have a great deal of penetration. But they're all good young footballers, they are a growing team. They are much like ourselves, which is why I thought playing young players would help us, as it would give them experience. Of course, I had to play some who needed a game badly. Phil Jones, Chris Smalling and Tom Cleverley have all been out for a long time so it was important to get them a game.'

For Smalling, progression masked a disappointing evening, and highlighted issues that needed to be ironed out before the weekend's trip to Norwich City. 'We're through to the next round,' said the defender. 'That's what we can take from it, but it was a very disappointing game. When we came off the pitch, we felt like we'd lost the tie. But at the end of the day we've made it through and we now have to make up for it in the next round. We'll have to look at the video from tonight and hopefully we'll play better at the weekend.'

Those hopes would have to factor in the absence of Tom Cleverley and Wayne Rooney, with the former sent for a scan on a foot injury sustained against the Dutch champions, while the latter continued to toil against a throat infection. Though Cleverley's absence was expected to be short-term, it represented another frustrating setback for the youngster. 'I'd hate to be getting the injury-prone tag,' reflects the midfielder, 'because the injuries I've had have all been contact, impact or reckless tackles. It's not like I'm picking up hamstring injuries or thigh injuries all the time. Hopefully, I'm getting all the bad luck out at the start of my career and I can go on to play as long as Giggsy; he's the perfect example.'

For the veteran winger, an outing at Carrow Road would mark his 900th appearance for the club he first represented at senior level 21 years earlier. 'Exceptional,' admitted Sir Alex Ferguson. 'An amazing career and an amazing man.' The boss also took time out of his pre-match preparations to sanction the loan of Tomasz Kuszczak to

Watford, and salute the work of a fellow Glaswegian, Paul Lambert, whose helmsmanship of the Canaries had earned widespread plaudits after a seamless transition to life in the Premier League.

'Norwich is an interesting club because they have a full house for every match,' said the United manager. 'It's in a lovely part of the world. They've got their own little empire down there. It's just like when I was at Aberdeen; it feels as though you're cut off from everywhere. Nonetheless they're being very successful with it.

'I think they have probably exceeded everyone's expectations. I knew Paul when he was a kid at St Mirren. He's had a great career. I think Norwich, for a young manager, is probably a good club to go to, where the expectation's not too high and you've got a full house every week. There's a lot of enthusiasm down there and I think it's suited Paul well.'

A stern challenge awaited the Reds at one of the league's least hospitable venues, but that merely set the scene for the most romantic outcome imaginable.

Barclays Premier League

26 February 2012 | Carrow Road | Kick-off 13:30 |
Attendance: 26,811

Norwich City 1 (Holt 83)
Manchester United 2 (Scholes 7, Giggs 90)

There are pivotal moments in every title race, and Ryan Giggs potentially served up another with an invaluable, last-gasp winner at Carrow Road on his 900th United appearance.

The veteran winger pounced to volley in a close-range finish in added time, prompting feral scenes of celebration among the United players and supporters, after the Reds had seemed set to drop points on an exacting afternoon in Norfolk. Grant Holt's late equaliser had deservedly hauled the Canaries level, after they had spent large portions of the afternoon penning back the champions, who had established an early lead through Paul Scholes' header.

Giggs flicked over from a Phil Jones cross with six minutes gone and, while that would have been a fairytale start, a goal was still forthcoming a minute later, as Nani whipped in a teasing cross from the right, which landed perfectly for Scholes to nod past the exposed John Ruddy.

A splendid move almost brought a second on 16 minutes, when Nani and Javier Hernandez ferried the ball to Danny Welbeck, only for Ruddy to usher the ball just past the post with his fingertips. Having survived that scare, Norwich retaliated, and David De Gea had to match Ruddy's excellence with a vital block from Anthony Pilkington at point-blank range.

The Spaniard preserved United's half-time lead with a cat-like catch from Holt's deft header, and there was no mistaking the signs that a difficult second period lay in store.

Despite impressive midfield work from Scholes and Michael Carrick, Norwich continued to press for a route back into the game. Bradley Johnson drilled wide following a stray pass out of defence by Patrice Evra, and Andrew Surman had a volley blocked, but the champions were also creating openings, as Zak Whitbread cleared Welbeck's gentle lob off the line and Giggs volleyed Jones' cross against Ruddy's bar.

A rare errant pass from Scholes was almost punished by Aaron Wilbraham, only for De Gea to spectacularly fend away the substitute's top corner-bound effort. From the ensuing corner, however, Norwich deservedly levelled as Holt adroitly controlled the ball, spun and crashed a finish high into De Gea's goal.

However, the champions mustered a spirited response and created a flurry of chances in the final ten minutes. Substitute Ashley Young had a shot blocked, Welbeck failed to meet Giggs' inviting cross and Elliot Ward almost diverted the ball past Ruddy, before Welbeck fired against the home stopper's legs after another incisive pass from Giggs.

It was left to the old stager to save the day himself, however, and Giggs timed and directed his run perfectly to meet Young's far-post cross and volley home the decisive goal from close range. With victory snatched from the jaws of a potentially damaging draw, the unhinged jubilation among United's players and fans underlined just how important a goal Giggs' could be.

The Teams

Norwich City: Ruddy; Naughton, Ward, Whitbread, Drury; Pilkington (Wilbraham 70), Fox, Johnson (Bennett 63), Surman; Holt, Jackson (Hoolahan 46)
Subs not used: Steer, Morison, Crofts, Barnett
Booked: Johnson

Manchester United: De Gea; Jones, Evans, Ferdinand, Evra; Nani, Carrick, Scholes, Giggs (Smalling 90); Hernandez (Young 63), Welbeck
Subs not used: Amos, Berbatov, Park, Fabio, Rafael
Booked: Evans, Ferdinand

'It is extra special when it's late and you know it's an important goal,' grins Ryan Giggs, looking back on his fairytale 900th appearance, 'especially if you're in front of your fans. If they're on the other side of the pitch, you're not going to run over there and I wouldn't have made it that far. But it is special because it just brings everyone up and you can see the excitement among the fans. It's a long way for them to go, so it was really nice to send them home with a win.

'It's always tough when a team comes up to the Premier League and they're playing Manchester United. It's the game they probably look for first: when they play United at home. We knew they'd be up for it, and Norwich certainly were that day. We played OK and I think throughout the season, whether it's from a defeat or for example in the Chelsea game going three goals down, we've come back well and there was a good response when Norwich equalised.

'We could have quite easily felt sorry for ourselves, but we created three or four chances after that and we could have won comfortably. But when the goal comes, it's excitement and more relief that I'd scored, and you saw that with the players, the fans and obviously the staff and the manager as well, that hopefully it would turn out to be a big goal in the course of the season.'

Amid the largely untamed celebrations among players and supporters, Jonny Evans admits he had to display a modicum of restraint. 'To go to Norwich and score in the last minute like we did was just an unbelievable feeling,' he smiles. 'You want to jump in with the fans, but I'd already been booked in the game! Obviously, it's different when you score, but referees book you as soon as you make contact with the fans, so it takes away a bit of their involvement in the celebration. We wanted to get as close as we could and celebrated in front of them. There were plenty of them at Norwich, which was fantastic. I'd have been in there with them if I'd scored!'

Regardless of who scored it, the winner and its late nature sent out a stark message to Manchester City, who remained two points clear but were unable to shake off the Reds during their taxing run of fixtures. 'It's a great result and it will have an impact,' warned Sir Alex Ferguson at Carrow Road. 'Everyone knows we never give in and no matter who plays us, they know they're going to have to play right until the very death.'

So far, so good amid an exacting time in the season, with games aplenty and an international break to end February. March would begin with a daunting trip to face third-placed Tottenham Hotspur, and there was no mistaking the crucial nature of the coming weeks.

'There was a run of games there that we looked at in the fixture list,' reflects Jonny Evans. 'And we had two tough away games against Norwich and then Spurs at the weekends and an international fixture in-between. Obviously, most of our lads are involved in international games, so that week was always going to be massive and we were thinking to ourselves to try and get through it, especially physically. We'd been playing a lot of games and it was really important to motivate everyone and make sure we got maximum points from those two away games.'

Coming round the bend and heading for the home straight apace, United would enter March having built impressive momentum: a key means to overcoming hurdles as imposing as Tottenham at White Hart Lane.

March – Title Fight

Until suffering a heavy defeat at Arsenal on the same day that United had pinched the points against Norwich, Tottenham had been regarded as contenders for the Premier League title, and the Reds' trip to White Hart Lane appeared set to test the champions' mettle as March began.

A further complication was the midweek international break, in which a clutch of United players represented their countries in friendlies. Chris Smalling arrived back at Carrington in the worst shape, ruled out of the Tottenham game after being hospitalised by a clash of heads with Klaas-Jan Huntelaar during Netherlands' victory over England at Wembley.

Otherwise, Sir Alex Ferguson was missing only Tom Cleverley and Antonio Valencia, both sidelined by injuries sustained during the two legs of the Europa League victory over Ajax, in addition to Nemanja Vidic, Darren Fletcher and Michael Owen. There was fatigue to factor into his selection policy, with several players completing 90 minutes for their countries, including Chicharito, who appeared for Mexico in Miami to feature in his fourth game in ten days.

Nevertheless, the United manager was relishing the chance to lock horns with Harry Redknapp in an invariably attractive fixture. 'Tottenham is always a tremendous highlight for us,' said Sir Alex. 'It's always a tremendous game given the history of both clubs. It's a very important game for us. Look at the rest of the season. You can certainly say we're building up to what could turn out to be a title decider with Manchester City.

'This is our hardest away game, no doubt. Hopefully we can navigate it. Harry Redknapp's added lot of players and changed things around. Kyle Walker is a tremendous full-back. He has great pace going forward and there's pace on the other side from Gareth Bale, while Rafael van der Vaart has cleverness off the front. As for Luca Modric, everyone realises what a tremendous player he is. So it's a team full of talent and they're having a great season.'

Those sentiments were echoed from within the dressing room by former Spurs midfielder Michael Carrick. 'We see this as a big game,' he admitted. 'Over the years, there have been some classic games. We have a decent record down there. It doesn't count for much on Sunday but, over the years, we have done quite well.

'At this time of the season, it starts getting serious. Wins and draws can make a huge difference. You saw [at Norwich] how we responded and won the game and what it meant to everyone. We will be looking to do the same again. Our away form has been terrific. It will be tested on Sunday and for the run-in. But if we get the right result and maintain the momentum, who is to know what will happen?'

Barclays Premier League

4 March 2012 | White Hart Lane | Kick-off 16:10 |
Attendance: 36,034

Tottenham Hotspur 1 (Defoe 87)
Manchester United 3 (Rooney 45, Young 60, 69)

United emphatically cleared a major hurdle in the race for the title, posting a priceless victory over Tottenham at White Hart Lane to remain hot on the heels of Manchester City. Wayne Rooney's header in first-half injury time followed a half of dominance for the hosts, while Ashley Young's brace of brilliant finishes ladled gloss on the scoreline for Sir Alex Ferguson's champions.

Tottenham had only Jermain Defoe's late consolation goal to show for their considerable efforts, and were dealt a disservice by the full-time deficit, having bossed matters for the first hour of the game. They found themselves thwarted, however, by a dogged display of resilience from David De Gea and his excellent defence.

The Spaniard produced the game's first save of note after quarter of an hour as he dropped to his left to parry away Emmanuel Adebayor's low, curling effort after he had been allowed to advance to the edge of the United area.

With both sides hounding each other out of possession throughout the first half, set pieces grew in significance. Spurs were given a free-kick from 25 yards, only for Younes Kaboul to drill just off-target, before Rooney hooked a low corner from Young goalwards, but straight at Brad Friedel.

The deadlock remained intact, but soon wavered in an almighty scare for the Reds as, amid a goalmouth mêlée, Adebayor controlled Louis Saha's shot with a combination of chest and arm, before flicking in a finish. To United's relief, referee Martin Atkinson promptly halted play for handball. The home support loudly bemoaned the decision, and their ire was only heightened when the champions moved into the lead in injury time as Rooney escaped Kyle Walker to emphatically head home Young's wickedly dipping corner.

Spurs would have drawn level soon after the restart, but for heroics from both De Gea and Jonny Evans: the Spaniard to instinctively block Jake Livermore's 20-yard effort which deflected off Saha, and the Northern Irishman for subsequently slashing the ball away from a packed goalmouth.

Benoit Assou-Ekotto then curled a 25-yard free-kick against the top of De Gea's crossbar, before United's lead was doubled on the hour-mark – and again it came from alertness at a set-piece. Phil Jones' quick throw-in found Nani on the Tottenham byline, and the Portuguese's cross was turned away from the goal-line by Walker, but Young dealt with the looping ball by brilliantly arrowing a volley inside the far post.

Within nine minutes, it was three. A sustained spell of passing and possession culminated in Patrice Evra slipping the ball to Young, who advanced on goal and exploited Kaboul's reluctance to meet him by curling a stunning, 25-yard effort high into Friedel's top corner. The clinical finish underlined the difference between the two sides, with United's ruthlessness in front of goal proving vital.

Tottenham salvaged deserved consolation late on as an errant pass from substitute Ryan Giggs gave Defoe the opportunity to advance on goal and thump a low, 25-yard effort past an unsighted De Gea. United otherwise ran down the clock, safe in the knowledge that there would be few greater hurdles to clear over the remainder of the Premier League season.

The Teams

Tottenham Hotspur: Friedel; Walker, Kaboul, King, Assou-Ekotto; Lennon (Rose 85), Sandro (Kranjcar 80), Livermore, Modric; Saha (Defoe 80), Adebayor
Subs not used: Cudicini, Dawson, Nelsen, Dos Santos
Booked: Sandro

Manchester United: De Gea; Jones, Evans, Ferdinand, Evra; Nani (Park 80), Scholes (Giggs 61), Carrick, Young; Rooney, Welbeck
Subs not used: Amos, Fabio, Rafael, Anderson, Hernandez
Booked: Evans, Jones

'As long as we stay as a team and a solid unit, which we did out there, then we know we can get a goal,' said Ashley Young, scorer of a decisive and brilliant brace. 'We nicked one in the first half and then came out and got another two. We weren't at our best in the first half, but we went one-nil up and went on the front foot in the second half.

'All of the players knew that we weren't playing to our full potential. We had to show it in the second half and we did well to get the two goals and the three points. We felt comfortable when the second goal went in. We just wanted to go on and we knew we could get more goals. We knew if we kept on working hard then we'd get a third, and we did that.'

Sir Alex Ferguson, meanwhile, expressed a degree of sympathy for the hosts, who on another day might have earned at least a point for their endeavours. 'We certainly carried a lot of luck today,' the manager admitted. 'It was a great performance from Tottenham in the first half and maybe we got our tactics wrong.

'We improved in the second half and pushed up. In the first period, we tried to drop off and bring them onto us a bit, but it didn't work. At half time I told the players to push up on top of their back four a bit more and not to allow them to build their play. We did much better at that, but it needed the second goal to give us the confidence in our game. After that, we played very well. It was a massive performance from our defenders. Their form at home has been absolutely fantastic, so it was a massive result.'

The Reds' tenth away win of the Premier League season represented a key evolution from the 2010-11 title triumph, which had been built on a foundation of near-immaculate form at Old Trafford, where only two points were dropped. Having registered just five away wins all term, to double that figure with two months of the 2011-12 campaign remaining was a baffling statistic.

'Last year, I don't know what it was,' said Rio Ferdinand. 'It could have been complacency, expecting to win games, whereas at the moment we're being very professional. We're hard to break down, hard to beat and we know that we've got players on the break who can beat anybody. White Hart Lane is a tough place to come. Spurs are a team with talented players. We've had that over the years; we've never had an easy win here. We knew we had to work hard and they made us work hard for the win.'

Conversely, the Reds' home form had appeared brittle in comparison to 2010-11 – especially in European competition. Basel and Benfica had taken Champions League draws from Old Trafford, while Ajax had exited the Europa League with at least a rare win in M16 for their troubles. One win in four European home ties was cause for concern for Sir Alex and his players, especially with Marcelo Bielsa and his highly rated young Athletic Club due at Old Trafford for the first leg of their last-16 Europa League summit.

'It's a very difficult tie,' warned the manager. 'All the work Bilbao have done has been very impressive. They're a very progressive team in Spain at the moment and it's going to be very difficult for us. We need to waken up, there's no question about that. Some of our European form has been disappointing.

'I don't know if it's because we're making too many changes in these games. Certainly against Ajax in the second leg we did that. We also made mistakes in the group stages. It's our own fault. The Basel game will always be remembered for the carelessness of our performance.

'We were a bit unlucky against Benfica at home but, at that point, we needed to beat them. It was a disappointment, but [against Athletic] I'm playing a strong team and I hope that makes a difference. But it's an opportunity to progress and we want to take that opportunity, although it's going to need a very good performance.'

Sir Alex was joined at his pre-match press conference by David De Gea. The Spanish goalkeeper had been showered with plaudits after a string of impressive and important contributions, and he confirmed that he was feeling the benefits of his taxing start to life in England.

'I did receive one or two bits of criticism at the start of the season,' he conceded. 'I think it only serves to make you a stronger person, though. It encourages you to keep fighting and keep working hard.

The important thing is to not let yourself get down. It can almost be a positive thing. You can turn it around. I waited for my chance and I've grabbed it. Now, fortunately, I'm showing some good form. Let's just hope this good form can continue right the way through to the end of the season.'

A Europa League winner with his former club, Atlético Madrid, De Gea added that he was delighted to be facing up to some familiar foes in the Athletic Club side. 'It's exciting because I never imagined I'd be facing Athletic when I came here,' he said. 'It'll be a special night for me. I have lots of good friends at Athletic; I've played with several of them for Spain at various age levels. They're all looking forward to the game too.'

Sadly for United, it wouldn't take long for Athletic to show just how motivated they were.

UEFA Europa League

8 March 2012 | Old Trafford | Kick-off 20:05 |
Attendance: 59,265

Manchester United 2 (Rooney 22, 90 (pen))
Athletic Club 3 (Llorente 44, De Marcos 72, Muniain 90)

Despite a pair of Wayne Rooney goals, United were left with an uphill task to stay in the Europa League after Athletic Club swaggered to an impressive victory at Old Trafford. Marcelo Bielsa's side adopted a free-flowing, energetic approach from the first whistle and thoroughly deserved their victory, procured by Fernando Llorente's header, a wonderfully worked strike from Oscar de Marcos and a late third from Iker Muniain. In response, United could boast only Rooney's close-range opener and injury-time penalty.

The visitors had never won in England, yet were clearly out to amend that statistic as they immediately flooded forward and snapped around the heels of any United player in possession. When they gained the ball, they broke in numbers in support of Llorente, who curled a shot just wide of David De Gea's left-hand post with the game's first effort.

Penned back for much of the first half of the opening period, United took the lead against the run of play when Javier Hernandez played a neat one-two with Ryan Giggs before firing in a shot, which Gorka Iraizoz could only parry. On the spot to convert the rebound was the onrushing Rooney.

Yet the opening goal failed to give the Reds a foothold in the game, as Athletic began to forge plentiful openings. Llorente headed over after a whipped cross from de Marcos down the right, Markel Susaeta carelessly lobbed wide with only De Gea to beat and then Andoni Iraola forced the United stopper to tip his low drive past the post.

A goal was coming, and the visitors nabbed it just before the break as the troublesome Llorente powerfully headed home Susaeta's right-wing cross. Straight after the break, the Spanish international striker was involved again, teeing up de Marcos to fire over from a handy position.

De Gea then drew gasps from the stands with two full-length saves: firstly finger-tipping Muniain's scorching 25-yard drive wide, then palming Llorente's curling effort over the bar, but he was powerless to stop de Marcos' effort on 72 minutes. Ander Herrera scooped a delightful ball up and over the United defence for de Marcos to volley into the far corner and, although replays showed the midfielder was in an offside position, the goal stood.

The hosts had scarcely made a chance all half, and Athletic seemingly wrapped up the tie in the final minute when De Gea parried out Llorente's early volley and Muniain capitalised on hesitancy in the United defence to nip in and power home the rebound.

Though de Marcos handled Hernandez's shot on the cusp of the area in injury time, giving Rooney the chance to blast home a last-gasp penalty, United's hopes of winning the Europa League had been severely dented.

The Teams

Manchester United: De Gea; Rafael, Smalling (Carrick 55), Evans, Evra; Park (Anderson 61), Jones, Giggs (Nani 75), Young; Rooney, Hernandez
Subs not used: Amos, Fabio, Ferdinand, Welbeck
Booked: Carrick

Athletic Club: Iraizoz; Iraola, Martinez, San Jose, Aurtenetxe; De Marcos, Iturraspe, Ander Herrera (Perez 84); Susaeta, Llorente (Toquero 81), Muniain
Subs not used: Raul, Ekiza, Koikili, Lopez, Gomez
Booked: San Jose

Once again, David De Gea was central to United's result, but this time the Spaniard had only been the difference between a damaging defeat and a humiliation. 'We were well beaten,' admitted Sir Alex Ferguson. 'Without David De Gea, we could have conceded four or five goals. He was superb. He made maybe four or five terrific saves in the game.

'Athletic Club Bilbao were the better team, they were very aggressive in terms of their attacking and pressing the ball. Their system caused us problems. All teams do that away from home – they overload the midfield, which can cause you problems. When we went to three midfielders in the second half, we seemed to get better and get a grip of the game and our attacking play was pretty good then. The attacking part wasn't a problem for us really, but our defending wasn't very good and it kept us on the back foot all the time.

'Bielsa's team probably mirror himself. The work ethic of their team is fantastic. They worked harder than us tonight. That's the way he's built his team to work as hard as that and press the ball every-where on the pitch. They never stopped running. They had a two-hour training session yesterday – one hour in the morning at our

Bouncing back: the away support makes a mockery of Manchester City's 'Poznan' celebration during United's thrilling FA Cup third round win at the Etihad Stadium.

Paul Scholes prepares for his shock return as a substitute at City, little more than an hour after his retirement reversal was announced.

Match-winner Danny Welbeck wheels away in delight after smashing home a late, decisive strike against Arsenal at the Emirates Stadium.

Patrice Evra returns to Anfield, where United are undeservedly knocked out of the FA Cup by Dirk Kuyt's winner for Liverpool.

From three goals down to parity, Chicharito rises to cap another barnstorming fightback from the Reds at Stamford Bridge.

United's point is preserved only by a stunning injury-time save from David De Gea, who claws away Juan Mata's top-corner-bound effort.

Wayne Rooney cannot contain his excitement after sliding home his second goal and securing an imperative victory over Liverpool.

After suffering silently during his ongoing racism row, Patrice Evra milks the victory at full time, while Luis Suarez trudges away.

United make a winning return to Europe, and Phil Jones enjoys an energetic comeback in Ajax's Amsterdam ArenA.

Milestone man Ryan Giggs marks his 900th appearance for United in fitting fashion, with a last-gasp winner for the Reds at Norwich.

Rio Ferdinand gets to grips with Emmanuel Adebayor amid United's hard-fought victory over title-chasing Tottenham.

United bow out of the Europa League as Athletic Club – winners of the first leg at Old Trafford – overpower the Reds in Bilbao.

The champions' Premier League title charge continues apace, as Jonny Evans fires home the first of United's five goals at Molineux – and his first for the club after 117 appearances.

David De Gea spectacularly keeps Blackburn at bay as relegation-threatened Rovers aim to complete a shock double over the Reds.

With time ticking away, Antonio Valencia powers home a scorching goal to set United on the road to three vital points at Ewood Park.

The return of Nani cannot prevent United slipping to a shock defeat at Wigan Athletic, a result that re-opens the title race.

Old Trafford is stunned as Everton's Steven Pienaar strikes to secure a 4-4 draw and severely dent the Reds' title defence.

Chris Smalling challenges Joe Hart at the Etihad Stadium, but the England goalkeeper is otherwise untested as City go top of the table.

Goalscorer Ashley Young and Chicharito have no time to celebrate as they chase goals galore against Swansea City.

The United players salute their supporters after beating the Swans, knowing that the title race is out of their control.

Wayne Rooney stoops to head United into the lead at Sunderland on a hugely dramatic final day of the season.

The Reds' stunned players can only applaud their supporters, as Manchester City's last-gasp win over QPR snatches the title at the death.

old training ground and one last night, so they trained for two hours and still put that effort in tonight. It tells you everything about them.'

The manager did, however, underline the dubious nature of Bilbao's second and third goals. De Marcos was clearly offside as he put the visitors ahead, while Muniain's late sucker-punch came from a free-kick given against Patrice Evra because his boot had slipped off.

'The second goal put us on the back foot again,' said Sir Alex. 'I thought it was offside and if it had been disallowed, I think we could have won the game. Maybe not deservedly, but I think we could have won it.' On Bilbao's killer third goal, he added: 'The ref said to the players that you can't play without a boot. It seems a bit bizarre as Patrice only passed the ball about three feet. It was a bit unfortunate.'

'Their [third] goal was a strange one,' echoed Michael Carrick. 'The referee had told us they were kicking it back to us, so we stopped and they scored. Then obviously we got the penalty straight back, but theirs counts for a little bit more, being the away goal.'

The midfielder conceded, however, that the Reds would have to quickly shift focus back to domestic matters, with Roy Hodgson's West Bromwich Albion due at Old Trafford three days later in another vital Premier League meeting.

'We'll be ready for Sunday,' he said. 'There'll be no carry-over from this. We'll regroup tomorrow, gather ourselves again and we'll go again. It's a disappointment, but we'll move on.'

The Reds' bid to maintain their breathless domestic pace was gradually being aided by a diminishing injury list. Chris Smalling was a doubt to face the Baggies after his stitches had opened up during the Bilbao game, but Tom Cleverley and Nani were fit again, while Sir Alex had rested Rio Ferdinand and Paul Scholes to safeguard their freshness to face a side who had won three successive league games.

'West Brom are in a bit of form,' conceded the manager. 'But we're at home and we're expected to win our games at home and hopefully we can put Thursday's result behind us. The players know the challenge is there and we have a great opportunity to kick on after the great result at Spurs and hopefully we'll manage to do that.'

Barclays Premier League

11 March 2012 | Old Trafford | Kick-off 14:00 |
Attendance: 75,598

Manchester United 2 (Rooney 35, 71 (pen))
West Bromwich Albion 0

Wayne Rooney struck in either half to give United a comfortable victory over ten-man West Brom and move the Reds to the top of the Barclays Premier League table.

Having survived a strong opening from Roy Hodgson's on-song Baggies, United took control of an entertaining game midway through the first period and rarely looked like slipping up after Rooney diverted home Chicharito's shot. The England striker then clinically converted a penalty after the lively Ashley Young had been felled, by which point Jonas Olsson had been sent off for garnering two yellow cards. United's victory took on added significance when news filtered through that Manchester City had lost at Swansea City.

Despite the Reds' need to bounce back from their home humbling against Athletic Club, it was the visitors who forged the game's first opening of note. After James Morrison pinched possession midway inside the United half, Liam Ridgewell curled a fine cross into the hosts' six-yard box, where the onrushing Keith Andrews could only steer the ball wide of David De Gea's goal.

Only a terrific block from Jonny Evans prevented Marc-Antoine Fortune from unleashing a shot deep inside the hosts' area, while Morrison blazed the rebound comfortably over the bar. United's first attempt came from Young, after a weaving run from Danny Welbeck, but the winger's shot was batted away by ex-Red Ben Foster.

Young was again involved in Rooney's first opening of the game. The winger profited on fine industry from Patrice Evra and Javier Hernandez before whipping the ball to the back post, where Rooney failed to gain sufficient purchase on his volley to do any more than tamely direct it to Foster.

There would be no such charity with the striker's next act, ten minutes before the break. A sustained spell of United pressure culminated in Paul Scholes spreading the ball wide to Chicharito. The Mexican cut inside Ridgewell and arrowed a left-footed shot towards goal, but Rooney intercepted the ball's flight and diverted it beyond the committed Foster.

For all the end-to-end excellence of the first period, however, the second period began with a muted five-minute period before bursting into life thereafter. Peter Odemwingie appealed in vain for a penalty after being clipped by Evra, immediately before Chicharito thundered a 20-yard shot against the top of Foster's post. The ex-United stopper then clutched Rooney's spectacular overhead kick, but was relieved to see Welbeck drag his left-footed shot agonisingly wide of the post after Foster had gone walkabout.

United's pursuit of a second goal was aided when Olsson, earlier booked for a challenge on Rooney, unceremoniously halted Chicharito's progress and earned a second caution. The Reds immediately pushed on and won a penalty when Andrews clumsily stopped Young's run near the byline and gave Rooney the chance to tie up the points from the spot and take the champions to the top of the table.

The Teams

Manchester United: De Gea; Jones, Ferdinand, Evans, Evra; Welbeck (Cleverley 77), Scholes (Pogba 73), Carrick, Young; Rooney, Hernandez
Subs not used: Amos, Rafael, Park, Giggs, Berbatov

West Bromwich Albion: Foster; Tamas, McAuley, Olsson, Ridgewell; Odemwingie, Andrews (Scharner 72), Mulumbu, Morrison, Brunt (Shorey 72); Fortune (Long 77)
Subs not used: Daniels, Tchoyi, Dorrans, Cox
Sent off: Olsson

'It's where you want to be and it's where you want to finish,' beamed Wayne Rooney, after putting United on top of the table. 'It's nice to be there now. I don't think we've had the credit we deserve over the last few months. Fair enough, our form in Europe has been disappointing. But in the Premier League we've had very tough games and played a lot of the big teams. Sometimes we haven't been at our best but we've got the wins. It's great credit to the team for the hard work and spirit we've shown to keep tallying up those points. I think we fully deserve to be top.'

Having watched his side demolish Manchester City's points advantage, Sir Alex Ferguson could only lament their failure to eat up more of the Blues' superior goal difference against the ten-man visitors. 'We could have scored a lot of goals today,' he said. 'If there is a criticism, then that is it. But we produced a stern performance; it was determined and there was a great will to win. I am really pleased with that part.

'We created a lot of chances and missed them. It becomes worrying because you need the second one to take the pressure off you. Fortunately, we got the second goal and we still missed chances after that, but we kept our drive for the whole game, which was good. The players didn't stop; they tried to score from every attacking situation, which is always pleasing.'

With Rooney notching his eighth and ninth goals in just six appearances, United's most menacing weapon was quite evident, and the manager was keen for his goalscoring talisman to extend his hot streak in front of goal, grinning: 'If he gets to forty [goals], I'll be absolutely delighted because we'll be in business then.'

Rooney's season haul stood at 27, still short of his personal best of 34, achieved in 2009-10, and it looked likely that the England striker would need to pack his shooting boots for the Reds' next outing: the return trip to Athletic Club. Needing a two-goal win or a single-goal victory in a high-scoring encounter, the Reds were up against it, but Ashley Young conceded that they would have to go for goals.

'It is unusual that we find ourselves in this position, but it is a very high-spirited camp,' he explained. 'Our form in general makes us believe we can score wherever we play. Our attacking play has been fantastic and we believe we can score the two goals we need. Everybody has been chipping in with the goals of late. Whoever scores the goals, as long as we get two, that is all that matters.

'Bilbao are an impressive team. We found that out last week. We had watched videos of them and saw how they played. I am sure if we are on our game one hundred percent, we can go there and get the win we need. I am sure, with the two goals we got and the different chances we created, we showed that we can score more. Our focus has not changed from the start of the season. Every competition that we enter, we want to win. We are in the Europa League to win it. That is what we will be looking to do.'

Young was among a 20-man party that jetted out to Spain's Basque country, while Phil Jones, Nani and Anderson remained in Manchester due to a variety of injuries and illness; Jones had 'flu, Anderson looked likely to miss a month with a hamstring pull and Nani was still nursing a foot injury.

Sir Alex explained their absence upon touching down in Bilbao, before also addressing the longer-term future of his squad's forgotten man: Dimitar Berbatov. Despite finishing 2010-11 as the Premier League's joint-top scorer, the Bulgarian had barely featured for the Reds during the course of the campaign, and appeared increasingly unlikely to remain at Old Trafford.

'Dimitar could play tomorrow, but I have good options with front players,' the manager told his pre-match press conference. 'His contract situation is we will be taking up the option on [extending] the contract [by one year] but, having had chats with him, he wants to get first-team football and we need to consider that at the end of the season. At the moment, he remains at United. But I'd listen to what he says. I think he's concerned he isn't getting enough first-team football. It's difficult for me to guarantee that. At thirty-one, you can understand he wants that. It may lead to him looking elsewhere.'

Addressing the decisive tie with Athletic Club, Sir Alex again underlined his admiration for his hosts' energy levels. He was flanked in the press conference by Ji-sung Park, one of his side's most willing runners, and the South Korean insisted the Reds were up for a breathless battle.

'It was a very tough game [in Manchester],' said Park. 'They played very well; they were aggressive and we should have been able to deal with that, but we couldn't and that's why we lost. But it's not over. We still have ninety minutes and we still have a chance, but we need to perform well.

'This time we have to show how Manchester United play, to be aggressive and fight. If we give everything, we can go through. We only have two trophies to play for, so we want to win the Europa League – and still believe we can, even though we're in a difficult situation now. It'll be a great atmosphere, but we have to quieten them. I'm looking forward to it.'

UEFA Europa League

15 March 2012 | Estadio San Mames | Kick-off 18:00 |
Attendance: 36,958

Athletic Club 2 (Llorente 23, De Marcos 65)
Manchester United 1 (Rooney 80)

The Reds were comprehensively ousted from the Europa League as Athletic Club completed a quickfire double over Sir Alex Ferguson's side to deservedly march into the quarter-finals. Marcelo Bielsa's Basque side wrapped up a 5-3 aggregate win with a comfortable 2-1 triumph in San Mames, in which Wayne Rooney's spectacular late consolation goal ultimately counted for nothing after Fernando Llorente's stunning opener and a deflected effort from Oscar de Marcos.

Just as they had at Old Trafford, it was the hosts who bossed matters from the first whistle. Buoyed by a raucous home support, Bilbao might have moved ahead inside three minutes, only for Markel Susaeta's deflected free-kick to hit the side-netting, while United were indebted to the woodwork and good fortune when Iker Muniain smacked a low shot against the post and de Marcos fired the follow-up over the bar.

The hosts' opening goal, when it came, was devastatingly simple, as Fernando Amorebieta's crossfield ball was brilliantly volleyed home on the run by Llorente to send San Mames into delirium. United now needed three goals to qualify, though one was almost immediately forthcoming as Ryan Giggs' header was deflected over the bar from Ashley Young's in-swinging cross.

Though Athletic lost Llorente to injury five minutes before the break, with Gaizka Toquero replacing him, they showed no signs of letting up after the restart, with de Marcos blasting a shot just wide. Right-back Andoni Iraola then embarked on a mesmerising slalom through the United defence before clipping his shot just past David De Gea's left-hand post.

Sir Alex introduced Chris Smalling and Paul Pogba at the expense of Rio Ferdinand and Michael Carrick, and the newcomers had barely taken to the field when the hosts sealed their progress. Iraola's cross was cleared by Smalling to de Marcos, whose low shot beat De Gea via a slight deflection off Jonny Evans.

The final goal of the tie belonged to the Reds, as Rooney patiently worked an opening and curled an unstoppable 25-yard effort into the top corner, but there would be no dramatic comeback. The home support generously applauded the United forward's superb strike, and then raised the roof at full time.

Comfortably and deservedly into the last eight at United's expense, it was difficult not to be impressed by Bielsa's side. As for the Reds, the exit capped a short-lived Europa League campaign that had merely reiterated the harsh lessons handed out in the Champions League. Roll on September 2012 and another tilt at Europe.

The Teams

Athletic Club: Iraizoz; Iraola, Martinez, Amorebieta, Aurtenetxe; Herrera (Perez 82), Iturraspe, De Marcos; Susaeta, Llorente (Toquero 40), Muniain (San Jose 88)
Subs not used: Raul, Ekiza, Lopez, Gomez
Booked: Susaeta

Manchester United: De Gea; Rafael, Evans, Ferdinand (Smalling 63), Evra; Young, Cleverley, Carrick (Pogba 63), Park, Giggs (Welbeck 68); Rooney
Subs not used: Amos, Fabio, Scholes, Hernandez
Booked: Rafael, Pogba

'There are always lessons to learn from every football match, whether you win or lose,' said Sir Alex Ferguson, after witnessing his side's season boil down to just their Premier League title defence. 'It's disappointing more than anything. We haven't progressed in the Champions League and now we're out of the Europa League. I think the best team went through. I don't think we can complain.

'They got a really soft goal to put them ahead, and that's the last thing we wanted. I can't believe we lost a goal like that. It was a really poor one. Otherwise, I thought it was quite even in the first half. I thought we did quite well. But at the start of the second half, Bilbao did very well. They could have scored two or three goals. Towards the end we had a bit of impetus – we scored a goal, but we didn't get anywhere near to winning it.

'It's not a sense of relief [going out of Europe], because we still have ten [league] games to play and that's a long way to go until you can win a title. Obviously, we now have to make sure we win on Sunday against Wolverhampton Wanderers. We decided to take off Rio Ferdinand, Michael Carrick and, eventually, Ryan Giggs because we have to think about Sunday.'

Patrice Evra demonstrated his trademark candour in the mixed zone immediately after the Reds' exit from their final cup competition of the campaign, telling the world's media: 'A big club like Manchester United should be able to compete in every competition. But now we have no choice, we have to focus on the league. We have to win the league to save our season. If we don't win the league, it will have been a really bad season.'

Looking back, Danny Welbeck rebuts suggestions that United struggled for motivation in Europe's secondary competition, having tasted only Champions League football for the previous decade and a half.

'Once we got knocked out and we were in the Europa League, it was just something where we just wanted to do our best in the tournament,' says the striker. 'But we came up against an Athletic Bilbao side who were very good home and away, so we couldn't really do much about that.

'Credit to them, because they were a really good team who knew each other's ins and outs. They'd clearly researched us well and it obviously worked very well for them. But it wasn't something that we went into thinking: "We're going to lose this game," it was just unfortunate that it didn't happen for us, because we would've liked to have progressed further in the Europa League.'

As it was, the Premier League was United's only focus, and the situation was simple: one point clear, ten games to go. Six more games would pass before the Reds travelled to Manchester City, in a Monday night derby already being billed as the probable title decider. With such a distance to go before the 30 April showdown, however, Ji-sung Park insisted he and his cohorts were remaining short-sighted.

'City is a massive game, but we have to concentrate on all our matches before then, otherwise the league could already be decided,' said the South Korean. 'The fixture list and debating who has the advantage does not matter. Our run-in may look easier, but we know it doesn't work like that as we've dropped points against the lower teams in the past, which can be painful. We're aware of that so we have to work hard, remember that it's a tight race no matter who we're playing, and give one hundred percent on the pitch to win the game. It's great to be top of the league, but we need to press on.

'We have experience of these situations, which will help us,' he added. 'It's a totally different kind of pressure now compared to the start of the season. We know how to deal with that and win these games – that's massive and could make the difference.'

United's trip to Terry Connor's Wolves fell three days before City's home clash with Chelsea, now under the temporary stewardship of Roberto Di Matteo, giving the Reds the chance to open up a four-point lead and heap pressure on Roberto Mancini's challengers.

'Wolves is a massive game for us, particularly given that Manchester City don't play until Wednesday,' said Wayne Rooney. 'We have a chance to go four points clear at the top of the table and we have to get the win. We've had tough games there in the last couple of seasons and we need to be at our best to win. Wolves are fighting for their lives after going through a bit of a sticky patch and seeing [former manager] Mick McCarthy leave.

'I'm sure it's been hard for Wolves to lift themselves, but from our point of view when you go to the home of a team fighting to survive, it's always very difficult. So we know we need to play well to win.'

Barclays Premier League

18 March 2012 | Molineux | Kick-off 13:30 |
Attendance: 27,494

Wolverhampton Wanderers 0
Manchester United 5 (Evans 21, Valencia 43, Welbeck 45, Hernandez 56, 61)

United mercilessly romped to victory at Molineux, bagging five goals in little more than an hour, to register an eighth win in nine Barclays Premier League games. Strikes from Jonny Evans, Antonio Valencia and Danny Welbeck had the Reds home and hosed by the interval, with the hosts further hamstrung by the dismissal of Ronald Zubar for two rash challenges. Chicharito bagged two clinical finishes after the break to emphasise the dominance of Sir Alex Ferguson's side, who cantered to victory.

Just three days after suffering a Europa League humbling in Bilbao, United began the match at Molineux eager to tap into the domestic momentum built since January's loss at Newcastle. Though Wolves were sprightly – motivated by their dreadful points return in 2012 – the opening goal doused the hosts' spirits.

The unmarked Evans bagged his first goal for the Reds by lashing home from close range, after Michael Carrick had calmly side-footed Wayne Rooney's deep corner through a maze of statuesque home defenders. It was a simple conversion, but nevertheless a moment to savour for the goalscorer.

When Zubar was dismissed – cautioned for careless challenges on Rooney, then Welbeck – the hosts were up against it, and United hammered home the advantage before the break. First, a lightning counter-attack culminated in Rooney releasing Valencia to bear down on goal and stab home an emphatic finish; then the Ecuadorian teed up Welbeck to sweep home from ten yards.

With Manchester City's longstanding lead on goal difference suddenly looking vulnerable, Sir Alex sent his side out to further erode the deficit. It took just over ten minutes for Chicharito to strike, heading home Rafael's superb cross amid more dispirited defending from the hosts, and five minutes later the Mexican doubled his tally.

Evans surged forward in possession and released Valencia, who played a tight one-two with Welbeck before standing up a back-post cross which Hernandez emphatically half-volleyed into the roof of Wayne Hennessey's net.

Though half an hour remained, the scoring was over. David De Gea routinely fielded a low shot from Michael Kightly and Hennessey denied Welbeck's close-range effort, but the chances dried up as United – for whom substitute Paul Pogba enjoyed a lively cameo – comfortably closed out the victory.

A five-goal win on a ground where United had come unstuck in two of three previous league visits represented a hugely satisfying afternoon, and another timely injection of impetus as the home straight moved ever closer.

The Teams

Wolverhampton Wanderers: Hennessey; Zubar, Stearman, Bassong, Ward; Doyle (Kightly 58), Davis (Jonsson 43), Edwards, Foley, Jarvis; Fletcher (Ebanks-Blake 77)
Subs not used: De Vries, Hunt, Johnson, Berra
Sent off: Zubar

Manchester United: De Gea; Rafael, Evans (Smalling 74), Ferdinand, Evra (Fabio 63); Valencia, Scholes, Carrick (Pogba 58), Welbeck; Rooney, Hernandez
Subs not used: Amos, Giggs, Park, Young
Booked: Welbeck

Goals, goals, goals. No wonder there were smiles all round in the United camp as they prepared to leave Molineux. 'What is significant is we've reduced the goal difference by five goals and that may make a difference at the end of the season,' beamed Sir Alex Ferguson, before adding: 'Chicharito got a couple that he needed to bring back his confidence, and it was good for Danny Welbeck to score as well after a few games without.'

'Before the game, I actually thought I do need a goal,' concurred Welbeck. 'Thankfully, it came. But you can't let these things play on your mind, you just play your normal game and, as long as the team keeps winning, that's the main thing.'

For one man, however, scoring added even greater gloss to the afternoon's work. Jonny Evans, having bagged the opening goal against the struggling hosts, was finally off the mark after 117 games for the Reds. Looking back, it's a moment the Northern Ireland international still recalls vividly.

'Rooney's played a deep ball and Carrers [Michael Carrick] has just knocked it back across, it's fallen for me and I was never going to miss that one – I made sure,' smiles Evans. 'I didn't want to just swing a foot at it, I wanted to make sure I got a good contact on it and made sure I kept it low. It was a weird feeling because I obviously knew I'd scored, but I looked up and saw Michael Carrick going off in the other direction and it was like: "Hold on a minute, I've scored here. Come and celebrate with me!" So I was kind of left on my own and I didn't really know what to do, but then I got a few of the lads around me. I remember Chicharito and Welbeck saying "Jonny, it's your first goal!"

'I remember Rio was probably one of the first ones on the scene, too. With Rio, he knows that, as a defender, you just want to make sure you get the first goal in a game, especially at Wolves, because it settles things down. It was nice to score the first goal, because if it had been the fifth goal it wouldn't have had the same reaction, I'd have just had to have walked off!'

Though Manchester City narrowly overcame Chelsea at the Etihad Stadium to move back within a solitary point of the Reds at the top of the table, the Blues' next fixture took them to Stoke ahead of United's Monday night clash with Fulham at Old Trafford. Though they had the chance to pile pressure on the champions, City could muster only a 1-1 draw at the Britannia Stadium to retake top spot on goal difference alone.

Now armed with a game in hand, United could begin to pull clear. Mercifully, Sir Alex Ferguson faced no further injury dilemmas, and the boss admitted: 'It's much better now. There was Jones getting that bout of 'flu, but he's back. He was actually back on Friday, but we didn't risk him at Wolves. He'll be available. So they're all training apart from Nani, who should not be far away and might start training this week, while Anderson and Michael Owen are the only other ones out. Nemanja Vidic and Darren Fletcher are obviously still long term.'

For Vidic, sidelined since December by his cruciate knee ligament injury, the second half of the season had been a time of frustration, but also a chance to ensure his readiness for the commencement of the 2012-13 campaign.

'The recovery is going well,' he said ahead of the Fulham clash. 'Obviously, the projection was I would be ready for the next season. I am on schedule and will hopefully start training again in July. I'm working in the gym mainly. Much of the stuff I'm doing in the gym I don't look forward to, but it benefits me. I have to say I'm doing more work now, while I'm injured, than I do when I'm playing. Because of that, I spend more time here at Carrington.'

Remaining around the squad kept the club captain abreast of the mood in the camp, and the Serbian was confident that when he returned to the side, the Premier League trophy would still be safely in the Old Trafford trophy room.

'If you look at the schedule of the games we have left to play, I would like to say we are the favourites,' he opined. 'We still have to win the nine games and we need to be focused. I would say we have nine Champions League final games now. But it's all in our hands. We have to focus and give our best. All the players are ready to perform, which is a good sign and a positive thing for the nine games ahead. We have the confidence – we've had the belief from the beginning.'

Vidic would again be perched in the stands for the visit of Martin Jol's Cottagers, as the champions sought to open up daylight between themselves and the challengers.

Barclays Premier League

26 March 2012 | Old Trafford | Kick-off 20:00 |
Attendance: 75,570

Manchester United 1 (Rooney 42)
Fulham 0

Wayne Rooney's solitary strike swung a nerve-shredding evening United's way, but the Reds were left relieved when Danny Murphy was denied a last-gasp penalty at the Scoreboard End.

The visitors were content to sit and soak up United's pressure throughout the evening – succumbing only to Rooney's close-range finish just before the break – and then piled on late pressure and might have had a spot-kick when Murphy fell under Michael Carrick's challenge. Referee Michael Oliver declined the award, however, much to the Cottagers' ire.

On the balance of play, the outcome was absolutely correct, as the Reds dominated throughout against a visiting side happy to sit in two massed banks of players. Though United controlled the early exchanges, the first effort on target did not arrive until the 11th minute when Ryan Giggs' header was plucked out of the air by Mark Schwarzer.

On the break, the visitors did carry some menace – Moussa Dembele dragged a shot wide, before Clint Dempsey shot too close to David De Gea – but the game was largely about United's attack against Fulham's defence. The Reds' defenders even got in on the act: Patrice Evra looped an ambitious overhead kick wide and fellow full-back Rafael shot straight at Schwarzer after cutting in from the right flank.

After a penalty shout for handball against Stephen Kelly was turned down by referee Oliver, the deadlock was broken three minutes before the interval. Ashley Young's in-swinging cross cleared Brede Hangeland's head and was missed by John-Arne Riise. Jonny Evans sharply slid in to hook the loose ball back for Rooney, who had the simple task of blasting his finish into the unguarded goal.

Still, Fulham remained encamped in their own half. Giggs' pass released Antonio Valencia, only for Schwarzer to deny the Ecuadorian, who then flung himself to his left to turn away Young's curling effort. Danny Welbeck made way for Javier Hernandez as Sir Alex Ferguson sought to wrap up the victory, and United's pressure continued to mount.

Giggs dragged a left-footed attempt well wide and Schwarzer made a superb double stop to keep out Young, following a cross from Valencia. Hangeland made another vital intervention to deny Giggs, and gradually nerves began to fray among the home support.

Fulham, having expended little energy in sitting so deep for 80 minutes, pushed on to try to force a shock climax to the game. There was drama, but it worked in United's favour as Murphy tumbled under Carrick's challenge without censure. It was a let-off for the Reds, but nevertheless a deserved and vital victory to remain at the head of the pack.

The Teams

Manchester United: De Gea; Rafael, Evans, Ferdinand (Smalling 73), Evra; Valencia, Carrick, Giggs, Young; Rooney (Scholes 77), Welbeck (Hernandez 62)
Subs not used: Amos, Jones, Cleverley, Berbatov
Booked: Giggs

Fulham: Schwarzer; Kelly, Hughes, Hangeland, Riise; Duff, Diarra (Murphy 70), Dempsey, Dembele, Frei (Ruiz 66); Pogrebnyak
Subs not used: Stockdale, Senderos, Briggs, Etuhu, Trotta

'I think they had a claim,' admitted Sir Alex Ferguson, in reference to Fulham's late penalty shout. 'No doubt. I think we had a claim for clear handball in the first half, maybe it was close to the attacker but it was a claim and Patrice Evra thought it was stonewall as he [Stephen Kelly] handled the ball going into the penalty box and denied an opportunity. Maybe the referee was thinking about that, certainly Carrick caught Murphy's heel as he's come back. But we deserved that because we completely dominated the game until the last fifteen minutes.

'It was a great game for us tonight, because that's exactly what it's going to be like for the rest of the season. Teams are going to be battling and fighting, trying to survive, and not be lambs to the slaughter to Manchester United, because they don't want to be seen to be laying down. Fulham put in a massive effort tonight. They're a very experienced team and were very difficult to break down. When you sit back, it doesn't matter if you've got eleven plumbers, joiners or footballers; it's hard to break down. We did enough to finish the game off, but didn't do it and nearly paid the penalty.'

With a three-point lead established, the Reds had a week to wait until their next outing: the traditionally taxing trip to face Blackburn Rovers at Ewood Park. United had won on Rovers' patch only twice in their previous 11 league visits, and still carried the scars of their shock home reverse to Steve Kean's side on New Year's Eve.

Amid the mounting pressure of the title race, it was decided that a mid-season break would prove beneficial for the entire squad. Sir Alex whisked his players away to Scotland's famous St Andrews golf course for the weekend, and the chance to swap football for fairways lightened the mood. So too did events at the Etihad Stadium, as members of the United squad congregated in their hotel to watch Manchester City host Sunderland. The Blues' hitherto perfect home record suggested a routine victory; instead, the hosts required two late goals to salvage a 3-3 draw, giving United the chance to open up a five-point lead if Blackburn could be beaten at Ewood Park.

Squeaky bum time had arrived.

10

April – The Twist in the Tale

After a weekend of shared confinement, the United squad was sufficiently primed for a taxing trip to face Blackburn Rovers at Ewood Park, imbued with a fresh dose of team bonding and suitably unwound amid the furore of another draining season.

'It was a really nice break,' recalls Wayne Rooney. 'We just went up to Scotland and relaxed before the Blackburn game. We just chilled out. Going away gets you away from the hype of the media and everything around the game. It takes your mind completely off it, which sometimes you need. Plus it's great for team bonding when you go away together. When you're there, you see the lads playing on FIFA, playing pool or table tennis, whereas when you come into Carrington you do your training, your gym work and whatever, then you go home and you don't really have that time to do anything with them. It's just something different and it's nice to have the players doing that together for a couple of days.'

With the scene set for the Reds to open up a five-point lead at the head of the table, Sir Alex Ferguson was keen to remind everybody that the trip to Ewood Park would be no gimme for the defending champions.

'The game at Blackburn is always a difficult type of game,' warned the manager. 'It has a local derby feeling about it and is always a bit feisty. Last season, we came back from a goal down to win the league, but we expect a difficult game. That's the way all the matches will be, but hopefully we can navigate them.

'Most of the players have had the experience: Ferdinand, Evra, Giggs, Scholes, Carrick and Rooney. There are some of the young ones that aren't accustomed to it, like Danny Welbeck, Ashley Young, David De Gea, Phil Jones and Chris Smalling. You've got the likes of Fabio and Rafael, who have been involved for two or three years so they're used to it; both have been in European Cup final squads as well. They gather experience that way. It hopefully helps them in the run-in.'

Still aiming to fend off the spectre of relegation, a pepped-up Rovers side was ready to test United's mettle.

Barclays Premier League

2 April 2012 | Ewood Park | Kick-off 20:00 |
Attendance: 26,532

Blackburn Rovers 0
Manchester United 2 (Valencia 81, Young 86)

In the penultimate game of the 2010-11 season, United fans in Ewood Park's Darwen End celebrated becoming English champions for a 19th time. Almost a year on, a relentless victory over Blackburn moved a potential 20th title into stark focus. Late strikes from Antonio Valencia and Ashley Young gave the Reds a rare away win over Rovers, capping a display of dogged determination to overcome the hosts' obstinate resistance.

Under pressure to capitalise on Manchester City's dropped points two days earlier, the Reds passed and probed against a team aiming to repeat their shock victory at Old Trafford earlier in the season.

Rovers had ensured this tense affair was in the balance until the late drama. David De Gea earned the acclaim of the baying away fans with three top-class saves in a first half his team had dominated. The Spaniard dived to tip away a piledriver from the lively Junior Hoilett and then produced superb stops to thwart Marcus Olsson and Grant Hanley towards the end of the opening 45 minutes.

Such openings were scarcer for United, who came no closer to scoring than when Chicharito's close-range effort struck a post, hit Paul Robinson on the back and dropped into the stranded goalkeeper's grateful grasp.

After the break, Morten Gamst Pedersen's free-kick worked De Gea again and then he had a goal correctly chalked off because Steven N'Zonzi had carried the ball out of play in the build-up. Though United dominated possession and had a clear territorial advantage, it also took a superb challenge from Rio Ferdinand to prevent Yakubu from tapping home the opener.

There was always a sense that United's chances would come. Robinson beat away a Wayne Rooney free-kick and a curling effort from Rafael, but was given no chance when Valencia raced into the Blackburn area and hammered a scorching cross-shot into the far corner of the hosts' goal.

The Darwen End bellowed and writhed with delight, and that sense of jubilation was only heightened when Valencia fed Young and the substitute cracked a fine low finish wide of Robinson to make the points safe.

Now five points clear at the head of the table, another victory procured in the dying embers of a game served a timely reminder that the reigning champions are in their element when pounding the home straight.

The Teams

Blackburn Rovers: Robinson; Orr, Hanley, Dann, Martin Olsson; Pedersen, N'Zonzi, Lowe, Marcus Olsson; Hoilett, Yakubu

Subs not used: Bunn, Dunn, Modeste, Formica, Petrovic, Rochina, Henley
Booked: Hanley

Manchester United: De Gea; Rafael, Evans, Ferdinand, Evra; Valencia, Carrick, Scholes (Young 80), Jones (Giggs 63); Rooney, Hernandez (Welbeck 61)
Subs not used: Amos, Smalling, Park, Pogba
Booked: Valencia

'Fifty-fifty,' laughed Antonio Valencia in his post-match interview, when asked whether his blockbusting opener had been a shot or a cross. However, the Ecuadorian's fellow goalscorer, Ashley Young, was happier to elaborate on events. 'It was a massive win for us,' grinned the England winger. 'We knew if we could win here then we would go five points clear at the top. It was a great result and a great performance.

'It's a crucial time in the season – everybody in the team knows that. It's a massive lead for us and it was a massive game for us. We knew we could get the first goal at some point. Whether it was a shot or a cross from Antonio, we were just delighted to see it go in the back of the net. It was a great feeling when the first goal went in.

'For us to come here and get three points was great; we knew it was going to be a tough game. Obviously, we just take each game as it comes. We have got another tough game on Sunday and we look forward to that one. We are five points clear, but we've just got to concentrate on each game as it comes.'

For Sir Alex Ferguson, the colossal efforts of the 7,000-strong Red Army congregated in the Darwen End played a major part in an invaluable victory, and the United manager was quick to pay tribute to their choral backing.

'They were fantastic,' he marvelled. 'They are unbelievable. They deserved the result tonight because they never stopped. They urged us on the whole way; they almost sucked the ball in. It's like the

Stretford End at times, in the last fifteen minutes of matches, and that's what it was like tonight.

'It was a long night. We just had to persevere and persevere, and in the end we got our reward for it. Coming so late in the game, [Valencia's opener] was important because it typifies the history of the club in a way. We've still got seven games left and my experience of these situations is that it doesn't matter what the points total is at the moment; what is really important is trying to win Sunday's game.'

With ailing Manchester City due to make the tricky trip to Arsenal on the same day United hosted struggling Queens Park Rangers, it looked like a potentially decisive weekend lay ahead. If both results went with form, the Reds would have an eight-point lead with just six games remaining. Though some bookmakers had taken victory at Blackburn as the cue to pay out on the champions retaining their crown, those who had been there and done it within the United camp knew there was still a distance to go.

'We are in the position we would like to be in at this stage of the season, but it is not over,' warned Rio Ferdinand. 'There is still a lot of football to be played between now and the end of the season, when the trophies are handed out. We have to make sure we apply ourselves in the right way for every game. If we do that, put in the performances and get the results we want, we will hopefully be lifting the trophy at the end of the season.'

'There are still twenty-one points to play for and we're going up against a very good team in City,' added Paul Scholes. 'They've had a fantastic season and they've got a great squad of players and they're capable of beating anybody. They're capable of going on runs and winning games.'

United's mission was to remain relentless. Victory in ten of 11 Premier League games had sent the Reds surging to the top of the table, and another win over QPR – from whom loanee Kiko Macheda had returned after injury – would merely be another step closer to the most coveted prize in English football.

Though the Reds had no fresh injury concerns for the Londoners' visit, Ryan Giggs was fully prepared for a difficult afternoon against a side helmed by a manager whose battling style remains etched in United folklore: Mark Hughes.

'Mark will have them well drilled and well prepared, just like the majority of teams that come to Old Trafford. They'll make it difficult for us,' said the veteran winger. 'He's a fighter and he has good staff around him. He made some good signings in the January transfer window and has a lot of quality in the side. QPR will be organised on Sunday and he'll have them working hard.'

Barclays Premier League

**8 April 2012 | Old Trafford | Kick-off 13:30 |
Attendance: 75,505**

Manchester United 2 (Rooney 15 (pen), Scholes 68)
Queens Park Rangers 0

Another game chalked off, another three points closer to the title, but another nervy and controversial afternoon for the champions against ten-man Queens Park Rangers.

Wayne Rooney broke the deadlock with a 15th-minute penalty before Paul Scholes assured the Reds of victory midway through the second period, but Rangers could rightly feel aggrieved by the award of Rooney's spot-kick. Not only was it given for a foul on Ashley Young, who was clearly offside, but referee Lee Mason immediately deemed Shaun Derry's questionable offence worthy of a red card, depriving the visitors of their captain.

Rooney's conversion merely reinforced Rangers' defensive resolve, and Mark Hughes' side battled commendably to frustrate the Reds. Paddy Kenny had already been called into action to field a Rooney free-kick, but the hosts were permanently fronted with a blue and white hooped thicket of bodies, ensuring an unexpectedly uneventful first period for the visiting goalkeeper.

Quieter still was David De Gea's afternoon. Bar a deflected Adel Taarabt effort, which looped up and required ushering over the bar, the Spaniard might have taken to watching the game from the stands, so underemployed was he.

Yet it was the hosts who were growing frustrated, demonstrated most glaringly when Scholes picked up the ball, 30 yards from goal, and was ordered to shoot by a collective bark from the Old Trafford gallery. He did, and only narrowly missed. That effort would prove to be a sighter.

Within two minutes of the second half's resumption, the referee's assistant flagged to correctly rule out Danny Welbeck's tap-in after impressive wing-play from Antonio Valencia. Moments later, on the opposite flank, the striker curled over the bar after an impudent back-heel from Young had teed him up.

Scholes then released Rafael with a lovely, disguised pass, but the Brazilian saw his low effort somehow turned onto the top of the post by Kenny. He soon had an assist, however, as he dispossessed Taarabt and teed up Scholes, who secured the victory by advancing and belting a low, 25-yard effort past Kenny.

The midfielder's brutal effort was bettered almost immediately when Michael Carrick unleashed a 30-yard scorcher, only for the shot to thunder against the inside of Kenny's post and rebound to safety.

Though Welbeck and substitute Tom Cleverley were both narrowly off-target with subsequent efforts, the outcome had long since been assured. The only question that remained was whether or not the Reds' profligacy in front of goal would ultimately prove costly.

The Teams

Manchester United: De Gea; Rafael (Jones 75), Ferdinand, Evans, Evra; Valencia, Carrick, Scholes (Cleverley 74), Young (Giggs 62); Rooney, Welbeck
Subs not used: Amos, Pogba, Park, Hernandez
Booked: Rafael

Queens Park Rangers: Kenny; Onuoha, Ferdinand, Hill, Taiwo; Mackie, Diakite (Wright-Phillips 71), Taarabt (Smith 71), Derry, Buzsaky; Bothroyd (Campbell 81)
Subs not used: Cerny, Gabbidon, Young, Zamora
Sent off: Derry

'Ashley was a yard offside, so I can understand Mark [Hughes] being angry and disappointed at that,' admitted Sir Alex Ferguson, upon seeing the replays which confirmed QPR's early misfortune. 'You see these kinds of decisions every week, though. The boy's just got a little tug on Young, not a great deal but enough to get us the penalty. And unfortunately he was the last defender and had to be sent off.

'The sending-off didn't help us at all. I was actually more confident before that, in terms of the speed of our play and the movement of the team, which was very good. The second goal from Scholes calmed everyone down. Before that we'd kept missing those vital chances. It just wouldn't go in. The important thing about today was we won.'

United's victory might not have been so slender with a little more care in front of goal, but also if Shaun Derry had remained on the field. Fronted with a visiting team hell-bent on protecting their area and keeping the score down, Michael Carrick admitted the situation, while familiar, was never easy to deal with.

'In some ways it's easier to play against eleven, because they might fancy their chances to come out and nick a goal,' said the midfielder. 'But when you're playing against ten men they've got the mentality to defend and protect the edge of the box. The space isn't there. But it's nothing new. We've been dealing with this for a while. Trying to find a pass, trying to be patient, making that decision whether to pass or shoot, trying to keep the ball and keep the pressure on. That's how it is and we score so many late goals by working on teams and breaking them down in the end. It's just patience, really; keeping a high tempo, but at the same time being patient and believing we'll get the goal.

'We've won the last two games two-nil, and if we'd been offered that we'd have taken it, so we can be satisfied with that. We've won the game today, we had a good win at Blackburn and we want another good win [at Wigan] on Wednesday night. If we keep winning games then the gap's going to be there still, so that's our aim. We'll have to wait and see what happens [to City] at the Emirates, but we've done our job.'

Sure enough, the potentially pivotal weekend in the title race went United's way, as City were beaten by a late Mikel Arteta goal at Arsenal. Now eight points clear with only six games remaining, the Reds would travel to Wigan Athletic three days later with the chance to move ominously closer to the title. Nani could finally make his return from a foot injury, while Tom Cleverley was expected to play some part against his former loan side.

Though the clubs had only ever met 14 times, United's record in the fixture provided cause for plentiful confidence ahead of the short trip to the DW Stadium: a 100 percent winning record, only four goals ever conceded to the Latics and none since 2009. However, with Roberto Martinez's relegation-threatened side earning widespread plaudits for their attacking football, Ashley Young warned the Reds that nothing could be taken for granted.

'Wigan is a tough place to go to – they're desperate for points and will want to win in front of their own fans,' said the winger. 'We've got to be on our toes and be ready for a tough game. I'm sure if we can show the confidence, desire and winning mentality we've shown throughout the season, we'll get the win.'

Barclays Premier League

11 April 2012 | DW Stadium | Kick-off 19:45 |
Attendance: 18,115

Wigan Athletic 1 (Maloney 50)
Manchester United 0

United's smooth passage to the Premier League title met an unexpected blockade when relegation-threatened Wigan Athletic bagged their first-ever victory over the Reds at the DW Stadium. Shaun Maloney curled home the only goal of an attritional game shortly after the interval, as a limp display from Sir Alex Ferguson's men was punished by a home side who looked sharper than their visitors all evening.

In another game punctuated by debatable refereeing decisions, Wigan were initially irate to have Victor Moses' header disallowed for a foul on David De Gea, but then benefited from the incorrect award of a corner for Maloney's goal and survived a pair of strong second-half penalty appeals for United.

From the off, Wigan were first to every ball and had United penned back. It appeared they had taken an early lead, but the 'goal' was controversially disallowed. Maloney's corner was headed in by Victor Moses, only for the goal to be chalked off for a foul by Gary Caldwell on David De Gea. The Scottish defender was clearly leaning back into the United goalkeeper, but the Latics players, staff and supporters considered themselves hard done by.

Even after the respite of half time, a Wigan goal seemed inevitable and, when it came, it summed up United's evening: they were collectively slow to react to a short corner, which was taken by Maloney and then worked back to the Scot, who cut infield, took advantage of space afforded to him and curled a fine finish inside De Gea's far post.

Lady Luck, having sported a red shirt in the first period, had clearly swapped sides at half time, as replays showed that the initial award of the corner was incorrect, as Jean Beausejour had kicked the ball against himself and out of play.

Phil Jones was the man unfortunately deemed to have conceded the corner, and the right-back was involved in another controversial episode with 20 minutes remaining, as his drilled cross was clearly handled by Maynor Figueroa, without censure.

The champions' sense of injustice was only heightened soon afterwards when substitutes Danny Welbeck and Tom Cleverley combined inside the Latics' area, and Caldwell escaped with a clear pull of Welbeck's shirt.

Then, with seven minutes remaining, United finally tested Wigan keeper Ali Al-Habsi as Cleverley fed Welbeck in the channel, and the Longsight striker's low effort was sharply beaten away by the Omani international. It was, however, too little, too late for the Reds and the hosts saw out a vital victory which aided their bid to remain in the Premier League, while denting United's hopes of topping it.

The Teams

Wigan Athletic: Al-Habsi; Alcaraz, Caldwell, Boyce; Beausejour, McCarthy, Maloney (Sammon 77), McArthur, Figueroa; Moses, Di Santo (Diame 70)
Subs not used: Pollitt, Crusat, Watson, Gomez, Stam
Booked: Di Santo

Manchester United: De Gea; Jones, Ferdinand, Evans, Evra; Valencia, Carrick, Giggs, Young (Cleverley 46); Rooney (Nani 65), Hernandez (Welbeck 58)
Subs not used: Amos, Smalling, Park, Pogba
Booked: Jones, Evans

'It was a disappointing performance throughout the game,' conceded Sir Alex Ferguson. 'We didn't reach the levels that we have in the last few months, so I think we got what we deserved. Wigan are a good team and they are very underrated. They play with three centre-backs, which gives them time on the ball and it was very difficult to stop their early possession.

'We decided to put three midfielders up against them in the second half and I think we were better to a degree, but we didn't deserve to win the game, so I have no complaints. We got a break [against QPR] on Sunday with the first goal, but tonight we didn't get one [with the penalty claim against Maynor Figueroa]. It evens itself out over a season and my experience of these things says it happens, so you just have to expect it.'

Similarly predictable was Manchester City's return to winning ways against West Bromwich Albion, a result that narrowed the Reds' lead to just five points. With the momentum suddenly arrested and reversed, the message to all within the United camp was clear: time for focus.

'It was a disappointment, but sometimes it can be a wake-up call just to remind us that anyone is capable of winning games in this league, against any opposition,' admitted David De Gea. 'We will be even more focused now going into these last five games, starting on Sunday, and carry on that battle for the title. We know there is still a little way to go yet and there is still plenty of work to do.'

Wigan had warmed up for United's visit with an unjust, narrow defeat at Chelsea that had followed victories over Liverpool and Stoke City. After beating the champions, the Latics also took three points from Champions League hopefuls Arsenal and Newcastle United. With the benefit of hindsight, Phil Jones admits Wigan's display should not have come as such a shock.

'Wigan were great against us,' says the England defender. 'I think the manager said they were in a false position and I couldn't agree more. They play some really good football and Martinez has them playing the way that they want to and they were a tough nut to crack. The results they had after that, against Arsenal, Newcastle and others, show that it was no fluke against us and that they were in a false position.'

'You get little reminders in this league that it's never easy to win games or leagues,' adds Ryan Giggs. 'You've got to be at your best. Every team has experienced it. Everyone was expecting City to win at home to Sunderland and Arsenal to beat Wigan, and we've had it this year with Blackburn and Wigan. If you're not at your best then you will come unstuck. We were disappointed with the result and the performance at Wigan and it was really important that we bounced back straight away.'

Alex McLeish's Aston Villa were due at Old Trafford for a game between two sides with wildly contrasting ambitions. From a mid-season position of apparent comfort to one of low-scoring freefall, the Villans were in danger of being sucked into an unlikely relegation battle, while United would see their lead further trimmed to just two points as Manchester City ratcheted up a 6-1 win at Norwich City.

Asked whether or not nerves may play a part in his side's play against Villa, Sir Alex Ferguson was quick to offer them his backing, declaring: 'I don't have any doubts about their temperament, to be honest. There's plenty of experience in the place. They always want to win and that's the mentality here. The attitude they've got is to win matches and they always try to win it.'

Barclays Premier League

15 April 2012 | Old Trafford | Kick-off 16:00 |
Attendance: 75,138

Manchester United 4 (Rooney 7 (pen), 73, Welbeck 43, Nani 90)
Aston Villa 0

United delivered a perfect response to their shock setback at Wigan with a resounding victory over struggling Aston Villa at Old Trafford. A Wayne Rooney brace, allied to further strikes from Danny Welbeck and Nani, took the Reds five points clear again after Manchester City's thumping victory at Carrow Road, and the champions might have had more on a one-sided afternoon.

The game began with Andreas Weimann immediately forcing David De Gea into a save, but that was not a sign of things to come. With only six minutes on the clock, former Villa star Ashley Young bypassed Alan Hutton and was tripped by Ciaran Clark. Though the winger fell dramatically, referee Mark Halsey duly pointed to the spot and gave Rooney the chance to calmly stroke home his 30th goal of the season.

As confidence flooded into United's play, Villa had to give their all just to stay in the game. Eric Lichaj and James Collins flung themselves to block a pair of efforts from Welbeck, and Rooney forced a smart stop from Shay Given; though Clark glanced Barry Bannan's free-kick just wide and Stephen Ireland also curled narrowly off-target on sporadic counter-raids to remind the hosts of the perilous nature of a single-goal lead.

A second goal appeared inevitable for the hosts, however. Paul Scholes came close with a pair of typically spectacular volleys direct from corners, while only a stunning reflex save from Given prevented Welbeck from turning in Antonio Valencia's cross. Just before the break, the striker's perseverance paid off as a neat midfield move released Patrice Evra, whose low cross was inexplicably left by Nathan Baker, allowing Welbeck a simple back-post conversion.

With the scoreline befitting United's dominance, the scene was set for more goals in the second period. It took a while for the hosts to replicate their first-half fluidity, but eventually chances began arriving, as Rooney dragged a clear opening wide and Baker escaped a strong shout for a handball inside his own area. With the visitors wobbling, Valencia and Rooney combined again, and the latter stabbed in a deflected finish after the former's incisive pull-back.

Given, who escaped a blatant handball outside his own area, then thwarted Welbeck and Valencia with impressive reaction stops from deflected efforts. The Republic of Ireland international was beaten once more as substitute Nani latched onto Jonny Evans' neat through-ball and slid home a clinical finish to cap a welcome return to winning ways for the Reds.

The Teams

Manchester United: De Gea; Rafael, Evans, Ferdinand, Evra; Valencia, Scholes (Cleverley 78), Carrick, Young (Nani 61); Rooney (Berbatov 74), Welbeck

Subs not used: Amos, Jones, Giggs, Hernandez
Booked: Scholes, Carrick, Nani

Aston Villa: Given; Hutton, Collins, Baker, Lichaj; Bannan,
Clark (Heskey 64), Ireland (Carruthers 75), Gardner, Weimann
(N'Zogbia 83); Agbonlahor
Subs not used: Guzan, Cuellar, Johnson, Delfouneso
Booked: Hutton, Bannan, Gardner

'It was a good result,' reflected Sir Alex Ferguson. 'We were careless at times but, at the end of the day, there was some terrific football and some good goals. I'm very satisfied. There could be twists and turns yet [in the title race]. I think the name of the game now is for us to enjoy ourselves and play with expression, like we did today. Hopefully we'll be all right. You can never be too confident in this game of football. My experience tells me there's always something can bite you on the bum, but hopefully we can avoid that and not drop any more points. The players accepted the fact they lost a game on Wednesday and did something about it. No panic. We played our own game and I'm pleased about that.'

For the second home game in a row, however, the post-match debate largely centred around Ashley Young. Sir Alex admitted that the former Villa winger had gone down 'quite easily' and 'made the most of' Ciaran Clark's challenge to earn the penalty with which Wayne Rooney opened the scoring, and though the United manager insisted that the award was correct, he did address the matter with Young.

'I've had a word with Ashley and he understands where we're coming from – hopefully it makes a difference,' Sir Alex later revealed, while also launching a staunch defence of his club against suggestions that they were favoured by officials.

'You get bad decisions and you get good decisions,' he said. 'It evens itself out, believe me. It's the same for everybody. We didn't get a penalty kick against Wigan last week, but we didn't scream from the rooftops about it. We realise it happens. We got a penalty kick against us when we played Newcastle that was never a penalty kick. We had an apology from Mike Riley for that. It happens.'

While the issue filled plenty of column inches, it was not allowed to become a distraction within the walls of Carrington. Five points clear with five games to go was a situation that, even a month earlier, had appeared impossible. For Danny Welbeck, back among the goals against Villa, the situation was one to savour, with the end of the season looming large.

'I definitely want to get among the goals,' said the striker. 'But the main thing is getting three points in every game. That gets us closer to the title. It was a good result for the team and we're looking forward to getting the next three points now, because those are going to be important.

'We know every game's going to be tight, but come kick-off we just want to get the three points. Getting three points is a necessity for us. Winning the title would mean so much to me. Words don't describe it. I'm really, really hungry for this title and I'd do anything to get it.'

Be it fate or a mere quirk of the fixtures generator, the possibility had arisen that United could even clinch the title at the Etihad Stadium: a dream scenario being talked up across the media. However, Everton were next up at Old Trafford, fresh from a heartbreaking FA Cup semi-final defeat to their arch-rivals Liverpool, and the Toffeemen – rather than City – were dominating United's thoughts.

'The key thing is that we have to win against Everton in order to even give ourselves that chance,' said Rio Ferdinand. 'All we're thinking about at the moment is that game, not what we can or can't do next weekend or the weekend after that. And Everton always give us a tough game, so we need to make sure we do the job properly. They're the sort of side who give their all.'

Those words would prove chillingly prophetic.

Barclays Premier League

22 April 2012 | Old Trafford | Kick-off 12:30 |
Attendance: 75,522

Manchester United 4 (Rooney 41, 69, Welbeck 57, Nani 60)
Everton 4 (Jelavic 33, 83, Fellaini 67, Pienaar 85)

United's title defence was hindered in shocking fashion as, having come from behind, the champions let slip a two-goal lead to take only a point from a pulsating encounter with Everton.

Nikica Jelavic capped an impressive start by the visitors with a superbly taken header, only for Wayne Rooney to bag a vital leveller for the hosts shortly before the interval. Danny Welbeck and Nani put the Reds two goals clear with brilliantly executed strikes, yet Marouane Fellaini reduced the arrears with a neat volley. Rooney then capped another fine move to seemingly put the game to bed, only for Everton to muster a grandstand finish.

Jelavic bagged his second after sloppy defending from the Reds, before Steven Pienaar restored parity from close range after the visitors had been allowed to stroll through the hosts' stunned ranks.

Though David Moyes' side might have been downbeat after their FA Cup semi-final defeat to Liverpool a week earlier, they were by far the brighter side in the opening exchanges as Leon Osman twice came close to scoring and David De Gea was forced into a smart save by Jelavic.

Amid a nervy atmosphere, United struggled to find cohesion. Nani chanced his arm from long range and both Rooney and Paul Scholes missed the target in quick succession, but the visitors registered the game's first goal when Tony Hibbert's deep cross was brilliantly headed back over De Gea by Jelavic.

Curiously, the goal liberated United from their nerves, and the hosts soon levelled. Nani took the ball from Patrice Evra and curled in a superb cross that cleared Phil Neville and dipped sufficiently for Rooney to nod in from close range.

After a slow start, the second period burst into life when Nani headed Darron Gibson's shanked clearance to Welbeck, just outside the area. The striker faked to shoot, totally out-foxing Johnny Heitinga, before nonchalantly curling a beautiful finish high into Tim Howard's top corner.

For good measure, another goal quickly followed, and once again its importance was almost equalled by its aesthetics. Patient play worked the ball to the edge of the Everton area, before Michael Carrick found Welbeck, who delightfully released the onrushing Nani to clip a delicate finish over Howard.

Just as United were coasting towards victory, Hibbert swung in a cross that fell perfectly for Fellaini to clinically volley past the exposed De Gea. No matter, as the Reds were almost immediately two goals clear again. Antonio Valencia played the ball infield for Welbeck, who dummied and raced onto a pass from the man behind him, Rooney, before sliding a perfect ball across the area for his strike partner to calmly convert.

United appeared in total comfort, and might have put the game out of sight when Rafael's cross was headed against the post by Evra at point-blank range, but instead the visitors somehow hauled themselves level in double-quick time.

Firstly, the Reds failed to clear the danger deep inside the penalty area, allowing Jelavic to slide home a simple finish. Then, with United again ragged defensively, the ball was worked down the Everton left and pulled back for Pienaar to convert at De Gea's near post.

Old Trafford was stunned. Time remained for Jonny Evans to head Nani's cross over the bar and Howard to tip Rio Ferdinand's shot over, but the shocking nature of Everton's comeback had sucked away United's momentum, and suddenly the champions faced the prospect of travelling to face Manchester City at the Etihad Stadium for what appeared to be a play-off for the Premier League title.

The Teams

Manchester United: De Gea; Rafael, Evans, Ferdinand, Evra; Valencia (Hernandez 88), Scholes (Jones 85), Carrick, Nani; Rooney, Welbeck
Subs not used: Amos, Smalling, Park, Giggs, Young
Booked: Evra

Everton: Howard; Hibbert, Jagielka, Heitinga, Distin (Cahill 83); Osman (McFadden 62), Gibson, Fellaini, Neville, Pienaar; Jelavic
Subs not used: Mucha, Gueye, Barkley, Stracqualursi, Anichebe
Booked: Neville, Distin

'I don't know what went wrong,' reflects Wayne Rooney. 'I think a bit of naivety played a part and, to be fair to Everton, they were a handful all day. Fellaini and Jelavic held the ball up all day. We knew that if we let them put balls into the box then they would cause us problems and we didn't close them down quick enough; maybe we sat too deep and we paid the price for that. We should never have let ourselves get into that position.'

'I think we were just lax,' echoes Rio Ferdinand, also reliving a gut-wrenching afternoon at Old Trafford. 'We went one-nil down, then we scored and after that it didn't look like anyone else was going to win the game. We came out, went three-one up and the problem was after each time we went two goals up, we conceded straight away. That was a killer and it gave them a bit of belief.

'We just didn't defend well enough in those situations. The balls came in from the areas too easily and we didn't defend them well enough when they got in there. I thought my shot was going to win it right at the death, but Tim Howard's got a bit of spring, so he made it. I should have hit it a bit harder, if I'm honest. I just tried to control it, and it was a clean strike but it didn't go in. I was up all night thinking about it afterwards but, at the end of the day, it's disappointing and we weren't good enough to get the win.'

That disappointment was exacerbated by Manchester City's win at Wolverhampton Wanderers which, as well as relegating the Midlanders, cut the Reds' lead to three points. With City now boasting a goal difference six greater than United's, the scene was set for a seismic Manchester derby at Eastlands in which defeat would cost the champions leadership with just two games to go.

'I suppose when the fixture list came out at the beginning of the season, all the roads pointed to this game,' admitted Sir Alex Ferguson. 'It was inevitable, maybe. But we are where we are and it doesn't matter what's happened before, who's dropped points or who hasn't dropped points. It really is all down to this game. It will be a fantastic atmosphere and I hope it lives up to the billing. I don't know how many countries are going to be watching it, but it will be considerable. Hopefully it's a very good game.

'We're smarting from throwing that game away [against Everton]. In the context of our history, we almost expected it. We tend to make it hard for ourselves. Our supporters have been subjected to that sort of drama for years and years. God knows what their nerves are like now but, hopefully, we'll make amends on Monday.'

With the spotlight burning so brightly on the fixture, Sir Alex and his coaching staff again sought to lessen the pressure on the players by whisking them away for a long weekend; this time in South Wales.

'It is a long weekend and I think we're doing the right thing,' said the manager. 'The training programme is exactly the same. We do our work. We do our preparation. The players have a fantastic work ethic and, hopefully, whatever happens in the training sessions transmits itself to the game situation.'

Given the high stakes of the game, both sides' tactical approaches would inevitably be carefully thought out and, while Sir Alex kept his cards close to his chest, he admitted that he had a variety of ways to take on Roberto Mancini's challengers. 'We've been working on two or three things in the last couple of days and I've got two or three options. Hopefully, I'll get it right,' he said.

Before heading down for the weekend retreat, time remained for the manager and his players to fulfil pre-match media requests. Ryan Giggs, a veteran of 35 Manchester derbies, was geared up for what looked likely to be the most important of his career.

'We're looking forward to the game more than anything,' he said. 'It's been a long week building up to it and as a player you just want to get out onto that pitch and perform. We just can't wait for Monday night to come.

'We're under no illusions that it's a tough game, but it'll be a tough game for City as well. They will be looking at it and fancying themselves to win, just like ourselves, because they're a good team and they're at home. But we're Man United, we're the champions and we'll be trying to put a statement out that shows we deserve to win this league.'

Barclays Premier League

30 April 2012 | Etihad Stadium | Kick-off 20:00 |
Attendance: 47,259

Manchester City 1 (Kompany 45)
Manchester United 0

On small margins, major consequences can hinge, and a solitary lapse in first-half injury time allowed Vincent Kompany to power home the header which wrestled control of the Premier League title race from United and put it firmly in the hands of Manchester City.

The Belgian escaped his marker, Chris Smalling, to head home the only glaring opportunity of a drab encounter that failed to match its plentiful hype, yet still spawned a resounding outcome. United's gameplan of containment and counter-attack failed to yield a shot on target, as City clinically closed out the second period, sparking scenes of wild celebration all around the Etihad Stadium.

Initially, it was the away support in finer fettle, as Sir Alex Ferguson's side, featuring a five-man midfield of Ryan Giggs, Michael

Carrick, Paul Scholes, Ji-sung Park and Nani, bossed possession and picked their way through the hosts' central areas. Set-pieces would feature heavily in the game, and from one half-cleared corner, Michael Carrick's shot struck Kompany on the hand, but the Belgian escaped censure. Within long, both Giggs and Park had seen shots fail to hit the target from well-worked corners.

However, City gradually began to pose problems. Sergio Aguero fired a volley wide and scuffed another effort off-target, while Pablo Zabaleta's effort dribbled straight to David De Gea. The Spanish goalkeeper had been superbly protected by his defence, but in the first of two added minutes, Kompany escaped the attentions of Smalling – who ran into traffic in the packed area – and powered home his header to give City a half-time lead.

With that, the entire dynamic of the game had shifted. City could afford to relax their approach and retain their impressive discipline as long as they had the lead. United, conversely, had to go for it. Mindful of being picked off, the champions were considered in their pressing, and waited until just before the hour-mark to introduce Danny Welbeck for Park. The striker's effectiveness was quickly compromised by a poor challenge from substitute Nigel de Jong, who picked up a booking, while managers Sir Alex Ferguson and Roberto Mancini traded views on the touchline.

Antonio Valencia and Ashley Young were introduced for Scholes and Nani in the dying stages, but City answered those changes by throwing on Micah Richards and James Milner and shutting up shop. Indeed, with Yaya Toure pushed forward in the Blues' reshuffle, it was City who threatened more. Toure capped one surging run by curling just wide, before Samir Nasri dallied inside the area and allowed Phil Jones to make a superb saving challenge.

The final whistle came before United could fashion a solitary chance to haul themselves back into the game and preserve top spot. Now level on points with the champions but eight goals clear on goal difference, City had snatched the lead in the title race with just two games remaining.

The Teams

Manchester City: Hart; Zabaleta, Kompany, Lescott, Clichy; Nasri (Milner 90), Barry, Y.Toure, Silva (Richards 82); Aguero, Tevez (De Jong 68)
Subs not used: Pantilimon, Kolarov, Dzeko, Balotelli
Booked: Kompany, Y.Toure, De Jong

Manchester United: De Gea; Jones, Smalling, Ferdinand, Evra; Nani (Young 83), Carrick, Scholes (Valencia 78), Park (Welbeck 58), Giggs; Rooney
Subs not used: Amos, Rafael, Berbatov, Hernandez
Booked: Jones, Carrick

'They're in the driving seat now,' conceded a stunned Sir Alex Ferguson. 'They only need to win two games of football [against Newcastle away and QPR at home]. It's not over. As long as there are games of football to play, it's not over, of course. We have the same number of points, but they have an eight-goal advantage and that's a big advantage at this time of the season. I think we have to look at last Sunday as the bad result for us – the Everton game.

'It was a feisty, competitive game, which we expected. There were not a lot of goal chances. I think David De Gea's made the only save in the match. We're disappointed we never tested their goalkeeper, to be honest. I thought City were more of a threat than us, simply because they had more action around our box. We had control in some parts of the game, but not enough to cause any damage.

'If you lose a goal at a set-piece at this level of football then you only have yourself to blame for that. It was a bad time to concede a goal, because there was nothing really happening at the end of the first half. We started off quite well for maybe ten to fifteen minutes and looked as if we were on top in terms of possession and creating opportunities around their box. But as the game wore on, nothing really happened. They had a lot of possession outside our box without really doing anything. Then they got a corner kick and scored. That was a bad time to lose a goal.'

No United player emerged from the pin-drop silence of the away dressing room to give their public reaction to the defeat but, looking back, defender Phil Jones concedes that the Reds were made to pay for a solitary mistake.

'We knew it was going to be a difficult game, but we were positive and confident that we were going to go there and get something,' he recalls. 'We didn't play the way we could've played and we know we can play, and looking back they didn't create any clear-cut opportunities themselves. They had a bit more possession than us, but you probably expect that when you go away to the Etihad, and you could never really see them scoring.

'Obviously we got done on a set-piece, but the problem was that we never looked like scoring either, so we cancelled each other out in a way and I'm sure that if we hadn't conceded just before half time then we'd have taken a point away at least. I don't think we went into the game wanting a point; we definitely wanted to go there and get all three. It's not an easy fixture and you have to go about attacking in the right way and we just didn't do that.'

In under three weeks, United had gone from a position of total control to one of requiring one of two things: a favour from either Newcastle or QPR, or two goal-laden victories over Swansea and Sunderland. Yet while there was no certainty, the champions could still cling to hope.

11

May – Hope Springs Eternal

The final month of the season commenced amid a haze of astonishment. Had United really conceded an eight-point lead in the space of four games to all but hand the title to their bitter rivals?

Carrington, inevitably, lacked its usual buzzing hubbub. The excited chatter of just a month earlier had vanished, lending an eerie atmosphere to the Reds' training base as everybody tried to come to terms with the ramifications of losing the Manchester derby.

'It's been quite muted and a quiet place to be,' admitted Sir Alex Ferguson. 'It's to be expected when we lose a game like that. Our job is to get the players up for the game on Sunday [against Swansea City], because it's such a big game for us.

'We have to analyse the derby as it's part of the game. Even when we win, it's to see good and bad points and we've done all that. It's over with. It's not something we address with the players, it's for the staff's knowledge – myself, Mike [Phelan] and Rene [Meuelensteen]. It's for our knowledge in terms of if we could have done something different. At the end of the day, there were some fantastic footballers on that pitch and we didn't do well enough.'

Stand-in skipper Patrice Evra summarised the collective mood among the playing squad, admitting: 'After the derby, I was really down and it was a massive blow because we always want to win the derby and, of course, it was an important game to win the league. It hurt me a lot because I love this club, and everyone was very down here because they love this club and it hurts when you don't win a game that's so important.'

Those emotions would have to subside in time for the impending visit of the free-flowing Swans if United were to inject a last jolt of momentum to try to reach the finishing line ahead of City. The league leaders would kick off their penultimate game of the season two hours before the Reds, with the unforgiving trip to Newcastle United on their agenda.

Alan Pardew's side had stunned Champions League finalists Chelsea with a victory at Stamford Bridge, and had the chance to cap an incredible season's work by taking third spot in the table with victory over City at the Sports Direct Arena. Their aim was shared by the United squad, who were praying for assistance from the Magpies in order to retain the title.

'Newcastle are a terrific team with some fantastic individuals,' said Phil Jones. 'Papiss Cisse's two goals the other night at Chelsea were terrific. They pressed us really well when they beat us [in January] and they are passionate fans in the North-East. Let's hope they can spur them on again and do us a favour on Sunday. I'm sure that game will be in the back of everyone's minds as we prepare to play Swansea, but we have to concentrate on what we want to do.'

'We must make sure we do our job,' echoed Evra. 'The belief and the hope is there, because I'm a United player and this is my spirit. That's why I believe we're going to win the title and we must make sure we do the job against Swansea. Let's hope for a miracle for Newcastle, but we must just focus on what we have to do – winning against Swansea and Sunderland.

'Everything is possible. I remember a game in the Champions League where Lyon had to win [against Dinamo Zagreb] by seven goals to qualify and they did it. When you play for Manchester

United, everything is possible. Don't look back because it's going to hurt you, knowing we were eight points clear. I don't want to look back, I want to look forward to winning against Swansea, winning against Sunderland and if we get that bonus of scoring a lot of goals then great, but we must just make sure we win the two games and after we'll see.'

The Reds went into the game shorn of the services of Danny Welbeck and Jonny Evans. Both looked likely to miss the remainder of the season; the former with the ankle injury sustained under Nigel De Jong's lunging challenge in the derby, the latter with the ankle injury that ruled him out of the defeat at the Etihad Stadium. Nevertheless, it was still a strong United squad named for the final home game of the season.

It was weakened, however, by events at the Sports Direct Arena. Newcastle held Roberto Mancini's Blues to a goalless scoreline for 70 minutes, before succumbing to a pair of goals from Yaya Toure that put City on the brink of the title. The Reds took to the Old Trafford turf knowing that they would have to register a hefty victory over Swansea in order to decimate their goal difference shortfall.

Barclays Premier League

6 May 2012 | Old Trafford | Kick-off 16:00 |
Attendance: 75,496

Manchester United 2 (Scholes 28, Young 41)
Swansea City 0

The required cricket score never materialised, but United still recovered admirably from the sickening blow of Manchester City's late win over Newcastle with a professional victory of their own at the expense of Swansea. First-half goals from Paul Scholes and Ashley Young secured the three points, but a succession of missed chances prevented the Reds from bagging the hatful of goals that were coveted.

The game began in understandably subdued fashion, following events on Tyneside, and Swansea forward Nathan Dyer had the first noteworthy attempt with a drive that was watched over the bar by David De Gea. That seemed to shake United into life and visiting goalkeeper Michel Vorm had to make a smart double save to thwart Patrice Evra and Wayne Rooney.

The Dutchman had no answer just before the half-hour-mark as United broke the deadlock. Antonio Valencia sped past his marker, Neil Taylor, with ease before pulling the ball back for Michael Carrick, whose measured shot was expertly back-heeled into the net by the lurking Scholes.

Though the veteran midfielder declined to celebrate his goal, it did spark a flurry of opportunities for the hosts. Carrick's cross was steered agonisingly wide by Javier Hernandez, who then nodded over Scholes' flick-on at point-blank range, before Rooney drifted an attempt off-target after collecting a Hernandez header.

A second goal duly arrived, however, shortly before the break. Sloppy play by the Swans gifted Scholes possession in a dangerous position and, although Rooney's subsequent shot was blocked by Angel Rangel, Young was on hand to precisely steer the rebound into the far corner of the net.

Phil Jones and Chris Smalling quickly chanced their arm in a bid to embellish the scoreline before the interval, but the visitors crucially reached the break without further concessions. Swansea emerged for the second period a changed team, sobered by their manager's words and more menacing in attack.

Gylfi Sigurdsson forced David De Gea to awkwardly palm his shot around the post, then drew a full-length save from the Spaniard with a curling free-kick. Dyer also fired off-target after losing his balance, and De Gea superbly readjusted to keep out Danny Graham's flicked effort.

Yet the chances still came at the other end as well. Dyer's diligence prevented Young from tapping home Rooney's cross, Chicharito headed over from another promising position and Rooney shot wastefully wide after being released by Carrick. Both Jones and sub-stitute Tom Cleverley forced Vorm into sharp saves late on, but there was to be no goal avalanche.

To their credit, the champions would fight until the final day. They would be relying on an almighty helping hand from Mark Hughes' Queens Park Rangers, however, if the title was to remain at Old Trafford.

The Teams

Manchester United: De Gea; Jones, Smalling, Ferdinand (Rafael 88), Evra; Valencia, Carrick, Scholes (Cleverley 68), Young; Rooney (Berbatov 79), Hernandez
Subs not used: Amos, Giggs, Park, Nani
Booked: Rooney

Swansea City: Vorm; Rangel, Caulker (Tate 89), Williams, Taylor; Gower (Britton 46), Sigurdsson, Allen; Dyer (Moore 71), Graham, Sinclair
Subs not used: Tremmel, Routledge, Monk, McEachran

'We watched it [Newcastle's defeat to Manchester City] anyway before the game,' admitted Michael Carrick. 'You can't hide from it. It's only natural that we were hoping they slip up, but obviously City have won the game so we had to get our heads on our game and, credit to the boys, we kept believing and we still believe any-thing can happen. It's not over. We'll keep believing and take it until next week.

'We created a number of opportunities. We wanted to start quickly and get on the scoresheet quickly and build from there. We did that, but didn't take our chances, although we'll take a win that gives us an opportunity to take it to next week. It would've been a big ask to score six, seven or eight goals. We tried, but we couldn't in the end, so we'll take the three points.

'We could've been three or four up at half time, so who knows after that? That was the aim, but it didn't quite work out. We can still hope. It's up to them now. We've got to go to Sunderland and win. It's still a tough game and it's not a given. We have to stay focused on that and hope QPR do what they've got to do and help us out. We're still in it, have still got a fighting chance. Until that's over, we'll keep fighting and keep believing. All our focus and energy is going into the last game.'

While the Reds regrouped and channelled their focus on storming the Stadium of Light, talk in the football media centred around a power-shift across Manchester. Were United, for much of two decades casting a shadow over the entire Premier League, about to be put in the shade by their closest rivals for a similar period of time?

'I know that if we don't win the league, then a lot of people will say this is the end of the empire and ask how we will survive,' said Patrice Evra. 'But there's a lot of talent at this club and we've had to deal with a lot. We lost players like Edwin van der Sar, Gary Neville and Paul Scholes last summer. It's never easy to find a solution immediately. But it's not over yet. I'll say it again: we're not dead.'

That calm, considered sentiment was echoed by Sir Alex Ferguson. 'Certainly Manchester City are not going away,' he conceded. 'That's for sure. But the great thing about this club is the in-bred discipline about what's needed to win the league. I think that's shown itself this season again.

'City are not going to go away, with the money they have got. They will buy more players for sure this year. But they can only buy so many and keep the balance for so long before they disrupt things. We've got our own ideas about where we're going in the summer. I think we'll be ready for the challenge. No matter whether it's as champions or runners-up, we'll be ready for it.

'We know how to challenge and accept a challenge. It's important we know we've got a challenge and that's a good thing. There are a lot of young players in the club who have been terrific this season. If we win it, or not, we know we've got a job to do.'

The United manager – fittingly, in a season underscored by horrendous injury problems – went into the final game of the campaign without a host of players. Chris Smalling would miss the trip to Sunderland, as well as England's Euro 2012 campaign, with a serious groin injury, putting him on the sidelines with Danny Welbeck, Nemanja Vidic, Darren Fletcher, Michael Owen, Anderson, Paul Pogba and Kiko Macheda.

City, conversely, didn't report a single absentee ahead of their biggest game in over four decades. A full squad, boasting a near-perfect home record, would host a QPR side that had registered only three league away wins all season. Short of United winning by nine or more goals at Sunderland, only Mark Hughes' side could save the Reds. Yet, against all odds, Patrice Evra retained optimistic.

'We were really down before the game against Swansea last weekend, because we expected a little miracle from Newcastle,' admitted the Frenchman. 'But it didn't happen. Now we just believe. We're level on points going into the final day.

'Maybe people will say I'm crazy or that I'm only saying this because I'm a Manchester United player, but I still believe we can win this title. I know the destiny of the title is not in our hands, but we will just make sure we start the game well against Sunderland. It won't be easy, but if we score first then maybe the City fans in the stadium will start to be nervous. When you are nervous then you can rush things and you don't do things as well as you'd like. That's why we have to make sure we beat Sunderland. I don't think City against Queens Park Rangers is an easy game. So, at the end of the day, we have to believe.'

Barclays Premier League

13 May 2012 | Stadium of Light | Kick-off 15:00 |
Attendance: 46,452

Sunderland 0
Manchester United 1 (Rooney 20)

United's reign as Premier League champions was ended in the cruellest of fashions, despite a battling victory over Sunderland at the Stadium of Light, as Manchester City took the title on goal difference with two injury-time goals against Queens Park Rangers.

Wayne Rooney's early header ensured the Reds ended the season on 89 points, and looked destined for an unlikely triumph, with City trailing ten-man QPR as injury time began at the Etihad Stadium. However, quickfire strikes from Edin Dzeko and Sergio Aguero ended City's 44-year wait to become champions in a remarkable turnaround. United were champions when the game finished at the Stadium of Light, only for City's late comeback to snatch the title a minute later.

It was a heartbreaking way to end an afternoon on which the Reds had comported themselves with class and concentration, registering a deserved victory at an inhospitable away venue.

From the off, United looked in the mood for victory. Ryan Giggs' floated corner was reached by Phil Jones ahead of Simon Mignolet, but the England defender's header agonisingly cleared the crossbar and dropped onto the roof of the net. Jones atoned within two minutes, however, as he teed up the game's opening goal.

The ball was worked wide to the Reds' right-back and, as Sunderland sat off, he curled in a magnificent deep ball which Rooney stooped to nod inside Mignolet's post, sending the small, but strident band of travelling supporters wild – especially with the scoreline still blank at the Etihad Stadium.

Just before the half-hour, United twice came close to doubling their lead. First, Mignolet showed sharp reflexes to beat away Giggs' prodded effort, before Rooney floated a beautiful free-kick onto the top of the crossbar from just outside the area.

Having equalled his personal best season tally of 34 goals with the opener, Rooney was in the mood to embellish his haul – and he should have done in the 34th minute. Impressive approach-play from Antonio Valencia teed up Ashley Young, and the winger's shot should have been swept in by Rooney, who somehow scuffed his effort off-target.

Sunderland quickly rallied, buoyed on by an increasingly tetchy home support, and might have drawn level when Fraizer Campbell stretched to volley goalwards, but could only skew his effort comfortably wide. The Stadium of Light was engulfed by cheers, however, when news filtered through that Pablo Zabaleta had put City ahead at the Etihad Stadium.

While the news was a blow to United's hopes of retaining the title, it didn't affect the pattern of play on the field. Valencia almost added a second goal in added time at the end of the first half, but his powerful shot deflected straight into Mignolet's midriff.

The Belgian stopper was called into action soon after the start of the second period, as a pair of lovely flicks from Giggs and Young culminated in the latter releasing Rooney, whose thunderous close-range effort thudded off Mignolet and away to safety.

Events for United hinged entirely on how City were faring at the Etihad Stadium, and the shock news soon filtered through that QPR – despite the sending-off of Joey Barton – had moved into the lead.

As the away fans dared to dream, United still sought a killer second goal to tie up their end of the bargain. A brilliantly worked move involving Young and Rooney released Paul Scholes just outside the Sunderland area, only for Michael Turner to cynically halt his progress at the expense of a booking.

Though Giggs curled the subsequent free-kick into the wall, both he and Scholes came close to doubling United's lead with 15 minutes remaining. Scholes' 20-yard effort thudded back into play off the upright, and Giggs' thunderous rebound from the edge of the area was spectacularly tipped over by the flying Mignolet.

United's job was simple: see out the final ten minutes without conceding and, if possible, add further gloss to the scoreline. Rooney came agonisingly close in the final minute with a free-kick which kissed the outside of Mignolet's post, but there were no further chances at the Stadium of Light.

Crucially, City managed to manufacture two more and bagged injury-time goals to wrench the title across Manchester and snatch their third domestic crown.

The Teams

Sunderland: Mignolet; Bardsley (Bridge 61), Bramble, Turner, O'Shea (Elmohamady 42); Gardner, Colback, Vaughan (Wickham 73), McClean; Sessegnon; Campbell
Subs not used: Westwood, Ji, Meyler, Kyrgiakos
Booked: Campbell, Bardsley, Turner

Manchester United: De Gea; Jones, Evans, Ferdinand, Evra; Valencia, Scholes, Carrick, Young (Nani 82); Giggs; Rooney
Subs not used: Amos, Owen, Berbatov, Park, Hernandez, Rafael
Booked: Giggs, Jones, Scholes

'I would like to say on behalf of Manchester United, congratulations to our neighbours,' said Sir Alex Ferguson, still digesting the dramatic denouement to the season. 'It is a fantastic achievement to win the Premier League. It's not easy to win; it's the hardest league in the world and anyone that wins it deserves it.

'We knew there were five minutes of injury time being played there, one of the assistant referees informed us of that. Our game had only three minutes, so for two minutes we didn't know that was happening. Of course, they got the break and won the game.

'It was a cruel way, but we've experienced many ups and downs in the twenty-five years that I've been here and most of them have been great moments. We have won the league three times in the last five seasons and we nearly did it again today.

'All we had to do – I said it before the game to the lads – was concentrate on our job, because you are going to get certain types of reaction from the fans – you saw that from our fans and from Sunderland's when City scored a third goal. You just have to put that to one side and concentrate on your own game, which I think we did pretty well.'

Having been there, done it, won it and also lost it before, the United manager was able to draw upon his experience to give a clear assessment of his side's season, as well as their bright future.

'We take great credit from the fact that we have had so many injuries this season and we've coped with that very well,' he said. 'They are only young players and they're a good bunch of lads. They've experienced what has happened today and they'll be around in five or ten years' time for Manchester United. The experience is good for them, even if it is a bad one. When you have a good character and a certain purpose about you, then you shouldn't fear the future.

'For us it's a challenge and we're good at challenges. We'll kick on from here.'

Epilogue

The emotion of the season's dramatic denouement was still etched across the faces of the United players as they trudged into the club's end-of-season awards bash at Old Trafford, little more than 24 hours after seeing their title snaffled away in the final moments of the campaign.

Even Antonio Valencia struggled to muster more than a fleeting smile as he thrice took to the stage to collect awards for scoring the goal of the season and being voted player of the season by supporters and team-mates.

Yet all around them, the voices of experience spoke words of reason. Bryan Robson and Sir Bobby Charlton addressed the entire audience, but aimed encouragement specifically at the crestfallen players.

'All I'd say to the lads is that yes, there's a massive disappointment from yesterday, but the points tally they achieved deserved to win the league,' said ex-Reds skipper Robson. 'It's an experience for them. What they've got to do is what United has always done: bounce back the next year, and that's their challenge. They'll bounce back and prove themselves next year.'

Sir Bobby elaborated: 'In football you learn you have to be prepared for surprises. We have an unbelievable club. The club without question is the best in the world. We have fantastic players, fantastic staff and I'm ever so proud. There'll be a lot of pressure put on the lads to do the best they can, but they've always done that and we will survive. We have the tools and we have the desire, and with that desire we're capable of doing anything, as we've already proved.

'We have the greatest manager that the world has ever seen, and with Alex and the squad that we have at the moment, we're capable of doing anything. It's a little blip, this, and at the end of the day we will survive and we will continue, because we have the right tools and the right people in the right places.'

Most rousing of all, however, was Sir Alex Ferguson's public address. Despite winning 12 Premier League titles, the manager had also seen a few slip through his grasp, and he drew on those experiences to deliver an impassioned battle-cry to his squad.

'What a day! We didn't deserve that,' he grinned, ruefully. 'I read an article in the paper this morning which says that we need eight new players. Why do I need eight players? I've got all the young players here evolving into the club. Of course, I've got the old masters: Giggs, Scholes and Ferdinand; and most importantly – and you'll maybe not understand this – I've got fantastic staff. The medical staff, the sports science staff . . . bloody hell, they're bright boys. They talk stuff I've never heard of before and hope I never hear again. They're beyond my intellect. I'm a dinosaur, an absolute dinosaur, but what I am . . . I'm a winner.

'I said this to all the players yesterday: when we lost the league to Leeds United in 1992, the young players came out that day and the Liverpool supporters were asking for their autographs and then tearing them up. I said to Giggs and the boys back then: "Remember this day," and that's exactly what I said to the players yesterday. Those Sunderland fans who were cheering for City, remember the day. We won't forget that, I'm telling you. Well done to the players, a fantastic group; they will be all right. Don't worry about them; they're a great bunch of lads. Well done, boys.'

No United player or supporter could have conceived a more harrowing climax to a campaign than watching helplessly as Manchester City snatched the title on goal difference, in injury time of the final day of the season. But that is what happened. Those gut-wrenching memories are etched for ever on the hearts and souls of everybody of a Red persuasion, and nowhere has it been carved deeper than within each member of Sir Alex Ferguson's squad.

Popular opinion away from Old Trafford and Carrington suggests that the limitless funding of the newly crowned Premier League champions will prove too much for United to overcome, and that a new era is upon us. But that was what they said when Roman Abramovich came to Chelsea, and many believed they would never be stopped. The Blue moon has risen, apparently, and it will take an almighty effort to eclipse it. But, with the finest manager in history, a balanced, talented squad and now the added motivation of avenging the cruellest of title races, a Red dawn may be closer than many think.

Appearances and Goals

Appearances

	Premier League		FA Cup		League Cup		Champions League		Europa League		Other		Total	
	Apps	Sub	Apps	Sub	Apps	Sub	Apps	Sub	Apps	Sub	Apps	Sub	Apps	Sub
Patrice Evra	37		2		0		5		2		1		47	
Wayne Rooney	32	2	1		0		4		3		1		41	2
David De Gea	29		1		0		4		4		1		39	
Michael Carrick	27	3	2		1		4		2	1	1		37	4
Rio Ferdinand	29	1	1		0		4		2		1		37	1
Jonny Evans	28	1	1		1		2	2	3	1	0	1	35	5
Phil Jones	25	4	1		1		4	2	3		0	1	34	7
Nani	24	5	1		0		4	2	2	1	1		32	8
Antonio Valencia	22	5	2		3		5		0	1	0		32	6
Danny Welbeck	23	7	2		0	1	1	1	0	3	1		27	12
Ashley Young	19	6	0		0		3		4		1		27	6
Chris Smalling	14	5	2		1		3	1	2	1	1		23	7

	Premier League		FA Cup		League Cup		Champions League		Europa League		Other		Total	
	Apps	Sub	Apps	Sub	Apps	Sub	Apps	Sub	Apps	Sub	Apps	Sub	Apps	Sub
Javier Hernandez	18	10	0	1	0		1	3	3		0		22	14
Ryan Giggs	14	11	2		1		3		2		0		22	11
Ji-sung Park	10	7	1		3		2	2	3		0		19	9
Paul Scholes	14	3	1	1	0		0		0	2	0		15	6
Rafael	10	2	1		1		0		3		0	1	15	3
Anderson	8	2	0	1	0		3		0	1	1		12	4
Fabio	2	3	0		3		5		2		0		12	3
Dimitar Berbatov	5	7	0	1	3		2	1	1		0	1	11	10
Anders Lindegaard	8		1		0		2		0		0		11	
Nemanja Vidic	6		0		1		2		0		1		10	
Tom Cleverley	5	5	0		1		0		3		0	1	9	6
Darren Fletcher	7	1	0		0		2		0		0		9	1
Ben Amos	1		0		3		0		0		0		4	
Michael Owen	0	1	0		2		1		0		0		3	1
Mame Biram Diouf	0		0		3		0		0		0		3	
Ezekiel Fryers	0	2	0		2	1	0	1	0		0		2	4

	Premier League		FA Cup		League Cup		Champions League		Europa League		Other		Total	
	Apps	Sub	Apps	Sub	Apps	Sub	Apps	Sub	Apps	Sub	Apps	Sub	Apps	Sub
Federico Macheda	0	3	0		2		0	1	0		0		2	4
Darron Gibson	1		0		1		0		0		0		2	2
Paul Pogba	0	3	0		0	3	0		0	1	0		0	7
Ravel Morrison	0		0		0	2	0		0		0		0	2
Larnell Cole	0		0		0	1	0		0		0		0	1
Michael Keane	0		0		0	1	0		0		0		0	1
Will Keane	0	1	0		0		0		0		0		0	1

Goals scored

	Premier League	FA Cup	League Cup	Champions League	Europa League	Other	Total
Wayne Rooney	27	2	0	2	3	0	34
Javier Hernandez	10	0	0	0	2	0	12
Danny Welbeck	9	1	0	2	0	0	12
Nani	8	0	0	0	0	2	10
Dimitar Berbatov	7	0	1	1	0	0	9

	Premier League	FA Cup	League Cup	Champions League	Europa League	Other	Total
Ashley Young	6	0	0	1	1	0	8
Antonio Valencia	4	0	1	1	0	0	6
Paul Scholes	4	0	0	0	0	0	4
Ryan Giggs	2	0	1	1	0	0	4
Ji-sung Park	2	1	0	0	0	0	3
Michael Owen	0	0	3	0	0	0	3
Anderson	2	0	0	0	0	0	2
Michael Carrick	2	0	0	0	0	0	2
Darren Fletcher	1	0	0	1	0	0	2
Phil Jones	1	0	0	1	0	0	2
Chris Smalling	1	0	0	0	0	1	2
Jonny Evans	1	0	0	0	0	0	1
Federico Macheda	0	0	1	0	0	0	1
own goals	2	0	0	1	0	0	3

Acknowledgements

MUTV
ManUtd.com
United Review
Inside United
Photographs: John and Matt Peters

Sincere thanks to everyone at the club for their co-operation and support during the writing of this book, especially Sir Alex Ferguson, his staff and players for their time, insight and candour.

Additional gratitude goes to John Allen, Nick Coppack, Rhea Halford, Ian Marshall, Karen Shotbolt, Paul Thomas and James White for their oodles of patience and help.